IN
DEFENSE
OF
LOOTING

IN DEFENSE OF LOOTING

A Riotous History of Uncivil Action

VICKY OSTERWEIL

BOLD TYPE BOOKS
NEW YORK

Bold Type Books
116 East 16th Street, 8th Floor New York, NY 10003
www.boldtypebooks.org
@BoldTypeBooks

Printed in the United States of America
First Edition: August 2020

Published by Bold Type Books, an imprint of Perseus Books, LLC, a subsidiary of Hachette Book Group, Inc. Bold Type Books is a co-publishing venture of the Type Media Center and Perseus Books.

The Hachette Speakers Bureau provides a wide range of authors for speaking events. To find out more, go to www.hachettespeakersbureau.com or call (866) 376-6591.

The publisher is not responsible for websites (or their content) that are not owned by the publisher.

Print book interior design by Linda Mark

Library of Congress Cataloging-in-Publication Data
Names: Osterweil, Vicky, author.
Title: In defense of looting : a riotous history of uncivil action / Vicky Osterweil.
Description: First edition. | New York City, NY : Bold Type Books, October 2020. |
    Includes bibliographical references and index.
Identifiers: LCCN 2020022054 | ISBN 978-1-64503-669-2 (hardcover) |
    ISBN 978-1-64503-667-8 (ebook)
Subjects: LCSH: Riots. | Pillage—Political aspects. | Pillage—Social aspects.
Classification: LCC HV6474 .O88 2020 | DDC 363.32/309—dc23
LC record available at https://lccn.loc.gov/2020022054

ISBN 978-1-64503-669-2 (hardcover), ISBN 978-1-64503-667-8 (ebook)

LSC-C

10 9 8 7 6 5 4 3 2 1

For Clark, Anna, and Pablo,
see you on the other side

Contents

INTRODUCTION

O F THE MANY FORMS OF POLITICAL ACTION IN TWENTY-FIRST-century America, it's hard to think of any less popular than rioting and looting. Voting and electioneering are widely respected as the baseline of political action; petitioning and lobbying elected representatives are not far behind. Labor action, despite four decades of propaganda and federal action against it, still has strong support in many quarters. Community organizing is at least theoretically the founding principle for thousands of nonprofits across the country. Liberals and conservatives alike grudgingly support demonstrations, at least when they're nonviolent and their people are doing it.

More extreme political actions also have widespread support. Both liberals and conservatives believe in war, considering it a necessary evil or a fundamental good. Liberals may oppose the death penalty, but they, like conservatives, believe in the efficacy of murder: they had little to say about Obama's extrajudicial drone executions, his death lists and Terror Tuesdays, and Democrats mostly critiqued Trump's 2020 assassination of Qasem Soleimani on procedural grounds: "He didn't consult Congress!" Torture is celebrated a thousand times a day on television in police procedurals and action flicks, and most people accept imprisonment—years of

1

unrelenting psychic torture—as a necessary fact of social life. Economic coercion on the international stage, through sanctions, trade agreements, and development loans, is a matter of course. At home, the threat of unemployment, homelessness, starvation, and destitution, along with debt, taxes, fines, and fees of all kinds, are so naturalized as to rarely even be recognized as a form of political domination at all.

But rioting and looting have few defenders. Conservatives, of course, oppose it utterly, rooting for the police to put down protesters, with the Far Right claiming riots are just professional troublemaking fomented by George Soros, Jews, and the "global elite." Liberals oppose rioting, too: because their love for law and order is much greater than their belief in freedom, they claim that rioters are "hurting their own cause" or are led by police provocateurs—agreeing with the fascists that rioters are paid troublemakers, just disagreeing about who signs the checks.

In the face of rioting and looting, even sympathetic self-identifying radicals sometimes balk. They claim that these more extreme actions are mainly the work of outside agitators, "opportunists," or out-of-step middle-class radicals. They claim that those doing the looting are "not part of the movement," that they are "apolitical" and ignorant, that their actions reflect "false consciousness," or even that they are acting as consumers and therefore furthering capitalism.

From within the movement, people tend to claim that what happened wasn't rioting but an uprising or a rebellion. No one wants to be associated with the idea of riot, and this is doubly true for looting. Even while a riot is going on, people in the streets often work to block looting. Many of them do so out of care for the struggle, worried about unfair media representation and hoping to advance the politically and ethically advantageous position. I understand that instinct, but it was to critique and push against that thinking, crucially in love and solidarity with those who pursue it and with looters the world over, that I began this project.

Other people, however—including local politicians, middle-class "leaders," political groups, and reactionary organizations—block looting in order to gain power for themselves. These peacekeepers and de-escalators cooperate with the police to derail and destroy uprisings to show the white power structure that they are responsible parties, that, because they can control and contain the unruly masses, they are the "natural leaders," the people who should be negotiated with. This book is spit in their eyes.

Looting is so unpopular not because it is an error or bad for the movement but because it is often a movement's most radical tactic. Looting attacks some of the core beliefs and structures of cisheteropatriarchal racial capitalist society, and so frightens and disturbs nearly everyone, even some of its participants. After all, we have all been raised and trained to hold, follow, and reproduce those beliefs every day. Looting rejects the legitimacy of ownership rights and property, the moral injunction to work for a living, and the "justice" of law and order. Looting reveals all these for what they are: not natural facts, but social constructs benefiting a few at the expense of the many, upheld by ideology, economy, and state violence.

That looting is one of the most racially loaded, morally abhorred, and depoliticized concepts in modern society should come as no surprise. From its very first usages, the word has served to re-enforce the white supremacist juncture of property and race.

The word *loot* is taken up from the Hindi word *lút*—similar to "plunder" or "booty"—which first appears in Anglophone contexts in 1788 in a handbook on "Indian Vocabulary" for English colonial officers.[1] In *loot's* first recorded appearance in the English language, it describes how an officer managed to gain consent and gather recruits for subduing Indian resistance: "He always found the talismanic gathering-word Loot (plunder) a sufficient bond of union in any part of India." The racialized idea of an "Indian" identity did not yet exist outside the minds of the colonizers, but a natural racial tendency, one overcoming tribal, religious, and cultural differences, could be "revealed" by the offer of plunder. In other words, a deviant relationship to property is the "sufficient" attribute that unifies and defines an otherwise disparate group under the sign of race. The earliest appearances of the gerund *looting*, meanwhile, refer to "hirsute Sikhs" and "Chinese blackguards."[2] *Looting* is a word taken from a colonized people and used to denigrate and racialize riotous subalterns resisting English empire. It would from the very beginning refer to a nonwhite and lawless relationship to property.

The looting that I am defending in this book is not that act that can be described by the synonym *plunder*. The looting of captured territory by armies, for example, or of colonial wealth by empire and its agents, can be equally well described by words like *robbery, pillage, booty*, and *spoils*. But the looting described, defended, and historicized here—that of a crowd of people publicly, openly, and directly taking things in the midst of riot and social unrest—has no easy synonym. I personally like the phrases "proletarian shopping" and "shopping for free" quite a lot and use the Marxist "expropriation," too. But all those phrases drain the idea of looting of its racializing character. Although it is understandable why people would want, in defending their movements, to find a less charged word, it is precisely the fact that looting exists at the nexus of race and class that gives it its tactical power.

Looting is a method of direct redistribution of wealth, from the store owners and capitalists to the poor. Looting, as scholar Delio Vasquez writes in "The Poor Person's Defense of Riots," "directly results (unless you get arrested) in your acquiring the things that you are seeking."[3] It is a practical, immediate form of improving life. Looting represents a material way that riots and protests help the community: by providing a way for people to solve some of the immediate problems of poverty and by creating a space for people to freely reproduce their lives rather than doing so through wage labor. Looting is an act of communal cohesion.

But looting is also an act of excess, of property destruction. When something is looted, that thing's nature as a commodity is destroyed by its being taken for free, out of the cycle of exchange and profit. Everything in the store goes from being a commodity to becoming a gift. Less abstractly, looting is usually followed up by burning down the shop. Looters also frequently throw items out onto the streets for anyone to take or pile goods chaotically in the middle of the store or pass bottles of liquor, bags of food, or goods between strangers and around the crowd. Looting involves not only taking wealth directly but also immediately sharing that wealth, which points to the collapse of the system by which the looted things produce value.

Looting is a communal practice: it cannot be done alone. Anthropologist Neal Keating argues that looting creates a similar relation to property as the potlatch, a communal practice of Indigenous nations in the Pacific Northwest. In the potlatch, held on a variety of special occasions—births, deaths, weddings, festivals—wealthy people compete to see who can give away the most possessions to the gathered celebrants and they vie with each other to destroy the most accumulated wealth in a massive bonfire. The potlatch works to level wealth in the community by consuming surplus, which might otherwise enable some to develop more permanent forms of power through excess accumulation. Rioting and looting similarly redistribute and reduce the wealth and the surplus, leveling material power differentials.[4] The potlatch was outlawed by the Canadian government as a part of its (ongoing) genocide of the First Nations: the potlatch was considered one of the most important obstacles to their becoming "civilized" and Christian. Like looting, this nonwhite, noncommodified communal approach to property was seen as a dangerous threat to capitalism and "civilization."

Though no single instance of looting is on its own sufficient to transform society, obviously, looting—at least when carried out by Black, poor, or Indigenous people—will always be strenuously and vigorously disavowed by the powers that be because it points to and immediately enacts a different relationship to property, a different history. There have been few instances of looting in the United States in the last quarter century; when it has appeared, it has been during brief and often one-off uprisings. Despite this fact, when the flames went up over a looted QuikTrip in Ferguson, Missouri, in August 2014, as antipolice rioting broke out after Michael Brown was killed, the media produced lines of argument and criticism that you might have just as easily heard in the sixties. Politicians and media outlets have a number of tried-and-true disavowals and defamations of looters at the ready. Before moving on to the historical narrative of looting in the United States, it's worth dealing with these common objections here.

"Riots Are Being Stirred Up by Outside Agitators"

The myth of "outside agitators" is used by conservatives and nonviolence champions alike to discredit militancy wherever it appears. This one is a white supremacist classic, going all the way back to slavery. Under slavery, plantation owners claimed that unrest, rebellions, and fugitives resulted from the influence of "uppity negroes" and pernicious Yankees who had come south to delude the otherwise content enslaved with ideas of freedom and equality. The completely racist assumptions at the base of this argument—happy dumb slaves duped into believing they are human beings by scheming Northerners—still forms the logic behind the "outside agitator," a phrase that emerged in force during the civil rights movement. Martin Luther King was the prototypical outside agitator, traveling the country fighting segregation, although white civil rights activists were also often tarred with this brush. These days "white anarchists," George Soros and the employees of his organization, "antifa," or "agent provocateurs" are likely to be the preferred outside agitating boogeymen.

This logic strips those who protest of their power, claiming that their experiences, lives, and desires are not actually sufficient to inspire their acts of resistance—implying that they don't know what they're doing. It also begins from the presumption that the world is fine as it is, and so only nihilistic or paid troublemakers could challenge it. But it is a racist idea on its face. What actually is wrong with an outside agitator? The concept is structured around the implicit racial logic of borders and citizenship through which an individual's status inside/outside is the main consideration that determines political legitimacy. Outside of what?

Why shouldn't we at least consider ideas or agitation from "outside" our most immediate environs? Isn't that what we call solidarity?

"Rioters Are Destroying Their Own Neighborhoods"

The "why do you destroy your own neighborhoods?" trope emerged in force during the dozens of uprisings in cities across the United States during the sixties. Here we see a willful confusion of geography and power. Though the buildings destroyed may be located in a predominantly Black or proletarian neighborhood, the losses go to the white, bourgeois building and business owners, rarely the people who live near them. Civil rights leader Stokely Carmichael (later Kwame Ture) had to challenge these logics to defend the riots: "In these cities we do not control our resources. We do not control the land, the houses or the stores.

These are owned by whites who live outside 'the community.' . . . White power makes the laws and enforces those laws with guns and nightsticks in the hands of white racist policemen and black mercenaries."[5]

Assata Shakur, freedom fighter in the Black liberation movement and the federal government's most wanted fugitive, describes having the same argument with white coworkers, who wanted Shakur to admit "what a shame it was" that rioters were destroying their neighborhoods and to disavow them. But Shakur instead put forward the positive case for the destruction: "They don't own those houses. They don't own those stores. I'm glad they burned down those stores because those stores were robbing them in the first place!"[6]

With the post-sixties emergence of a Black business class and, later, a Black president, and with the legal dismantling of Jim Crow, the logic that rioters are destroying their own neighborhoods has only grown stronger. Because a higher (though still small) percentage of owners, businesspeople, and politicians are likely to be Black, it becomes even easier to imagine looting and rioting as somehow striking internally within the Black community. As Tyler Reinhard wrote in the wake of the Ferguson uprising: "I'm not sure how people who make this argument imagine 'owning' a neighborhood works, but I'll try to break it down: we don't own neighborhoods. Black businesses exist, it's true. But the emancipation of impoverished communities is not measured in corner-store revenue. It's not measured in minimum-wage jobs."[7]

As a Ferguson rioter put it in a viral Instagram video, "People wanna say we destroying our own neighborhoods. We don't own nothing out here!" This could be said of most majority Black neighborhoods in America, which have much higher concentrations of chain stores and fast food restaurants than non-Black neighborhoods. How could the average Ferguson resident really say it's "our QuikTrip"? Indeed, although you might hang out in it, how can a chain convenience store or corporate restaurant earnestly be part of anyone's neighborhood? The same white liberals who inveigh against corporations for destroying local communities are aghast when rioters take their critique to its actual material conclusion.

Only a cop, in this case Baltimore police commissioner Anthony Batts, prosecuting an arsonist from the 2015 Freddie Gray uprisings, could say without irony "Raymon Carter burned a CVS—our CVS—to the ground." Nowhere is the absurd hollowness of modern American populism more clear than in a police commissioner's heartfelt pause, then plea: not just any CVS; "our CVS."

"Looters Are Opportunists and Criminals, Not Protesters: They Have Nothing to Do with the Struggle"

When protesters proclaim that "not all protesters were looters, in fact, most of the looters weren't part of the protest!" or words to that effect, they are trying to fight a horrifically racist history of Black people depicted in American culture as robbers and thieves: it is a completely righteous and understandable position.

However, in trying to correct this media image—in making a strong division between Good Protesters and Bad Rioters, or between ethical nonviolence practitioners and supposedly violent looters—the narrative of the criminalization of Black youth is reproduced. This time it makes criminal and moral divisions between certain kinds of Black youth—those who loot (bad) versus those who protest (good). The effect of this discourse is hardening a permanent category of criminality on Black subjects who produce a supposed crime within the context of an "acceptable" protest (though those protesters would be just as quickly slandered as criminals in less confrontational protest scenarios). It reproduces racist and white supremacist ideologies, deeming some unworthy of our solidarity and protection, marking them, subtly, as legitimate targets of police violence.[8]

If looters are "not part of the protest," then why do they appear again and again in liberatory uprisings? In fact, a number of sociological studies from the seventies showed that, against the commonsense narrative, those who participate in rioting and looting tend to be the most politically informed and socially engaged in the neighborhood, while the most apathetic, disconnected, and alienated people riot at the lowest rates. This suggests that looters and rioters understand the stakes and meaning of the struggle, have been active within it, and see looting as a sensible escalation of possibilities.

"Rioters Hurt the Media Coverage, They Make Us/Our Concerns Look Bad"

Rioters are often accused of being the cause of negative media coverage. But this claim is always made after the cameras have arrived, without recognition of how or why those cameras got there. If it were not for rioters, the media would probably pay no attention at all. If protesters hadn't looted and burnt down that QuikTrip on the second day of protests, would Ferguson have become a point of worldwide attention? It's impossible to know, but all the nonviolent protests against police killings across the country that go unreported seem to indicate the answer is no. It was the looting of a Duane Reade, and not the vigil that preceded it, that brought widespread attention to the murder of Kimani Gray in New York City in 2013. The media's own warped procedure instructs that riots and looting are more effective at attracting attention to a cause.

But the point of a protest isn't media attention, anyway. As a 1967 editorial on press coverage of urban riots in the Student Non-Violent Coordinating Committee's *The Movement* magazine put it: "The white-run daily press in America is not an objective, critical viewer of events. Newspapers are industries. They are private property, not public utilities. When black people revolt against their conditions, they are also revolting against the mass media; the press."

The essay reproduced and analyzed guidelines on covering future instances of unrest that were given out to CBS reporters in the wake of Watts. The editors highlight one of those guidelines, which says: "At the outset of the disorder, broadcast newsmen should be dispatched to law enforcement command posts, rather than directly to the scene, where their presence may heighten the disturbance or interfere with efforts to establish control. An authoritatively staffed command post will undoubtedly be in communication with the scenes of disorder and be capable of providing newsmen with any desired information."[9]

During the LA riots of 1992, national news broadcast nonstop footage of the violent beating of white truck driver Reginald Denny by four Black teens that was captured by news helicopters. The news did not provide the context—that the National Guard had just driven through that intersection, firing live rounds at rioters, meaning Denny was in the wrong place at the wrong time—or the aftermath, in which other Black rioters ran out, tended to his wounds, and got him to a hospital, saving his life, though both were also captured on camera. Instead, the violent beating was shown on loop, out of context, across the country.

During the UK riots in summer 2011, which saw people rise up in response to the police murder of Mark Duggan, the BBC, which had mostly relied on helicopter and police footage, did a live interview with a man from Croydon, one of the London neighborhoods where rioting was intense. That man, Darcus Howe, was a respected broadcaster and writer originally from Trinidad. The presenter asked him leading questions about how terrible the riots were, but Howe clearly and angrily laid out the stakes of the riot. "What I was certain about, listening to my son and my grandson, is that something very serious was going to happen in this country. Our leaders had no idea. . . . But if you listened to young Blacks, and young whites in this country . . . you would know that what is hap-pening to them is wrong." The presenter then interrupted him, insulted him, and accused him of being a rioter himself. The BBC was forced to issue an apology, but it also scrubbed the footage from its websites and future broadcasts, preferring not to allow this accidental moment of rad-ical clarity to continue.

No matter how peaceful and "well-behaved" a protest is, the domi-nant media will always push the police talking points and the white su-premacist agenda. Although it can sometimes be leveraged strategically, the mass media is the enemy of liberation, and when we shape our ac-tions to conform to its opinions or perspectives, we will always lose. If we riot, they will slander us. If we behave politely, peacefully, legally, they will simply return to ignoring us.

"Rioting, Looting, and Property Destruction Justify Police Repression"

People are told not to escalate, that nonviolence will prevent police from being excessively violent toward activists. But this reflects a shoddy analy-sis of state violence in the face of the very thing these uprisings are about: Black people being killed for walking in the middle of the street, selling

CDs or cigarettes, driving with a broken taillight, wearing a hoodie, etc., etc., etc. How is it that we can go to the streets to protest that violence still believing that our behavior dictates police response rather than recognizing that the police will brutalize whoever they want, whenever they want to, unless we can stop them?

"Looters Are Just Being 'Consumers,' They Are Acting on False Consciousness"

Many people—self-styled "revolutionaries"—criticize rioters for looting flat-screen TVs or expensive sneakers. These people often claim they would support looters stealing medicine or food, life necessities, but because they are stealing expensive commodities it reveals that rioters are just "consumerists," "materialistic." As Evan Calder Williams wrote in his essay "An Open Letter to Those Who Condemn Looting," this analysis was particularly prevalent around the 2011 UK riots. Even during the riots, the entire white UK Left, from the left-liberal media establishment to the "revolutionary" political parties, basically told rioters to drop dead. As Williams asks, are these revolutionaries to have us believe that "the poor are not supposed to understand the fundamentals of exchange-value? That they should have been loading shopping carts with flour and beans, rather than with computers which could, in theory, be sold for a much larger quantity of flour and beans?"[10]

The failure isn't merely an economic one: when people make this argument, they reveal a fundamental contempt for the poor. They share a moral logic with conservative antiwelfare talking heads and pull-up-your-pants respectability politicians who claim that poor people are poor because they spend their money on smartphones or fancy clothes. These so-called revolutionaries, who support the looting of bread, but not of liquor, reveal that they are only willing to support poor people in struggles for bare survival: in other words, in struggles that keep them poor. They withdraw their solidarity when the proletariat act on desires to have their lives be more pleasurable and more worth living.[11]

These reactionaries don't want the poor to have nice things any more than the police who execute looters do. They see the masses as fetish objects in their feverish revolutionary abstractions, who should only rise up in some pure proletarian struggle, perhaps led by them at the vanguard of a glorious Party.

All of these different slanders contain a connecting thread: that looting and rioting are not *really* about the issues (usually but not always police violence) that initiated them. Riots are instead minimized as criminal disorder, sudden outbursts of "tension," or somehow objective markers of the state of race relations or poverty.

At the basis of this criticism is the idea that poor Black or working-class folks don't know what they're doing: that when they riot and loot, they're acting outside of reason, outside of "real" struggle. Unlike strikers or nonviolent protesters, the people who rise up in rage and destruction are exiled from recognition as a real revolutionary subject, as people. Philosopher Sylvia Wynter critiqued this notion harshly when analyzing the LA riots:

> This category [of the New Poor], unlike the working class jobholders, cannot be seen, within the economic logic of our present organization of knowledge, as contributors to the process of production. . . . this New Poor, seduced too, like all of us, by the clamor of advertisements which urge them to consume, so that frustrated in their consumption goals, they turn on one another, mutilate and kill each other, or "damage themselves with alcohol and drugs" convinced of their own worthlessness, or in brief episodes of eruption, "fire the ghettoes, riot, looting whatever they can lay their hands on," means that today's intellectuals, whilst they feel and express their pity, refrain from proposing to marry their thought with this particular variety of human suffering.

Instead, Wynter goes on, the rising of these masses has created the possibility of thinking through a new, revolutionary ethics. "The eruption . . . in South Central Los Angeles has again opened a horizon from which to spearhead the speech of a new frontier of knowledge able to move us toward a new, correlated human species, and eco-systemic, ethic."[12]

It is Wynter's admonition to marry our thought, learning, and theorizing to this group and their actions that shapes the work of this book.

Any meaningful forms of struggle derive from the oppressed communities that need that struggle most, not from the minds, forms, or theories of the most successful activists or revolutionaries. As much as any of us can, rioters and looters know exactly what they're doing. This book, the thinking and study I've done here and the essay it expands on, would have been impossible without the uprising in Ferguson. The rebels of Ferguson have taught me more than I can ever hope to teach, and this book is meant as an act of gratitude to them for that teaching.

IF RIOTS ARE SEEN AS INCHOATE, SENSELESS OUTPOURINGS OF ANGER and resentment, it is also a commonplace that famous historical riots "give birth" to movements. The Stonewall riots gave birth to the gay liberation movement; the storming of the Bastille gave birth to the French Revolution; the Boston Tea Party, the American Revolution. This, of course, is just meant as a simple claim of cause and effect, a rhetorical flourish. But birth is in fact an excellent metaphor for rioting and its relation to social movement and revolution.

Homo sapiens are quite unlucky evolutionarily. In almost all mammals, pregnancy and birth are safe and simple processes: gestating mothers basically never die in childbirth. Indeed, if there are insufficient resources or the gestator is unable to care for a baby at that moment for some reason, the fetus can easily be aborted. But in humans, birth is violent and dangerous, life-threatening to both gestator and fetus.[13]

With that understanding in mind, we can begin to analyze riots as births. Riots are violent, extreme, and femme as fuck: they rip, tear, burn, and destroy to give birth to a new world. They can emerge from rising tensions and lead to nothing—a miscarriage—or be the height and end point of a given movement. In most instances, however, they transform and build a nascent moment into a movement: rioting, as the Black trans women of Stonewall showed us, is a form of queer birth.

As a mode of struggle, riots are marked by many characteristics traditionally defined as feminine: not driven by rational argumentation or "proper" political dialogue, they are instead driven by desire, affect, rage, and pain. They are disordered, emotional, and chaotic. Importantly, too, riots struggle within the sphere of social reproduction: looting makes day-to-day life easier by changing the price of goods to zero, relieves pressure by spreading wealth within the community, and reinforces bonds of solidarity and kinship through mutual struggle and action.[14] It is important to remember that, for the most part, riots are experienced as celebration, as joyous and cathartic releases of emotion: police and politicians who enter riot zones often cite this atmosphere as the thing that terrifies them the most.[15] But riots are also driven by anger and loss. They emerge as an alternative form of care and remembrance for those the state's patriarchal violence has destroyed: rising up in mourning for lost children and in outrage at the domination of daily life. They can be ugly, bloody, and frightening.

They are often protective, defensive struggles, but they are always about reproducing a community; as the study of riots in the United States makes clear, one of the main aftereffects of riots is a sense of unity, togetherness, and joy not normally experienced in the urban neighborhood, a unity that leads to the blossoming of dozens of political, social, and economic projects. Riots are communicative, but unlike protest, they do not aim their speech at those in power, at leaders or the state; instead, they are a form of direct communication and knowledge transfer among those outside the traditional avenues of power. As Black Panther Party minister of defense Huey P. Newton put it, "In Watts the economy and property of the oppressor was destroyed to such an extent that no matter how the oppressor tried in his press to whitewash the activities of the Black brothers, the real nature and cause of the activity was communicated to every Black community."[16]

Conceiving of riots as birth does not manage to contain everything important or worth understanding about riots—it is not a perfect or total metaphor. But it can help us to understand and analyze the role rioting has in movement and revolution and the way that riots work for their participants and the towns and cities where they occur. Rather than seeing riots as either totally apolitical, chaotic, or beside the point, instead of seeing them as one-off rebellions, uprisings, or insurrections that have little interaction with everyday forms of social transformation, we can instead see them as crucial moments in the course of revolution and as fundamentally transformative experiences for everyone involved.

And it is this book's contention that we need a total transformation of our society. The society we live in under capitalism is entirely structured around the production and circulation of commodities. It is a cruel system, built for the creation and reification of things, not for the flourishing of people. Commodities are not just any things, but a special kind: goods and services that can be given a price and sold for more than it cost to make them so that they produce more value, an excess: profits. Under capitalism, those profits go to the owner of the "means of production." But the owner doesn't and can't make commodities on his own; he must have people—workers—run his factory, farm his land, or excavate his mine. Rather than sharing the profits among the people who created them, however, the owner keeps as much as he can, instead paying workers a wage, almost always the lowest he can get away with, in exchange for the workers' time and effort. In other words, he exploits them. The profits he gains from their work he uses to live lavishly and to invest in more commodity production, increasing the amount of profits he can grab.

The workers get the privilege of not starving to death.

This is all completely natural to us: in our daily lives, we don't often question that a store or factory owner should be allowed to steal the profits we create when we work or that we should have to spend money to have things people like us created. We don't question that we should have to work for a boss and pay a landlord to keep our stomachs full and a roof over our heads. We accept that the police and the state, through laws, courts, and violent armed action, guarantee that the owners of stores, companies, and apartment buildings can take our money and time on their terms, and that the boss can fire us and the police can evict us, arrest us, or even kill us if we try to live otherwise.

But this society built around the "natural" laws of commodities and profits is both historically novel and relatively young. It is also structurally unambiguously colonial and white supremacist. For three hundred years, as capitalism and commodity society developed in this hemisphere, the great wealth of the European empires was built on slave-produced commodities: the silver mined from Peru and Mexico, the sugar and tobacco raised in the Caribbean, the cotton grown in the American South. African people were enslaved to produce commodities on lands stolen through the genocide of the Indigenous people of the Americas. The two great forms of property of the New World were land and slaves, both racialized. Historian of settler colonialism Patrick Wolfe argues that as the concepts of the commodity and private property were established, the primal, ideal commodity was the enslaved African—she existed exclusively for the further production of commodities and profits—and the purest property was stolen Indigenous land—it could be exploited, profited from, and expanded without concern for its historical and social role.[17] It was the wealth of the New World that produced sufficient surplus for the creation of capitalism.

Racial settler colonialism is thus at the core of all modern notions of property. All our beliefs about the righteousness of property, ownership, and commodity production are built on the history of anti-Black violence and settler-colonial extraction. The right to property is innately, structurally white supremacist: support for white supremacy involves a commitment to property and the commodity form.

To protect this system of property and commodity, to stabilize this racist violence and patriarchal domination, the owners and ruling classes organized and developed nation-states to enforce their will where the "laws" of the market failed to do so. Their particularly novel innovation for this task was the police, the first citywide bureaucracies in the West, evolved from slave patrols and colonial administrators, and instituted to protect property, control urban crowds, and repress slave revolts.

Looting, especially when committed by racialized people rising up against the police and the state, cuts straight through the heart of that history. It shows that goods can be had for free if we all fight together, and that we would be able to live without a wage if we freely shared the products of society. It publicly and communally disregards the store owner's property rights and demonstrates that those rights are only upheld by the violence of the police. That is why looting, which is, after all, akin to mass shoplifting, is treated as a crime deserving of the death penalty: during riots, police shoot looters on sight. The police exist to prevent Black people and poor people from threatening rich white people's property rights: abolishing property is a direct attack on their power.

In striking a blow against the laws of the commodity, looters also strike against white supremacy: in an antipolice uprising for Black liberation, looting is a directly effective and sensible tactic. No wonder it is so despised.

To support the arguments and claims made here, to understand the use of looting at this moment and in the future, this book takes the perhaps paradoxical-seeming turn toward history, more specifically the history of looting, from slavery to the present. In doing so, I follow in the footsteps of the Black Radical Tradition, as well as many other (sometimes overlapping) veins of liberatory and revolutionary thought, from Indigenous and anticolonial thinkers to anarchist and communist revolutionary traditions.

Throughout his life, across his body of work, James Baldwin returned again and again to a certain way of reckoning with history: "History . . . is not merely something to be read. And it does not refer merely, or even principally, to the past. On the contrary, the great force of history comes from the fact that we carry it within us, are controlled by it in many ways, and history is literally *present* in all we do." For Christina Sharpe, scholar of English literature and Black studies, Black life and racial capitalism today must be understood as existing "in the wake" of the Middle Passage, in the ongoing processes, violences, and social forms of anti-Blackness initiated in that genocidal kidnapping across the Atlantic and echoing down into the present. As a reflection of these facts, political prisoner Mumia Abu-Jamal has said, "True history tells us more about today than about yesterday."[18]

This conception of history is consonant with the Jewish tradition in which I was raised. Every year at Passover, one of the two most important holidays of the calendar, Jews gather together with family and friends to retell the story of Jewish enslavement and Moses-led deliverance in Egypt. This ritual, the annual act of remembering the horrors of slavery and the joys of emancipation, is one of the most important traditions

holding a diasporic people together *for three thousand years.* If this has
been the long historical wake of slavery and emancipation for Jews, how
could we begin to understand the ongoing effects of four centuries of
industrial chattel slavery, which only ended—and even then, only technically—a mere 150 years ago? It appeared to me that any Jewish ethics
must directly prioritize Black liberation.

Without reckoning with the direct, lived, *present* past, no movement
can truly change, heal, or care for our present, let alone produce a liberated future. And studying history has other advantages: with the benefit
of an overview of long historical durations, the accumulation of docu-
ments, and consistent study, it is in some ways easier to highlight the
meanings and effects of riots.

Studying history also has a vital abolitionist role. Ideology would have
us believe that capitalism, the nation-state, the police, prisons, and other
violent forms of oppression are timeless, infinite facts. If there have always
been police, across cultures, then there can never be a world without
them. But by understanding how recent these things are, and by tracing
strategies of resistance, struggle, and revolt against them, we can begin
to imagine a world otherwise.[19] This book is mostly a work of history,
a history based in the desire to break with this world and destroy all its
monstrous continuities.

But the study of history also has some serious problems and limits,
problems that are doubled in the study of rioting and looting. Resistance
is consistently underreported in the historical record. Those with power
over discourse and documentation, those in the media, universities, government offices, churches, and corporations, prefer not to widely report
or record forms of militant struggle for fear of its spreading and inspiring
others. If they record it, they slander it, underestimate its size or power,
misinterpret it, or exaggerate its failings. Meanwhile rebels and revolutionaries are often illiterate, isolated, imprisoned, killed, or otherwise
prevented from making sure their struggles end up in the archive the
way they lived them. So history must rely on stories passed down through
generations, accounts and interviews with participants, and the work of
radical archivists, historians, and academics.

Looting makes this problem of underreporting even deeper. During the Great Depression, for example, store owners were loath to even report organized looting *to the police* for fear that that would help it spread.[20] Few looters, meanwhile, are willing to discuss their own participation in looting. Rarely asked to speak, they are faced with universal condemnation from friend and foe—not to mention serious legal consequences—and so they rarely argue their own case in public after the fact.

I am not, myself, a trained historian with institutional access. As such, my methods have largely been to rely on secondary sources, online archives and videos, and the work of other historians, academics, and revolutionaries.[21] I have also focused almost entirely on looting in the so-called United States of America, a serious flaw that it would take at least another few book-length studies to correct. I hope that the effect of encountering the stories, theories, and accounts I've traced and gathered together might help comrades in the struggle and inspire others to do the work, research, and critique necessarily lacking herein.

We are again living through historically transformative times, in an era of looting, of riot, revolt, and revolution. This time we face a resurgent global Far Right and ecological disaster beyond our comprehension. We cannot afford to leave the revolution half-done: the planet simply cannot survive it. But we needn't be afraid. The future is ours to take. We just need to loot it.

chapter one | # THE RACIAL ROOTS OF PROPERTY

T HE UNITED STATES OF AMERICA IS BUILT ON AFRICAN SLAVERY AND
Indigenous genocide. This simple fact is the premise from which any
honest study of American history must begin. Property, state, government, and economy in America rise from these pillars of racialized dispossession and violence—slavery and genocide—and any change made
that does not upend this history, that does not tear these pillars to the
ground in a process of decolonization and reparations, does not deserve
the name justice.

Although US history is predominantly the story of the continuation of
this violence, it is also full of moments, movements, and images of a life
lived otherwise, of resistance, liberation, and transformation. One of the
most consistent images from this other world to come, one that terrifies
even many of those who claim to be partisans of that world, is of the Black
looter, who finds her antecedent in the escaped and fugitive slave.

To fully understand this, it is necessary to trace how this image developed, to see how white supremacy and the racial regime of property—what
preeminent historian Cedric Robinson calls racial capitalism—evolved
out of Euro-American chattel slavery and (ongoing) settler colonialism.[1]

The first slaves in the "New World" were not Africans but Indigenous Americans. Columbus had barely disembarked in the Bahamas before deciding that the people there "would make fine servants." It was Indigenous slaves who built the great wealth of the Spanish empire, mining silver from Potosí in Bolivia and from the Mexican plateau throughout the sixteenth and seventeenth centuries. Much of this specie was siphoned off by Dutch, Genoan, and German bankers and merchants, who had grasped the nature of the coming market economy much better than the Spanish monarchy did.* This mineral wealth was the material basis and political focus of European mercantilism, the system that would give rise to the bourgeoisie and lay the groundwork for industrial capitalism. This wealth was produced by enslaved Americans (and Africans) under a genocidal slave labor regime that would reduce the Indigenous population of the Spanish colonies from fifty million at "first contact" to four million by the end of the seventeenth century. From its very beginnings, capitalism was built on the backs and the graves of the enslaved.[2]

In what would become known as the United States, the first colonial slave trade also traded in Americans, because it was considered best practice to ship Indigenous "servants" far away from their native land, where their knowledge of the local terrain and proximity to friends and family encouraged both escape and violent retribution. Thus, Indigenous peoples were swapped between New England and the Carolinas or sold from the continental colonies to the West Indies, and vice versa. This trade was crucial for the early colonies; Indigenous servants were one of the main exports during the first century of British colonial rule.[3]

Despite these precautions, Indigenous escape, insurrection, raiding, and war proved a constant threat to profit and stability. Combined with the fact that they were a "labor supply" succumbing to genocidal depopulation caused by both disease and systematic colonial policy, the Indigenous peoples of America were only temporarily the enslaved basis of the British colonial economy.

---

*Indeed, the fact that the Spanish paid in specie and thus increased the "real" wealth of England would be a major defense made by English slave traders of selling Africans to the Spanish colonies, despite the fact that, according to the economic commonsense of the period of mercantilism, trading with opposing empires was to be avoided at all costs.

This, historian Patrick Wolfe argues, is consistent with the labor logic of settler colonialism. A settler colony relies on the promise of "open land" or "virgin territory" as the material and ideological basis of its existence. The problem is that this "open land" is always already occupied. Thus, to capture the land, the settler colony must eliminate the Indigenous population through genocide, first by outright murder, later, by cultural destruction and assimilation. Yet, at the same time, laborers are required to transform that "virgin territory" into value for the colonizers, and a large and ever-expanding population of laborers is required to produce profits.

These two requirements—genocide of the Indigenous to take their land and justify the colony's existence and the expansion of the pool of laborers to increase profits—are obviously incompatible. As a result, Indigenous labor cannot be relied upon in a settler colony. Thus, in the early continental colonies, the colonists emphasized Indigenous "unsuitability" for the brutality of plantation labor, an unsuitability that would not, of course, protect Indigenous Americans from continued forced labor, dispossession, and ethnic cleansing.[4]

But more labor *was* desperately needed by the planters and merchants of the colonies, who had come to the New World, after all, to get rich. The answer to this problem, for the first sixty or so years of what would become the United States, was largely found in the system of indentured servitude. Working alongside enslaved African and Indigenous peoples, white and Black "indentured servants" toiled in the tobacco fields and built the towns of colonial America.

But these servants were not yet distinguished as "white" and "Black." Though the word *Negro* appears in Virginia's colonial records, it is used as a national, not racial, descriptor, deployed in the same way that people's nationality (Scotch, Irish, English) was.[5] In this "national" definition that used "Negro" to interchangeably refer to Africans of any provenance, be they from the Spanish Caribbean or recently kidnapped from West Africa, we can see that the collapsing of various African nationalities into Blackness already existed. But whiteness had not yet been fully formed in the early seventeenth century, nor the fatal equation white-over-black that would give both racial identities their full force in America.[6]

These indentured servants came to the colonies with contracts lasting generally from three to seven years, during which time they were to
serve at the absolute dictate of their master. After these terms expired,
they were promised not only freedom but also land and wages from their
former masters, called freedom dues. But for the first four decades of the
US-American colonies, working conditions were so dire that few servants
survived the length of their contracts.

In many ways, the peculiarly American systems of African slavery
would be tested and designed around indentured servitude, which would
expand rapidly during the tobacco boom in the mid-seventeenth century.* Servants were bought, sold, traded, kidnapped, or awarded to early
colonists by the Crown, other settlers, and various companies.[7] Though
some servants signed on voluntarily, hoping for a new start in America,
many were exiled criminals, orphaned children, or anti-English rebels
captured in Scotland and Ireland. Many, too, were kidnapped off the
streets of English cities by a particularly hated class of entrepreneurs
called "spirits."† Laboring on monocultural plantations, servants were
beaten, starved, branded, maimed, and killed with near impunity. Even
some of the horrors of the Middle Passage were practiced on English
servants, who, at the height of the servant trade from 1650 to 1680, would

---

*I should note here that the servant trade, though it took on many of the aspects of the
African slave trade, never reached the size and levels of technical organization present
in the African trade in later centuries. Nor would it last nearly as long or touch even a
fraction as many people. The servant trade was over before the end of the eighteenth
century. Even at its zenith, European servants were never enslaved indefinitely or hered-
itarily, could represent themselves in court, and became full citizens after their indenture. There exists a white supremacist myth about the horrors of the "Irish slave trade"
that contends that enslavement of Irish people lasted well into the nineteenth century
and was equally as violent and vicious as the African slave trade. This is a historical false-
hood—a white supremacist manipulation of the facts of indentured servitude. For more
on the Irish slave trade myth, see the work of Liam Hogan, in particular: "Debunking the
Irish Slaves Meme," a four-part series on Medium.

†Spirits would befriend and feed the gullible, drunk, or vulnerable on English city streets,
who would wake up the next morning not in their new friend's home but in a cage, to be
shipped to America (hence the phrase "spirited away"). So common and so hated were
spirits that in the late seventeenth century, to accuse someone on a Bristol or London
street of being one was sufficient to start a riot.

be "packed like herrings," locked belowdecks for weeks with barely any food and only a few feet to move.[8]

Similarly, Africans in the colonies had not all been reduced to chattel slavery. Though life terms were sometimes enforced in the Caribbean colonies in this period, many Africans in the early United States were not enslaved for life, but only under indenture contracts, and eventually went on to receive freedom dues, own land, even own white servants. As historian Barbara Jeanne Fields writes, "African slaves during the years between 1619 and 1661 enjoyed rights that, in the nineteenth century, not even free black people could claim."[9] African and European servants worked together, married, and escaped tobacco plantations together. It was not some preracial utopia of equality but rather a period of violent domination and frontier colonialism in which the specific tenets of white supremacy had not yet been fully developed, what Lerone Bennett Jr. calls an "equality of oppression."[10]

As the seventeenth century wore on, conditions in the colonies improved, and indentured servants started surviving their terms—and receiving their freedom dues—much more regularly, thus becoming more expensive. Plantation owners tried to squeeze more profit out of their workers, finding increasingly spurious reasons to extend the length of servitude, driving servants harder and harder in the fields. However, as Fields argues, English servants were crucially "backed up" by the history of struggle between British laborer and landowner, by centuries of conflict and negotiation passed down into the present as culture, precedent, and norms of treatment. Furthermore, news of servant mistreatment that reached England made it harder, and therefore more expensive, to capture or recruit new servants. There was thus a limit to how much planters could exploit English workers: they could not be made slaves for life; their progeny would not be born into permanent bondage.[11]

Africans had no such power in the English colonies, no such backup. And enslaving someone for life became more ghoulishly attractive when "life" meant more than just a few miserable years. This logic was reinforced by the threat of servant revolt. Bacon's Rebellion, the largest rebellion in the pre-Revolutionary colonies, taking place in 1676–1677, saw armed and aggrieved free Englishmen, joined by slaves and servants, loot

and burn the capital of Virginia and briefly take over the colony. This revolt, in which freemen joined servants in insurrection, increased distrust
of English servants among the planters and colonial governorship. Thus,
"the importation of African slaves in larger and larger numbers made
it possible to maintain a sufficient corps of plantation laborers without
building up an explosive charge of armed Englishmen resentful at being
denied the rights of Englishmen and disposing of the material and political resources to make their resentment felt."[12]

Though African slaves were present in the colonies from the beginning, "the law did not formally recognize the condition of perpetual
slavery or systematically mark out servants of African descent for special
treatment until 1661."[13] By the end of the seventeenth century, African
laborers were cheaper, served life terms, and had children born into slavery. Without the same history of struggle and thus a customary level of
expected treatment, an ocean away from their comrades, families, and societies, Africans were alone in America. White and Indigenous servitude
would continue through the eighteenth century—nearly 10 percent of
the white population of the colonies were still servants at the beginning
of the Revolution—but they were slowly and surely being replaced on
the plantations by African laborers.[14]

If, legally and socially, there was a space and time in which race-based
chattel slavery did not exist in the colonies, could American capitalism
have developed some other way? Some claim that Europeans acting as
tenant farmers, yeomen, and merchants might have been perfectly viable in Virginia and the Carolinas, much like they were in the Northern
colonies, and that, therefore, slavery was not necessary. But the Northern
colonies' economies were built almost entirely upon exporting their food,
livestock, and small commodities to the sugar colonies of the West Indies, which, as a result of slavery-based plantation monoculture, did not
produce enough of their own. Northern merchants, meanwhile, made
much of their wealth building ships for the Triangle Trade and making
rum and molasses from slave-produced sugar. New York City's insurance
and financial institutions—Wall Street—were largely built through providing capital for the slave trade. Without the support of the continental
colonies, Britain could never have developed its sugar monopoly, but the

reverse is also true: without the sugar monopoly, the continental colonies would have ended in failure. Quite simply, there is no American economy, North or South, without slavery.[15]

Indeed, the incredible profits reaped from the English slave economies in the Caribbean and on the North American continent—a surplus of 50 percent or more on investments made by British capital—were the cash basis of the growth of industrial production occurring in England and the European continent through the period, and, thus, a key factor in the growth of European capitalism. Planters deposited their incredible wealth with bankers and bought new luxury goods from merchants, who would then reinvest this money in infrastructure, entrepreneurial firms, and agricultural improvements in England. Back in England, where the majority of the population was still transitioning out of subsistence agriculture, the goods produced in the colonies helped form an incentive to drive peasants into cash markets and capitalist labor relations. As historian Robin Blackburn writes, "The availability of tobacco, brightly coloured cotton goods, sweetened beverages, cakes and preserves, helped to tempt Britons into greater participation in market exchanges and greater reliance on wages, salaries and fees."[16] Thus slavery strengthened the English bourgeoisie, enriched British and continental banking and merchant firms, and helped create the modern English working class.* It's not just America: industrial capitalism is impossible without New World slavery.

But capitalism is a system ideologically committed to free labor—though the freedom in "free labor" is the freedom to starve. The maximum development of profit for the bourgeoisie relies on a free labor market, on the reproduction of a proletariat with nothing to sell but their labor power. It is necessary that individual capitalists be able to manipulate their workers' labor hours, for example, via hiring and firing, to

---

*As Cedric Robinson points out, even this "English working class" was hardly a unified subject but was, as it formed, deeply riven by racial hierarchy, with Irish laborers at the bottom, and Scottish, Welsh, and more recently West Indian and Asian workers below "English" workers proper. These divisions, though briefly overcome in the Chartist movement, were a crucial factor in limiting English working class radicalism in the nineteenth century (Cedric Robinson, *Black Marxism*, 2nd ed. [Chapel Hill: University of North Carolina Press, 2000], 45–52).

respond to developments in the productive forces and swings in demand
within the market.

What Southern agriculture discovered is that this can be achieved
without free laborers. Plantation owners frequently "hired out" farm-
hands to other owners or temporarily hired skilled slaves from other areas or industries. Southern cities of the nineteenth century were filled
with communities of such laborers, who earned a wage much like a
free worker did, the difference being they did so only at their enslavers'
pleasure and they were required to turn over most of their income every
week—as many proletarians in America today turn over all their wages to
debtors and landlords.

Frederick Douglass spent some of his bondage working as a ship
caulker in Baltimore and, like many others, deceived his enslaver about
how much he was actually making, thus secreting funds for his escape.
Many of these workers lived miles distant from their enslavers—indeed,
it is precisely these urban communities of relatively independent Black
people that would lead to the earliest development of police departments,
as gangs of slave catchers evolved into formalized slave patrols designed
to keep these "slave quarters" under surveillance and control.[17]

Still, the main way capitalists increase profits is to drive down the cost
of production, of which the largest part is usually the price of labor. This is
done by maintaining a large body of unemployed proletarians, thus making workers replaceable and allowing employers to fire insubordinate,
disabled, sick, or pregnant workers, while using the threat of unemployment to coerce the rest into working more hours for less pay. Agricultural
slave labor, therefore, intuitively seems hard to make cheaper. With no
threat of losing their wage nor any real promise of advancement, and
with no unemployed people liable to take a slave's position—slavery is a
system of 100 percent employment, after all—the enslaved tend to work
the bare minimum required to avoid punishment and are less reliably
coerced by speedups and expanded managerial demands.

But research increasingly reveals that, rather than merely delay profit
growth, this "dilemma" of enslaved labor saw overseers develop some of
capitalism's most powerful (and erroneously considered modern) man-

agement techniques. The earliest examples of employee surveillance, individual performance assessment, traceable units of production, detailed record keeping, and employee incentivization—all key concepts in modern management theory—occurred on slave plantations.[18]

Nevertheless, certain models of historical teleology persist in calling slavery "pre-capitalist," or just primitive accumulation, a necessary condition for capitalism's growth but something ultimately overcome by actual, real industrial capitalism. This relies on a definition of capitalism that considers the wage the most important defining feature of capitalism, a definition that underestimates the importance, for example, of the totally necessary unwaged reproductive labor that predominantly falls to women under capitalism: housework, emotional care, and the literal reproduction of the working class. In these models, unwaged labor becomes not a central component of capitalism but a supporting side effect, an arbitrary management tactic.

Other scholars have argued that capitalism eventually abolished slavery as inefficient, unprofitable, or immoral. But they ignore the fact that, even though formal slavery and the slave trade ended in the Americas in the nineteenth century, the enslavement of prison populations in the United States continues to this day, not to mention that colonial slave regimes in Africa and Southeast Asia expanded vastly at the very moment of American emancipation. When Brazil abolished slavery in 1888—the last country in the Americas to do so—King Leopold II of Belgium's genocidal domination of the Congo was but three years old. From 1885 to 1908, almost all the people of the Congo Basin, along with thousands kidnapped from other parts of Africa, were forced into slavery.

The sinisterly named "Congo Free State" saw fifteen million people worked to death on rubber plantations, starved by monoculture-produced famine and drought, murdered by colonial overseers for failing to meet rubber or ivory quotas, killed on forced marches, or executed by militias for rising in rebellion. The rubber thus accumulated enabled the mass production of the bicycles and automobiles that would transform daily life in the Global North. Across the nineteenth and well into the twentieth century, capitalist development relied on enslaved, colonized labor.

Though one of capitalism's defining features is free labor, unfree and unwaged labor are endemic features of capitalist profit production, not holdovers from previous economic systems.

Still, slavery and capitalism are not identical regimes: slavery has existed across cultures and time periods, under various names, with differing centrality, at different levels of violence, and supporting divergent societies, whereas capitalism is a modern development that tends toward a global and homogenous social organization. And there is no question that the experience of the enslaved is fundamentally different from that of the worker. So then, how do we reconcile these two separable yet materially integrated and coproductive regimes without simply collapsing one into the other and thus losing sight of their specificities? One helpful step is to recognize the absolute centrality of race to the development of private property, and vice versa.

Racial domination is not a by-product of capitalism, nor one of a number of available strategies plucked from the ether of potential management paradigms, conveniently to hand. As we have seen, slavery and settler colonialism were necessary components of the formation and maintenance of capitalism. And slavery and settler colonialism couldn't be carried out, day by day, instinctively and across centuries, by millions of Euro-Americans, both rich and poor, without the formal, legal, psychological, and ideological frameworks of racism, white supremacy, and anti-Blackness.

Many historians have shown that strong, explicit racist ideology does not appear in the historical record in America until the revolutionary period, when the rights of man (and it is indeed man) became the defining philosophy of US politics. If the rights to liberty and property are inalienable, then what to do about all these people who are, very clearly, not in possession of liberty or the capacity of property ownership? What of these people who are the property of the men claiming all men have inalienable rights? Much like gender naturalizes and "explains" why women are not granted these inalienable liberties, the white Founding Fathers resolved this contradiction through race: Black men are not men, not really. As Fields writes, Black people "resolved the contradiction more straightforwardly by calling for the abolition of slavery."[19]

This contradiction finds its roots deep in European history and philosophy. The emergence of modern, explicit racial ideology is built on centuries of implicit racial and racialized power, a form of power absolutely fundamental to creating the division of labor, the construction of "Europe," whiteness, and the very possibility of private property.

Cedric Robinson demonstrates that racialized hierarchies were crucial to medieval European notions of nobility and the formation of serf and slave populations—for example, in Russia, serfs were imagined to have black bones, as opposed to the white ones of nobles. Myths about the bloodlines of Normans, Irish, and Scots justified differing levels of work and privilege in medieval and mercantilist England. Proto-racial hierarchies, as framed around notions of barbarians and outsiders, were also the key tool for structuring and disciplining the mercenary armies and the immigrant and migratory working populations of sixteenth- and seventeenth-century mercantilist statecraft.[20]

The contradiction between racial power and the liberal concept of inalienable rights to life, liberty, and property is visible throughout American history. One striking example occurred one hundred years before the Revolution, in the racialized conception of freedom visible in Bacon's Rebellion. In the infamous 1676 Virginia uprising, enslaved and servant, Black and white fought side by side, and some historians therefore celebrate this rebellion as a proto-democratic and revolutionary uprising. Much like the Civil War was about slavery, but with neither side originally fighting for emancipation, so was Bacon's Rebellion originally about "Indian policy," with a disagreement about how quickly genocide of the Indigenous people should be carried out. And, as in the Civil War, slaves joined the fight, changing the meaning of the struggle in their attempt to win emancipation.

The conflict was sparked by Nathaniel Bacon, a backcountry planter and settler living on the border of "Indian territory." He wanted to seize more land, and to do so advocated a more aggressive and immediate genocidal policy than that of the colony: total war on the natives. Berkeley, the English governor of the colony, disagreed. He recognized the strategic imperative to maintain provisional and relative peace—until, of course, the next time the colony needed to expand westward—rather than risk an all-out war they would almost certainly lose.

Bacon ignored Berkeley, and in the first act of the rebellion, in May 1676, gathered a militia to attack a group of Indigenous Americans. Not even attacking a "hostile" nation, Bacon's militia massacred a village of the British-allied Occaneechi. Governor Berkeley declared Bacon's mustering of the militia illegal. In response, armed supporters of Bacon stormed the capital and forced Berkeley to change his ruling and approve Bacon's commission as militia leader. This indicated the functional end of Berkeley's power, and Berkeley and his governmental assembly would eventually flee the capital.

Bacon's Assembly, the first and only formal government of the rebellion, was held in June 1676. It passed a number of new acts into colonial law, the most famous removing property restrictions on suffrage and giving democratic electoral control over parish priests to all free men of the colony, regardless of race. Bacon's sudden death in October 1676, followed by a series of military defeats—ending in a famous last stand made by a mix of Black and white servant-rebels—concluded the uprising, and the acts of Bacon's Assembly were repealed. Still, some historians hold up their expansion of voting rights and popular control as examples of early democratic policy in America.

Bacon's Rebellion is thus seen as an antecedent of the America Revolution. And, indeed, it is, though not in the way its defenders usually intend but because the first three acts of Bacon's Assembly all focused on pursuing total war against Indigenous Americans and confiscating Indigenous lands theoretically protected by British treaty.* European and Black servants fought together in the rebellion, which points to the fact that whiteness had not fully developed by then, but we can see in the first three acts of Bacon's Assembly that racialized structures of freedom-for-some were already well established.

This contradiction, between legal and social structures of racial oppression and democratic liberty, is the central epistemological frame-

---

*J. Sakai calls this contradiction "the dialectical unity of democracy and oppression in developing settler Amerika" (*Settlers* [Chicago: Morningstar Press, 1989]).

work of the modern European worldview. As philosopher Sylvia Wynter demonstrates, it is the constitutive principle of Rational Man; for Wynter, the key transition from feudal thought to enlightened reason centers around the replacement of God versus Man as the structuring dichotomy of society with that of reason versus lack of reason. Because, under feudalism, all people were subservient to the law of God, everything in "nature" served to verify the glory, power, and existence of God: nobles and kings were divinely ordained, the sun rotated around God's earth, and so forth. But once nature was no longer needed to perform this affirmation of the divine,

> another mode of nature, human nature, would now be installed in
> its place. The representation of a naturally ordered distribution of de-
> grees of reason between different human groups enable what might
> be called a homo-ontological principle of Sameness/Difference,
> figured as a by/nature difference of superiority/inferiority between
> groups, and could now function tautologically as the verifying proof
> of a . . . naturally caused status-organizing principle, a principle based
> on differential endowment of Reason (rather than of noble Blood)
> and verified dynamically in the empirical reality of the order.[21]

The emergence of reason and the subsequent reification of reason as the fundamental attribute of human nature is therefore completely premised on the creation of hierarchies of reasonable and unreasonable people. The enlightened, reasoned man can only exist in distinction to the (African, Indigenous, nonmale) person who lacks reason; the idea of universal humanity is premised on human difference from and opposition to the less- or nonhuman person, a racialized and racializing difference.

In practice, this means that anything is justified in introducing reason to those who lack it, because, lacking it, that person is cast outside what Wynter calls the "sanctified universe of obligation"; in other words, they are not entitled to those same protections colloquially referred to as basic human decency. This principle, "verified dynamically in the empirical reality of the order," is the ideology of progress: domination, colonialism, and the expansion of capitalism become justice, the end of poverty, and the spread of culture, science, and truth. As Wynter shows, in the colonial period this humanist structure was used to justify genocide of Indigenous Americans. Spanish colonists encountering what they understood as senseless human sacrifice (as opposed to rational, sensible wars of religion or conquest) used it as proof that the Indigenous societies they confronted lacked reason. In the name of God, yes, but as He is now the God of reason and un-reason's innocent victims, Spanish colonists claimed they not only could but also were morally obligated to conquer this society.

This is the same logic that allows Bacon's Rebellion to expand the franchise while advocating wiping out the "primitive" Indians. The concepts of the individual and the human that constitute the basis for all rights, for all law, for "life, liberty, and the pursuit of happiness" were already and always built on a racial definition. But the phrase is an adaptation of a John Locke quotation that did not mention happiness: it was "life, liberty, and the pursuit of estate." This inalienable right to "estate," to property, would be the marker of the kind of subject recognized by this new government. But this also works in the other direction: to be able to own property is to be human, so those who cannot own property—be they enslaved, Indigenous, or even the children and wives of settlers—need not be recognized as fully human by the state.

In the early decades of the colonial era, it was illegal to enslave Christians in perpetuity. But as the theological explanation of the world gave way to reason, the justification for enslaving people also transformed: only barbaric, uncivilized, and "reason-lacking" people can be enslaved. And, as Wynter shows us, because this is a tautological structure that verifies itself through what has already come to pass, Africans, who were by the turn of the seventeenth century "easier" to enslave than Europeans, became just such a "reason-lacking" people. Africans came to stand for lack of reason itself. Because people lacking reason were not human, they were only capable of *being* property, not owning it. Although the more liberal-minded settlers believed that with education and uplift some select Black people might become capable of humanity, they did not challenge the basic framework by which most Africans were deemed inhuman. Black people became, legally, socially, and ideologically, property.

American power and property developed along two racial axes: the genocidal dispossession of the indigene and the kidnap and enslavement of the African. As historian Patrick Wolfe writes in *Traces of History*, this is core to the worldview of John Locke, preferred property theorist of the Founding Fathers, who argued "in texts that would profoundly influence Euro-American colonial ideology, private property accrued from the admixture of labor and land. As this formula was color-coded on the colonial ground, Blacks provided the former and Indians the latter."[22] Property in America is only possible through this racial accumulation.

The stolen land and enslaved people were together by far the most valuable property in America, from the earliest days of the colonies up to 1860. The establishment in American jurisprudence of absolute rights to property and the inviolability of contract would occur in an 1810 Supreme Court ruling, *Fletcher v. Peck*, that centered around a massive expansion of slave territory in Georgia. That is why legal scholar Anthony Paul Farley argues that "the black is the apogee of the commodity." Blackness, he writes, is a way of marking certain bodies as owners and certain bodies as owned. Simone Browne calls this mutual process of racialization and propertification the "making and marking of blackness as property."[23]

Just as Blackness marks a person as (potential) property, whiteness also cannot be understood outside of property relations: the characteristic of "whiteness" is the thing white people have that makes them legal subjects, owners, and human beings. We tend to think of property as tangible things, items or commodities, although we also understand ideas of intellectual property and copyright. *Property*, in other words, also includes rights, protections, and customs of possession passed down and ratified through law. Whiteness emerges as the race of people who are neither Indigenous nor enslavable—national identities are increasingly collapsed around the distinctions of slave/free and Black/white. As legal scholar Cheryl Harris writes in her seminal text "Whiteness as Property," "Whiteness defined the legal status of a person as slave or free. White identity conferred tangible and economically valuable benefits and was jealously guarded as a valued possession, allowed only to those who met a strict standard of proof."[24] Property law emerges to codify, formalize, and affirm white enslavement of Africans and conquest of the Americas, to protect, project, and strengthen whiteness.

This can be seen as white settlers came in conflict with Indigenous landholders. Settlers claimed, absurdly, that they were the "first possessors" of the land. "Only particular forms of possession—those that were characteristic of white settlement—would be recognized and legitimated. Indian forms of possession were perceived to be too ambiguous and unclear."[25] Law develops to codify whiteness and to give technical description and explanation to the genocide-accomplished fact of settler-colonial conquest. Access to certain forms of power, legality, and personhood—property-in-whiteness—was a prerequisite for access to property in land or slaves: whiteness became the meta-property from which all other private property flows and is derived.*

Not only is capitalist development completely reliant on racialized forms of power, but bourgeois legality itself, enshrining at its center the right to own property, fundamentally relies on racial structures of human nature to justify this right. Private property is a racial concept, and race, a propertarian one.

But what happens when this ultimate commodity, the slave, refuses to be property? This refusal, practiced over and over again, across and against the whole history of the United States, expressed in art, music, poetry, and dance, in religious fervor and revolutionary organization, in violent confrontation with the state and the cunning avoidance of it, in prison breaks and intellectual breakthroughs, has not yet been fully consummated. That is because the owners have always victoriously reasserted their great big YES, that yes of the police, the prisons, the plantations, redlining, borders, Jim Crow, failing schools, gang injunctions, slave patrols, cultural appropriation, housing courts, lynch mobs, unemployment, and the countless other aggressions, micro and macro, that reassert the commodifying mark every day in all its violence. As Blackness became a way to signify and describe those who can be and had become property, the radical consummation of that refusal would mean

---

*A similar process occurs through patriarchal domination, whereby being head of household—legal ownership of a family's children and women—was the basis for citizenship.

at minimum the abolition of the entire system under which things can be commodified. Revolution.

Such a revolution, against white supremacy, property, and their fundamental intersection, was taken up by the enslaved of the United States, en masse, with the strategy of refusal that had proven most successful across the preceding centuries: escape from the plantation. And though this revolution would only destroy legal slavery and not everything it meant, defended, and reproduced, it is evidence of the revolutionary potential of abolishing property, of joining together and expropriating the owners. The revolutionary potential of looting.

| # LOOTING EMANCIPATION

WHO FREED THE ENSLAVED? ANY SCHOOLCHILD CAN TELL YOU IT was Abraham Lincoln. Most adults would agree, perhaps adding that it was what the Union fought for in the Civil War.

The social revolution in the South that ended slavery might have been impossible without the Civil War and the Union Army, and it's true that the *legal* end of chattel slavery was brought about by Lincoln and the Thirteenth Amendment.* But it was despite the intentions and desires of Lincoln and the North, not because of them, that the enslaved achieved emancipation, dragging Lincoln and the Union Army kicking and screaming behind them. The enslaved freed themselves.

They did so with an act of mass looting and strike that shook the regime of white supremacist capitalism to its core: they stole themselves from their masters and, in so doing, abolished a huge percentage of America's wealth, a wealth, according to historian David Roediger, "equal to the combined value of all capital invested in manufacturing, railroads,

---

*The Thirteenth Amendment left an exception allowing forced labor in the situation of legal and carceral punishment. As many in the prison abolition movement have argued, this work-in-jail-for-free clause means slavery has never actually legally ended in America.

and banks, as well as all currency in circulation and all federal expenditures."[1] Almost entirely illiterate, forcibly barred from gathering and organizing, ostensibly kept ignorant of current events, they nevertheless recognized, well before the planters who enslaved them or the Union generals who would be the instruments of their liberty, what opportunity the Civil War really held: Jubilee, the end of slavery, and the coming of their emancipation. They took it.

Though we may question it and struggle against it, our default sense of history, like our default idea of politics, is a story of leaders, laws and wars, important dates and formal treaties. Such a historical lens can't help but misrecognize the political will and communal intelligence behind the massive, decentralized direct actions that mark all revolutionary moments. Instead, five hundred thousand enslaved persons escaping in the span of four years is treated like some individualistic, apolitical phenomenon called "opportunism"—a crime rioters and looters are always accused of. The history of the Black Atlantic, however, reveals that enslaved populations across the centuries have always recognized political crises among their enslavers as the best moments to organize and get free.

The most famous example of this, of course, is the Haitian revolution. News of the French Revolution's beginnings in 1789 sent the French sugar colony of Saint-Domingue into turmoil. While different political factions struggled, both in Saint-Domingue and in the revolutionary National Assembly back in Paris, the enslaved workers, the vast majority of the island's population, watched, waited, and formed a plan of revolt. On the night of August 21, 1791, the enslaved rose up in a coordinated and furious attack and, within ten days, had burned dozens of plantations and taken over the entire Northern Province of the colony.*

These masses would eventually form great armies, overthrowing the colonial government and taking over the island. By 1804, after defeating the colonial government, the Spanish, the British, and Napoleon Bonaparte, the independent Black nation of Haiti had been established. The Europeans and the United States have never forgotten this history of lib-

---

*The signal to rise up was famously given a week before, on August 14, at a Vodou ceremony in Bois Caïman, attended by representatives from the surrounding plantations and led by a fugitive: revolutionary leader and high priest Dutty Boukman.

erty at their expense, and the tiny country of Haiti, the result of the first victorious anticolonial and antislavery struggle in the Americas, has been punished by economic sanction, debt, invasion, war, boycott, and neocolonialism ever since.

But it wasn't only Haitians who used political conflict to break their bonds. The overthrow of the July Monarchy in 1848 and the rise of the Republic of France saw an abolitionist government installed in Paris. Though this new government would formally abolish slavery in the remaining French sugar colonies, the enslaved of Martinique did not wait for Paris's help. They deserted plantations in the thousands, forcing the colonial administrators of Martinique and Guadeloupe to abolish slavery *before* the order from the new government to do so could arrive across the Atlantic.[2]

In the United States, meanwhile, as many as a hundred thousand people, near 20 percent of the colonial slave population, escaped slavery during the course of the American Revolution—including some slaves of Thomas Jefferson and George Washington, fugitives who no doubt had a more expansive idea of freedom than their enslaving Founding Fathers—making it the largest slave revolt in United States history until the Civil War.[3]

The American Civil War is largely remembered as a clash of armies, but its historical meaning and significance were mostly determined by a social revolution in the South, what W. E. B. Du Bois called the "general strike of the slaves." The enslaved rose up, fled the plantation, picked up arms to destroy their former enslavers, and took history into their hands. The fight for emancipation in the United States did not begin in the Civil War, and neither did it end at the war's conclusion.[†] The fugitive escaping slavery is as old as the colonies. Her history is necessary to understanding the course of and possibilities for revolution in the United States.

[†]Nor, indeed, did the Civil War simply begin in 1861 at Fort Sumter and end at Appomattox in 1865. For the "Civil War" here, I use Du Bois's expanded period of revolutionary transition and social instability, from 1854—with Bloody Kansas and the fight to expand/contain slavery—to 1877—when the Republicans betrayed and ended Reconstruction and withdrew troops from the South in exchange for the Hayes presidency.

Similarly, the Confederate Army did not spring from thin air, but evolved from what Du Bois called the "armed and commissioned camp to keep Negroes in slavery and to kill the black rebel," the proto-police state the antebellum white South became after the Revolution.[4] Nor was this armed camp destroyed utterly in the crucible of war and defeat, but rather reformed itself as the white vigilantes and police forces (themselves often indistinguishable) of the following Reconstruction and Jim Crow eras. The white industrialist North, labor and management alike, had gone into the war not to abolish but to contain slavery (and thus Black people) in the agrarian South, and it would continue afterward to attempt to restrict Black movement and resist Black migration north and westward.

White people north and south thus united after the war to maintain what theorist Saidiya Hartman calls the "tragic continuities in antebellum and postbellum constitutions of blackness."[5] These continuities would mean—after a brief and often revolutionary interregnum known as Reconstruction—such economic, social, and political oppression that Frederick Douglass, in 1888, only eleven years after the end of Reconstruction, would denounce emancipation as a "stupendous fraud."*

Still, despite these bleak facts, the decades of the Civil War and the self-emancipation of the enslaved are a crucial hinge point in American history. The violent collapse of slavery dramatically accelerated a series of economic and political transformations already under way: a market driven by the rural production of agricultural staples giving way to one driven by urban industrial outputs; political power shifting from south to north and west, from planters and merchants to bankers and industrialists. The results of these changes would form the cornerstones of the modern American state.

More important to our story and the possibility of revolution in America is the legal and ideological transformation of Black people from slaves

---

*As Saidiya Hartman asks: "How does one adequately render the double bind of emancipation—that is, acknowledge the illusory freedom and travestied liberation that succeeded chattel slavery without gainsaying the small triumphs of Jubilee?" (Saidiya Hartman, *Scenes of Subjection: Terror, Slavery and Self-Making in Nineteenth Century America* [Oxford: Oxford University Press, 1997], 12).

into criminals, the formal transition of slave patrols into police, and the increasing organization of Black people in America as a political, social, and revolutionary force.

In the center of all these transformations is the fugitive slave. Winning her emancipation singly, in groups and en masse, stealing through dark swamps and across busy roads, dodging the slave catchers and outwitting police patrols, she moves unseen on the edges of history, changing it inexorably with her flight. To find herself, she must steal and abolish white property, must abolish herself-as-property. She strikes fear into the heart of white society because she reveals just how flimsy their regimes of property, power, and domination can be in the face of her jailbreak for freedom.

This specter of slaves freeing themselves is American history's first image of Black looters.

IN DESCRIBING THE ORGANIZED FREEING OF THE ENSLAVED AS "LOOT-ing" I am committing an anachronism. As we saw, *loot* does not appear as an English word until 1845, and the word *looter* first appeared in 1858. Nevertheless, it is easy to imagine that Nat Turner, John Brown, Harriet Tubman, and other revolutionaries—already referred to as robbers and criminals—would have been called looters. For they were engaged in nothing less than the open, organized, and criminal expropriation of white property.

The enslaved themselves, more than their putative masters, even described what they did as stealing. As Saidiya Hartman writes: "When the enslaved slipped away to have secret meetings, they would call it 'stealing the meeting,' as if to highlight the appropriation of space and the expropriation of the object of property necessary to make these meetings possible. Just as runaway slaves were described as 'stealing themselves,' so, too, even short-lived 'flights' from captivity were referred to as 'stealing away.'"[6]

As Hartman analyzes, even "small" acts of liberty and pleasure, such as going to a prayer meeting, a dance, or visits with families and lovers, were understood as having to be stolen. This produces a helpful and liberating contradiction, for "property can't steal property." In looting themselves and in "stealing away," the enslaved not only abolished themselves as property but also pointed to the absurd paradox implicit in property itself. The act, Hartman notes, challenges and threatens the entire regime; it "reconsiders the meaning of property, theft, and agency."[7]

However, much like a single riot or a single instance of looting does not in itself endanger the system of property, a single fugitive did not in herself threaten the total system of slavery. Robin Blackburn argues that "to run away . . . could still impose a cost, but a very unequal one. The owner lost the value of the slave but was rid of a problem."[8] Of course, the power of the owner is crucial. A CVS store is certain to be riot-insured and operating with a huge margin, whereas a struggling business might not be able to afford an extended closure and thus could be ruined by a riot; similarly, a large plantation owner might be okay with seeing his most rebellious property away, whereas a small white farmer who enslaved only one or two people might be ruined. And though individual enslavers might do whatever they could to recapture a fugitive, some of them understood that, as a class, owners benefited from the way escapees functioned to relieve pressure within the plantation. Individual instances of rioting and looting can similarly have a medium-term positive effect for the regime of racial capitalism if they are not soon repeated or taken further, instead functioning as "safety valves," diffusing anger and releasing tension. But this benefit is utterly lost in the long sweep of history.

Just as riots and uprisings produce a new generation of revolutionaries, so too did the fugitives provide the basis for the abolition movement of the antebellum period. As W. E. B. Du Bois writes in *Black Reconstruction*: "Not only was the fugitive slave important because of the actual loss involved, but for potentialities in the future. These free Negroes were furnishing a leadership for the mass of the black workers, and especially they were furnishing a text for the abolition idealists. Fugitive slaves increased the number of abolitionists by thousands and spelled the doom of slavery."[9]

This doom was finally brought upon the South at the height of the Civil War. From 1861 to 1865, five hundred thousand slaves escaped the

plantations, throwing down tools and often crossing Union lines to emancipation. As many as two hundred thousand of them served in the Union
Army. It is this incredible act of revolution that would both decide the
war and give it its meaning.[10] Du Bois called this movement the general
strike of the slaves.

This tremendous political action, this general strike, this mass looting did not appear from nothing or materialize "opportunistically" in the
face of war. Indeed, by 1860, before the general strike began, the number
of escapes had reached perhaps fifty thousand annually—many of those
escapees staying in maroon or free Black communities in the South and
some escaping for only a short time—meaning the general strike was
an acceleration and intensification of a movement already in process.[11]
The number of fugitives steadily grew from 1830 onward, with a marked
increase in militancy after the Fugitive Slave Act of 1850.*

Fugitives played a crucial role in the end of slavery well before
their great revolutionary moment. In the face of the movement of ever-
increasing maroonage, the Democratic Party pushed the Fugitive Slave
Act into the Compromise of 1850: this law was a central component of
the political crisis that led to the outbreak of the Civil War. The act not
only made harboring a fugitive in a Free State a federal crime, not only
gave slave catchers jurisdiction over the entire North, not only removed
any legal proceedings beyond the enslaver's testimony, but also *obliged
all citizens* to actively participate in capturing fugitives.

This law didn't stem the tide of fugitives, but it did galvanize the abolition movement, which grew increasingly militant in the face of the law's
overreach: across the North, former slaves and free people armed themselves and started speaking not just of abolition but of revolution. And it
convinced many Northern white politicians, intellectuals, and capitalists
of the fearful rise of the great "Slave Power," an anxiety not about slavery
itself but about a lack of Northern political sovereignty within the federal
government. This fear helped lead to the rise of the Republican Party and
the political crisis that would become secession.

---

*Recognizing the role of the enslaved in their own emancipation is one reason to join
Du Bois in seeing the Civil War as beginning in the partisan combat of Bloody Kansas
in 1854.

And so the fugitive, finding her emancipation by escaping the plantation, pulled the tides of history toward emancipation for all.

FUGITIVES ON THE EVE OF THE CIVIL WAR WERE DRAWING ON A TRA-
dition of revolt and resistance that was hundreds of years old. Across
the Americas, throughout the centuries, the sleep of white plantation
owners, merchants, and governors was made fitful by the nightmare of
slave revolt. The enslaved, armed with guns, hoes and scythes, flaming
torches and unimpeachable vengeance, marched unceasingly across
their unconscious. As the years progressed, these dreams took on a less
spectral and more nameable shape: Toussaint L'Ouverture, Jean-Jacques
Dessalines, Denmark Vesey, Nat Turner, Gabriel, Haiti, Bahia, Stono,
Amistad.

Violent insurrections were only the most spectacular form of resistance. Poisoning enslavers, their kin, and their livestock, sabotaging
equipment, and burning buildings to the ground were common night
terrors of the enslaver. Suicide was also a common, tragic form of struggle against the slave regime. Less dramatic, more everyday resistances
abounded. Working slowly and inexpertly, pretending ignorance or in-
comprehension—despite the widespread use of the hoe in African agriculture—oversleeping, and other ways of rejecting the enslaver's labor
regime and lowering his profits were practiced wherever Africans were
enslaved.[12]

The most reliable form of resistance was flight. The very first known
enslaved Africans in what would become the United States, kidnapped
and brought to a small Spanish colony in the area of the Carolinas
around 1526, revolted, escaped their bondage, and lived out their lives
among Indigenous tribes.[13] Flight was not always permanent: the record
is full of the enslaved leaving only to visit family members and friends
on nearby plantations, to attend social events and religious gatherings, or
sometimes to strike, refusing to return to the plantation until demands
were met.[14]

In the early colonial days of what would become the United States, those who escaped permanently fled to Indigenous tribes to the uncolonized west or to the sparsely colonized Spanish territory of Florida to the south.* These fugitives also formed or joined secretive communities of escaped slaves in the swamps and hills around the plantations— maroon communities. Although maroonage is a more historiographically centered phenomenon in Brazil, Suriname, and the West Indies—for example, in Jamaica, where maroon communities fought famous guerilla wars with the colonizers—it was still considerably practiced in the United States.

During the colonial period, European, African, and Indigenous enslaved and indentured peoples escaped the plantation together to form maroon communities, with European maroons conveniently able to pass as legal citizens and thus trade with the colonies on behalf of the larger settlement.[15] Particularly large communities formed in the mid-Atlantic Great Dismal Swamp and across more sparsely colonized Florida.

The maybe six-thousand-square-mile Great Dismal Swamp, running through the borderlands of North Carolina and Virginia, was a known free and hostile community in the center of slavery's heartland. Maroons from the Dismal Swamp sent units to serve alongside the British in the Revolutionary War, and during "peacetime" they went on looting raids out into the surrounding slave country, stealing supplies and freeing the enslaved. In doing so, they developed guerilla tactics that would help them to free *thousands* during the Civil War.

In Florida, between 1817 and 1858, the federal government waged four decades of war to uproot the powerful autonomous Seminole communities, made up of African maroons and Creek Indians. These communities often sent looting raids into Virginia, Alabama, and Georgia to free family members and comrades, and their settlements were the destination of many fugitives from the Deep South. Remembered in history as the Seminole Wars, the federal government's military campaigns against

*Even in this early period, when Indigenous tribes attacked settler communities, they often left Black people unharmed. Though in some places Indigenous people enslaved Black people, in other places solidarity, co-maroonage, and rebellion were the norm.

them, which lasted for almost the entire antebellum period, started as slave-catching expeditions.

The so-called Second Seminole War, from 1835 to 1842, included the largest slave rebellion in American history outside of the Revolutionary and Civil Wars. The role of maroons in this war has been mostly left out of standard histories, but at least four hundred enslaved people looted themselves from Florida plantations to join the Seminoles in fighting the US government. A government terrified by Indigenous and Black solidarity waged the Seminole Wars, and these conflicts represent an important moment in the long tradition of armed self-defense in both insurgent communities. It is a tradition that liberal historians often try to explain away, but armed self-defense against the white supremacist state has always been a crucial part of movements for liberation.

Despite some victories, these protracted wars, at great cost to the US government in lives and money, eventually saw most of the Seminoles killed or forced to migrate to Oklahoma, Texas, or Mexico. Though the Seminoles were never fully defeated, these campaigns, along with the concomitant growth of plantations and white populations in US-American Florida, meant that as the nineteenth century wore on Florida became a less viable destination for fugitives. So, instead, many captives stole themselves North.[16]

THANKS TO THE CENTERING OF THE CIVIL WAR IN OUR STUDY OF THE history of slavery, and the telling of that history predominantly by the liberal white descendants of the Union—who like to pretend that white supremacy is a Southern condition—slavery is often wiped from the history of the Northern colonies. But Black and Indigenous captives of the Dutch built the first European settlements on the island of Manhattan;* Rhode Island was home to the two largest and most important colonial

---

*Indeed, the Dutch gave a large area of the west side of Manhattan, from what is now the West Village to Herald Square, as freedom dues to their African captives. But after the English took over, their colony of New York passed a law against African land own-

slave markets of the eighteenth century; and people were auctioned on the market squares and advertised in the newspapers of Philadelphia, New York City, and Boston.

The North's rocky soil and cold climate could not support large-scale cash-crop plantation agriculture—though something resembling it emerged in the fertile coastal areas of Rhode Island—so the Northern colonies never had nearly the same numbers of enslaved Africans living within them as did the South. But they still had slaves. And, as we've seen, the famous small farmer and independent merchant of New England, central to the story of the American Revolution, did most of his business with the slave colonies of the West Indies: New England often replaced Britain as the third point in the Triangle Trade.

The North did not abolish slavery out of some liberality of spirit. Instead, it saw slavery mostly materially destroyed by fugitives in the years of the American Revolution. Early in the war, the British promised emancipation to any slaves who joined their cause. Eventually, seeing the incredible effectiveness of this promise, so did colonial forces. Wherever the war went, the enslaved escaped behind its lines. But, as Russell Maroon Shoatz writes, though liberal historians "are fond of reminding everyone that Blacks provided over five thousand fighters to the colonist cause during that struggle," the enslaved favored the British, joining with them over the colonials at a rate of more than ten to one. At the war's end, some ten thousand Black people fled the colonies with the defeated army they had fought alongside, leaving the new United States on British ships.[17]

This does not mean that the British, still reaping massive profits from the slave trade and enslaving hundreds of thousands across their empire, had suddenly become the friends of the enslaved: the Crown's forces were merely the simplest and easiest vehicle of emancipation. Those who joined neither army fled otherwise. Tens of thousands used the confusion to flee to Indigenous and maroon communities, if not to Florida, then to Canada. Perhaps one hundred thousand, or 20 percent of the entire

ership. "Manhattan was thus twice stolen from oppressed peoples" (J. Sakai, *Settlers* [Chicago: Morningstar Press, 1989], 8).

colonial enslaved population, escaped during the conflict. And because much of the fighting happened in the North, a much higher percentage of the enslaved in New England, New York, New Jersey, and Pennsylvania, though a smaller absolute number, made it to freedom.

Northern slavery, thus considerably reduced from its relatively small position, was legally abolished in the years following the Revolution, with the last state to formally do so New Jersey in 1804. And yet, even this economically safe, mostly after-the-fact legal abolition was not carried out immediately and totally but was rather instituted gradually and partially by state governments. The law that abolished slavery in New York, passed in 1799, protected enslavers such that slavery only actually ended in the state in 1827. There were still hundreds of legal slaves in Pennsylvania and New Jersey in the 1840s.

And as African slavery began to disappear from Northern states, white people installed laws and practices discouraging free Black people from settling there that, to the modern eye, look an awful lot like Jim Crow. These included disenfranchising Black men, banning them from professional trades, and instituting harsher criminal sentencing for Black people. All this happened against the backdrop of extensive vigilante white violence. Frederick Douglass, escaping bondage and settling as a free man in New Bedford, Massachusetts, was barred from practicing his highly skilled trade of caulking. Despite the flourishing shipbuilding business in this major whaling port, Douglass was forced into low-waged general laboring. And New Bedford was an abolitionist stronghold! As a result of these proto–Jim Crow practices, despite the fact that many maroons would come to settle in the North, they were greatly outnumbered by white American birthrates and European settlers, and the percentage of the Northern population that was Black decreased by more than half between the signing of the Constitution in 1787 and the forming of the Confederacy in 1861.

At the same time, the enslaved population in the South grew exponentially, particularly after the introduction of the cotton gin and the resultant cotton boom of the early nineteenth century. With the expansion of slavery to the south and west, as America colonized Florida, the

Louisiana Territories, and Texas, fugitive routes to freedom increasingly pointed north.

MUCH AS POPULAR HISTORIES OF THE BLACK LIBERATION MOVEMENT of the 1960s often reduce it to MLK's dream, Rosa Parks, sit-ins, and Freedom Rides, the general sense of the antebellum abolition movement is as a largely white protest movement that mostly worked to change the hearts and minds of Northerners. It's true that propaganda campaigns, slave narratives, public rallies, and Northern organizing were crucial parts of the movement. But in the years leading up to the Civil War, it was a movement equally focused on militant direct action, whether through opposition to the fugitive slave laws or by the Underground Railroad.[18]

The Underground Railroad was equally not some group of friendly white Quaker homeowners who helped fugitives by hiding them in their extra rooms. Though such people existed, they were a minority of the decentralized network of militants, many of them fugitives themselves, most of them Black, who would come to be described by the umbrella term Underground Railroad. The Underground Railroad was extensive in the North, but it also led into Mexico, a western branch aided and organized in large part by Indigenous tribes and displaced Seminole maroons. This route became less viable, however, after the Compromise of 1850 made Texas an official slave state.

Lacking any overarching organization, illegal from the very outset, from the early nineteenth century until the Civil War, the Railroad laid its track all across the country. This widespread, horizontal group of freedom fighters was not a formal party or organization but, as historian Eric Foner describes it, an "interlocking series of local networks."[19] The Underground Railroad is believed to have helped as many as one hundred thousand fugitives to freedom in the North, with thousands more escaping to Mexico.

Underground Railroad stations stood as waypoints in a series of logistically and geographically distinct routes to freedom. The first station a

fugitive might encounter, if they fled slavery by foot, was a home at border points between slave and free territory, such as on the northern banks
of the Ohio River, where fugitives could hide out and wait for passage
farther north.

Their next stop might be facilitated by an urban "vigilance committee." Vigilance committees were among the most important stations on
the railroad and were set up as major hubs in cities such as Boston, New
York, Oberlin, and Philadelphia. These small, local action committees
sometimes comprised only a handful of people and were in constant
need of funds. Nevertheless, their records furnish much of the surviving
documentary history of the Underground Railroad. When things went
easily, committee members would receive word from stations farther
south or west and greet arriving fugitives as soon as they landed. But
they also scoured the neighborhoods around ports and train stations for
apparent fugitives who had managed to gain access to transport out of the
South and who had arrived alone or without a plan.

Upon arriving in a free town or city, many fugitives described asking
for help from the first Black person they saw, who often directed them to
the vigilance committee or a local station of the Railroad. Though the records are obviously biased toward those who successfully found the committees, evidence still points to the fact that this knowledge was widely
spread in free Black communities. Urban Black communities practiced
mutual aid, protection, and self-defense: abolitionist action was not only
taken by those who considered themselves activists.

The committees gave the fugitive shelter and food, investigated
whether they were being hunted, and organized legal counsel if needed.
They set up fugitives with work and housing locally if it was safe and
the fugitive wanted to remain, or they bought them rail tickets or ship
passage farther north. Fugitives frequently went on to Canada or to cities with a strong abolitionist community—such as New Bedford, where
Frederick Douglass settled—which meant they would be better protected
from slave catchers. When they arrived, they were then helped by activists who organized work and housing for them and often reunited them
with family or friends who may have been expecting them.

But vigilance committees didn't just protect the newly emancipated. The fugitive slave act of 1793 gave enslavers and their inheritors the permanent power to capture fugitives, no matter how long the fugitive had been free. And because the evidence required was minimal (and even this tiny legal hurdle was cleared by the Fugitive Slave Act of 1850, under which law, as historian Nell Irvin Painter writes, "a slaveholder need merely swear that a particular black person was his slave, and appointed commissioners and federal marshals would seize the purported fugitive"[20]), Black people born free were frequently kidnapped under this law and sent into slavery.

Vigilance committees would thus track the marshals and courts closely. With only nineteenth-century communication technologies, they had to mobilize quickly, because the legal proceedings to send a "fugitive" South often lasted less than twenty-four hours from the moment the person was kidnapped by slave catchers—American courts can work quickly when that speed serves white supremacy. Even so, the committees often prevailed upon lawyers to delay proceedings long enough for the kidnapped person to escape to freedom, and sometimes crowds gathered and physically attempted to free them from marshals and enslavers. These slave-freeing riots, these lootings, though they didn't always succeed, happened frequently enough in Manhattan to be a major impetus in the creation of the New York City Police Department.[21]

This entire "railroad journey" was done with great speed, seriousness, and secrecy and under the constant threat of danger and violence. When it went smoothly, it appeared a simple logistical procedure, but assisting fugitives was a federal crime and Underground Railroad militants were the declared enemies of the enslavers and the state. Many were jailed, (re)enslaved, or killed.

No role in the Underground Railroad was more dangerous than that of "conductor," however. Many of those souls who organized raids into the hearts of slave country itself, free men and women who led military incursions into hostile territory to help free the enslaved, never came back. And no conductor is so widely known as Harriet Tubman.

Tubman was recognized as a great leader, referred to by the enslaved and free alike as "Moses," an important and powerful designation in a time and among a population, as many have noted, that thought quite literally and directly in biblical references. But even during her life, white supporters described Tubman as "superhuman," as somehow fundamentally different from other ex-slaves. As biographer Butch Lee writes, "This made her less dangerous to them. Easier to handle. Less awesome. After all, picture a nation of Harriet Tubmans."[22]

Indeed, just as bourgeois history uses the most visible and famous movement leaders to obscure the great masses who make their leadership possible and legible, so does Harriet Tubman's heightened visibility serve to hide the thousands of operatives who ventured into slave territory every year to free slaves. As J. Sakai writes: "In 1860 we know that five hundred underground organizers went into the South *from Canada alone*."[23]

Harriet Tubman was only the most famous of a generation of militant warriors who fought for the total overturning of slavery by any means necessary. She lived a life of direct action. Born into slavery, Tubman never learned to read, but she became a brilliant military tactician. She planned and carried out nineteen separate raids into slave territory, usually going twice a year, often on foot, without ever being caught: one of her major strategic insights was to continue moving south some distance with the newly fugitive before heading north, because enslavers never suspected groups would head deeper into slave territory. Tubman bore a massive bounty on her head until the fall of slavery; she was the most wanted, and hated, woman in the South.

Tubman falling ill delayed John Brown—who called her "General Tubman"—from attempting to loot the armory at Harpers Ferry on the planned date of July 4, 1859. Had she been present when Brown carried out their plan on October 16, 1859, some have argued, she would have prevented Brown from making the tactical blunders—most notably, allowing a mail train to leave Harpers Ferry and thus bring news of the raid to the federal government—that led to his becoming a martyr and symbol rather than a victorious freedom fighter. And had Tubman and Brown's raid succeeded, the terms of the Civil War might not have been set by the slavocracy's secession but rather by a revolutionary slave army, as Terry Bisson imagines in his speculative historical novel *Fire on the Mountain*. But, much as the enslaved have been removed from the narrative of their own liberation, Tubman is erased from or made a footnote in the popular history of John Brown's raid.*

So, too, is her role, and the role of the enslaved in general, during the combat of the Civil War. Tubman is known as a spy for the Union Army, but again this is individualized and taken out of context. She is seen as "a lone superwoman spy for the white man's army," when instead she organized an intelligence network of river pilots, Black scouts, and slaves that kept the Union Army informed of enemy movements. Indeed, the importance to the Union effort of maroon intelligence and knowledge, both of local terrain and Confederate movements, cannot be overemphasized.

And Tubman's most dramatic military action, the Combahee River raid, is sometimes left out of popular histories altogether. In June 1863, during the height of Civil War combat, Tubman guided three hundred Black soldiers up the Combahee River in the middle of the night, deep into South Carolina plantation country. As a reporter's dispatch at the time described it, they "struck a bold and effective blow, destroying millions of dollars worth of commissary stores, cotton and lordly dwellings, and striking terror into the heart of rebeldom, brought off near 800 slaves and thousands of dollars worth of property, without losing a man or receiving a scratch."[24]

They set fire to four plantations and six mills and looted property and slaves from wealthy Confederates. Such an act, within the context of war, was celebrated by white supporters of the Union Army. But had it been carried out under "peaceful" circumstances, would it have been celebrated or seen as an act of violent looting, rioting, arson, and rebellion? The reaction to John Brown's failed raid, only four years earlier, gives us our answer: the US Senate set up a committee to prosecute anyone who had aided Brown, Abraham Lincoln called him "insane," and many

---

*It's not just Tubman: when I visited the John Brown museum in Harpers Ferry in July 2015, the exhibit about the Black men who fought beside him during the raid was relegated to a small, hard-to-find room away from the main halls.

liberal white abolitionists reacted with shock and outrage against his violent methods.

It is only the 20/20 hindsight of history—a vision corrected by the actions of the enslaved—that allows us to see property in human beings as the evil it was. At the time, it was as natural as the prisons and police are today. Only the thousands of abolitionists like Tubman, the millions of enslaved who rose up in revolt, flight, and strike and who overthrew the system of slavery, have allowed us to see slavery clearly.

WHEN THE SOON-TO-BE CONFEDERATE STATES WITHDREW FROM THE Union, starting with South Carolina on December 20, 1860, they did so ostensibly in response to the election of Abraham Lincoln. Lincoln was the presidential candidate of the six-year-old Republican Party, which had formed out of the ashes of a number of political parties—the Whigs, the Know-Nothings, and the northern half of the Democrats—all of whose national bases had fractured during the 1850s over the question of slavery.[25] But the Southern states that rose in reactionary secession against the United States did not do so because Lincoln threatened to end slavery but because he intended to keep it from spreading into the new territories of the American West.

The general strike of the enslaved meant that the Civil War would become a struggle over the existence of slavery, but, up until their great revolt, the total and immediate abolition of slavery was an extreme and unpopular political vision. Beyond the enslaved themselves, it was held mostly by freeborn Black people, ex-slaves, maroons, and a tiny handful of radical whites who had joined the abolitionist movement. The mainstream political battles over slavery in the 1850s were rather between the plantation class, who wanted slavery to expand into the territories of the West, and those who wanted the western territories to join the Union as "Free Soil."

The plantation owners, with pretensions of being European gentlemen, believed they were creating a New World historical slave empire and cultural center akin to Rome or Greece. To prove this, they spent money well beyond their means, imagining elaborate displays of conspicuous consumption and architectural splendor made them akin to European aristocrats. The massive, chronic debt thus accumulated—perhaps the main attribute they really shared with nineteenth-century European nobility—combined with increasing market pressures, meant that they needed to expand available plantation territory to increase their profits. They looked hungrily toward Mexico (which then included much of today's southwestern United States), California, and the Caribbean, where they saw the promise of endless plantations filled with African laborers. They rejected the Northern model of development, believing that the industrialist production of a professional middle class would mean less wealth accumulation at the top and that, furthermore, reliance on a massive white proletariat promised class war from the bottom.

The Free Soil movement, for its part, represented a cross-class alliance that, though it included abolitionists, was mostly made up of Northern capitalists, merchants, recent European immigrants, and organized labor. Capitalists looked to Haiti with horror and believed that it was *slavery* that produced unmanageably rebellious subjects. Some of America's first Nimbyists, they wanted to keep profiting off of plantation slavery as it existed, restrained to the South, but to use the "new" territory for mixed agricultural and industrial development carried out by a predominantly immigrant white settler workforce. The workers, who wanted to settle the land as homesteaders, joined them in this white supremacist vision: the expansion of slave plantations across the territory would leave no space for them to homestead.* Furthermore, just like racist anti-immigrant rhetoric holds today, many white workers and organized labor unions of the antebellum period believed that the mere presence of Black workers, enslaved or free, drove down wages.

---

*They did not foresee that Free Soil would betray them all the same and that the best land would be consolidated overwhelmingly by railroads and various corporations, leaving poor soil and hardscrabble lives for the homesteaders, who would by debt and manipulation largely be transformed into tenant farmers in the decades following the Civil War.

Neither side saw any problem with the fact that these territories were to be added to the United States by the violent conquest of their Indigenous residents, many of them already multiply displaced by America's genocidal expansion. The political conflict around slavery that precipitated the Civil War was, in other words, between two different white supremacist, pro-slavery, settler-colonialist visions of America's future.

Throughout this period, all branches of the federal government remained steadfastly pro-slavery. Congress passed the series of bills making up the Compromise of 1850, which, along with enacting the Fugitive Slave Act, guaranteed that slave states would retain their disproportionate power in the federal government. That compromise was the diplomatic coup of the moderate liberal president Millard Fillmore, but such mealy-mouthed liberal white supremacy would give way, in 1853, to a fiercely pro-slavery executive branch led by Democratic president Franklin Pierce. Pierce shepherded the disastrous Kansas-Nebraska Act through Congress, an act that would overturn federal restrictions on slavery's expansion and lead to the first stage of the Civil War, when guerilla combat between enslavers and abolitionists exploded in Kansas. Not to be outdone by the other branches of government, the Supreme Court in 1857 issued the Dred Scott decision, which ruled that Black people had never been allowed to be nor ever could be American citizens, that Congress was constitutionally unable to ban slavery in the territories, and that the federal government had no legal ground to free slaves whatsoever.

But this strong governmental support for slavery, driven by Southern Democrats, wasn't enough for the constantly anxious plantation class, who feared that the actual unification of Free Soilers within a single political party—the Republicans—threatened their goals and their future power in Washington. Still, Lincoln's election was more pretense than cause. Tubman and Brown's insurrection had flared up only a year previously, in October 1859, and, combined with the constantly growing movement of fugitives—reaching fifty thousand maroons per annum by 1860—and the always increasing "disorder" among urban communities of enslaved Black workers, insurgency seemed a much more immediate threat to slavery's existence than Abraham Lincoln. The planters believed they would be better armed legally and normatively to repress slave uprisings if they didn't have to confer with a North that just didn't understand the necessities of their peculiar institution.

Slavery was simultaneously more successful than it had ever been—the cotton crop of 1859 was almost twice the size of that of 1850—and facing more organized and concerted limits than ever before. Southern plantation owners believed they would not be able to compete politically or economically forever without the expansion of slavery's territory, and they believed that this was a fortuitous moment to force the issue. Arrogant in the face of their legislative successes, the planters overestimated their power and their popular support. And so the enslavers made their great historical gambit, counterrevolution by secession, and sealed their fate as a doomed class.[26]

WHEN THE SLAVE STATES OF SOUTH CAROLINA, MISSISSIPPI, FLORIDA, Alabama, Georgia, Louisiana, and Texas seceded from the United States and formed their own federal government, the Confederacy, in the winter of 1860, they did so under the banner of states' rights, with the aim of protecting and expanding slavery.* They hoped that their secession would be recognized by the North and that they would be allowed to split away.

The Confederate leadership's reasoning wasn't totally wrong-headed. They anticipated that Lincoln and the North quite possibly might accept a peaceful secession. And, in case of war, they felt confident in the gallantry of Southern gentlemen and the support of the French and the English empire, an empire whose global domination was built in substantial

---

*Virginia, Arkansas, North Carolina, and Tennessee would secede and join the Confederacy as soon as the war fully broke out.

part on profits in textiles made from plantation cotton.* Much as the North, they foresaw any martial conflict being short-lived and relatively bloodless. Even when war broke out, they had no immediate reason to fear the coming end of their system.

This is one of the most important interventions Du Bois's *Black Reconstruction* makes: to clearly lay out that the Union did not intend to free the slaves and that emancipation was against the Union's economic, political, and social interests. The abolitionists of the time knew this well. As Frederick Douglass famously put it in a speech in 1865, the war was begun "in the interests of slavery on both sides. The South was fighting to take slavery out of the Union, and the North fighting to keep it in the Union; the South fighting to get it beyond the limits of the United States Constitution, and the North fighting for the old guarantees;—both despising the Negro, both insulting the Negro."[27]

As Du Bois argues, not only could the North never have fielded an army under the slogan "Abolition of the Slaves," it did not want to. Nor did Free Soil, the political argument unifying the Republican Party, make any sense in justifying a war with the South, where there was, after all, no new "Free Soil" to settle. "On the other hand, the tremendous economic ideal of keeping this great market for goods, the United States, together with all its possibilities of agriculture, manufacture, trade and profit, ap-

---

*This is one of the many ways that the Confederacy underestimated the power of the people. When England did not immediately support the Southern cause, the planters organized a boycott against selling cotton to England, which was then made moot by a Union blockade of the southern coast. Though many planters continued selling their cotton on the black market to the North, England, and Europe—as with all capitalists, their patriotism ended abruptly at their pocketbooks—this sudden drop in supply resulting from the blockade meant the price of cotton exploded in England. The textile factory owners in northwest England cut back dramatically on textile production, sending thousands of English workers into unemployment, an event referred to as the Lancashire Cotton Famine.

But rather than give in to this blackmail on the part of both their bosses and the slavocracy, in one of history's great moments of international solidarity the working people of northern England organized mutual aid to see themselves through the crisis—including a series of riots that had them looting bread—held protests demanding their employers and the English government remain steadfast against the Confederacy and slavery at any cost, and sent declarations in support of emancipation to Lincoln. This unrest helped keep the English out of the war until the Emancipation Proclamation, at which point English entry on the side of the Confederacy became politically impossible.

pealed to both the West and the North; and what was then much more significant, it appealed to the Border States."[28]

Lincoln, despite whatever tale liberal historians or Hollywood hagiographers want to tell, was no abolitionist. Had the war not broken out and had his most ambitious antebellum emancipation proposal gone into effect, he would have set slavery in America on a course to legally end . . . in a hundred years. In 1958. Furthermore, Lincoln believed that the best course of abolition would be to "convince" Black people to emigrate from the United States, a historical position called "colonization." The same day that Lincoln finished drafting the Emancipation Proclamation, December 31, 1862, he also signed a contract funding the relocation of five thousand Black men, women, and children to Haiti as an experimental test case for total colonization.[29] The experiment failed miserably, but he was still arguing for colonization as late as 1864. And even in 1865, with emancipation all but completed, Lincoln opposed giving Black men the vote.

But the Civil War was that rare historical period—a revolutionary period—in which the desires and goals of the powerful are swept aside utterly by the vision and action of the masses. Just as through their self-emancipation the enslaved gave the Civil War its meaning, so it was their belief that Lincoln would be the Great Emancipator that would make him appear so to history.

Lincoln's transformation was, ironically, aided by the most rabid Southern ideologues. In both the 1860 presidential contest and in the state-by-state campaigns for secession in the winter of 1860–1861, the slavocracy's propagandists painted Lincoln a dangerous enemy of the peculiar institution. Though this was a provocation that Lincoln would continuously deny, it had unexpected consequences. The political campaign Southern nationalists waged to confer legitimacy on peaceful secession, held in the big houses of the plantations and the central squares of Southern cities, was based on the (false) claim that Lincoln's election would mean abolition, and the campaign couldn't be waged without revealing this logic to the enslaved. So when secession instead came with war and chaos, not an orderly and peaceful legal split, the enslaved did not see some grim tale of "brother fighting brother" but rather Jubilee, the Bible-ordained day of emancipation, and they fled the plantation in their hundreds of thousands.

But they didn't go all at once. As Du Bois argues, a mass move-ment among a largely illiterate, geographically dispersed, and isolated population like that of the four million Africans enslaved in the United States builds slowly and in fits and starts. And it was unclear at the outset whether the Union Army was indeed an army of emancipation.

In 1861, as Union generals advanced into South Carolina and Vir-ginia, they made assurances to the local owners that slavery would not be threatened. Union general Ambrose Burnside returned fugitives to their plantations, and many generals allowed civilian enslavers to enter their lines and retrieve their "property." Throughout the first years of the war, the administration refused Black volunteers, and Lincoln was deliberat-ing with his cabinet whether or not to attempt an *army-wide return of all fugitives*. Even through 1863, after the Emancipation Proclamation, the Union Army was returning fugitives in the border states to their enslavers (the proclamation had not freed border-state slaves anyway).*

But the enslaved kept striking. Fugitives arrived in the tens, in the hundreds, some fully fit, many in terrible physical condition. What was to be done? General Benjamin Butler hit upon a happy solution in Fort Monroe in Virginia. When asked by enslavers to return three men who had escaped to the fort, he refused, declaring the fugitives "contraband of war" and putting them to work. As the war turned more serious, and as the Union Army desperately needed labor, the soundness of this strategy was recognized, and it was taken up for the year and a half of combat pre-ceding the Emancipation Proclamation. The fact that the Union Army at first would only accept emancipation on terms that continued to regard fugitives as property—contraband or not—reveals just how little this war began as one of emancipation. David Roediger puts it more optimisti-

---

*Four slave states, Delaware, Kentucky, Missouri, and Maryland, never declared seces-sion and thus remained part of the Union, although allegiances within the states were split and some white men from there fought with the Confederacy. These are known as the border states, and as a result of their presence the Union always contained slavery within it.

cally: "The policy preserved the norms of slave property even as it opened new possibilities to resist bondage."[30]

However, as soon as it became clear that the Union Army would accept fugitives, "the movement became a general strike against the slave system on the part of all who could find opportunity. The trickling streams of fugitives swelled to a flood."[31] In many places, fugitives did the crucial labor in the construction of Union Army infrastructure; elsewhere they did equally important agricultural work, gathering the crops on abandoned plantations behind Union lines for the army to sell. Elsewhere, many more refused to work for the Union as a condition of their liberty, instead squatting and claiming land, setting up agricultural communes, or joining maroon communities. Through their flight and strike, they dramatically transformed conditions on both sides of the front lines.

The next logical step, literally unthinkable to both sides only a few years previously, was to arm the fugitives and hire them to serve in the Union Army, a measure that followed quickly on the heels of the Emancipation Proclamation. Virulent racism in the Union meant Black people were seen as unfit for service, but the Union was facing an enlistment crisis.

By 1863, two years into the combat, both sides, despite instituting a draft, confronted considerable problems recruiting soldiers. In the North, the poor, largely immigrant populations that represented the majority of Union conscripts resented serving in a bloody and seemingly intractable war fought on behalf of industrialists. But this class resentment merged with a resurgent Northern anti-Blackness, and Black people, rather than the slavocracy, were blamed for the conflict.

The New York City Draft Riots, among the most violent riots in American history, began as working-class, predominantly Irish men rose up against the draft's incredible class bias. The law allowed a man of draft age to hire a substitute for $300 (more than $6,000 in 2020 dollars) rather than serve, and as a result few rich men wore the Union blue. But the riots turned into an anti-Black pogrom, killing over one hundred Black people and burning down abolitionists' homes, Black bars and theaters, and even the Colored Orphan Asylum. In the aftermath of the riots, almost the entire Black population fled the city, many of them settling in Brooklyn. Though they never reached such violent extremes elsewhere, in 1863 antiwar riots spread and racist antiwar sentiment ran rampant in the North.

But classed resentment of the war was even more pronounced in the South. As Armstead L. Robinson argues in his seminal *Bitter Fruits of Bondage*, the very fact that the war was being fought to preserve slavery doomed the Confederacy's cause from the outset. To show this, Robinson traces the social composition of the Confederacy, whose class makeup was oligarchic in the extreme. Out of the total population of the South—around ten million people—four million were enslaved and six million were free. But of those free families, only 25 percent enslaved Africans, and, of that 25 percent, only 10 percent had enough land and human property to qualify as "planters." Yet, thanks to the Three-Fifths Compromise, that tiny cohort of planters had voting power equivalent to perhaps two million citizens in the North. A similar form of disenfranchisement continues in 2020, as imprisoned people are stripped of their right to vote, even though the census counts them as residents of the (overwhelmingly rural, white) counties where they are caged rather than the (mostly Black, urban) communities from which they are captured.

As Robinson shows, when the Confederacy seceded, despite making paeans to states' rights and individual sovereignty, the planter class doubled down on their oligarchic power, with planters and their allies taking almost every seat in the Confederate congress and cabinet. Confederate president Jefferson Davis was a plantation owner, as was Vice President Alexander Stephens and General Robert E. Lee. Though the vast majority of Confederate citizens were poor backcountry yeoman farmers with no human property, many living very far away even from plantation country, they had no representation in the Confederate government. The planters' interest was the only interest truly represented in Richmond, the seat of the Confederate government from May 29, 1861, just after the war began, until April 3, 1865, when it fell to Union forces.

This meant that in session after session the Confederate government passed draft exemptions for planters, overseers, and their families. Meanwhile, planters used their influence in local militias to keep corps of men at home for defense against fugitives and slave rebellion. At the very moment the Confederate cause needed all able-bodied men on the front lines, the planters schemed to increase the numbers of the slave patrols on the home front instead.

The general strike of the enslaved made these patrollers' presence on each individual plantation even more necessary as, at the same time, it made their efforts in aggregate totally fruitless. On plantations where work continued, slowdowns and disorder increased dramatically. "Morale" completely collapsed on many plantations, where the enslaved simply stopped working, fled en masse, or even took control themselves. Much was made in the Confederate press of the Black sexual menace threatening the wives and daughters of planters left alone during wartime, a cruel and twisted propagandistic tool considering the centuries-long endemic rape of African women by their enslavers. However, the record shows remarkably little violence committed against planters or their families in the period—Du Bois explains this by suggesting it was simply easier to run away.

But even as plantation production began to break down, and with it the economic backbone of the Confederacy, so too did soldier morale. Hardly the popular cause its white supremacist defenders today like to pretend, after an early burst of excitement in 1861, the yeomen of the South began to see the Confederate struggle for what it was: "a rich man's war and a poor man's fight." Though this phrase describes most of the wars ever fought in history, as Robinson shows, in the South this particular slogan was widespread and had devastating consequences. Entire Confederate companies melted away to desertion. In some places, dissident white yeomen assisted fugitives and spread intelligence about the war, serving as Union spies alongside enslaved people. In other regions, like the highlands of Eastern Tennessee, poor white Unionists resisted the Confederacy with guerilla warfare, opening up internal fronts that spread Confederate military forces thin. However, it is important not to confuse our current understanding of the Civil War with the motives of all who fought against the Confederacy: although some of these yeomen were abolitionist, many of these Unionist forces were just as racist as their Confederate enemies. Nevertheless, they played a crucial role in bogging down the Confederacy and destroying its power.

Thus, a war fought to preserve slavery produced the conditions under which the enslaved could escape and destroy it. In attempting to stop this social upheaval and preserve the slave system, Confederate policy exacerbated class tensions, guaranteeing the Confederacy couldn't win the military struggle, either.* By the time Black fugitives finally put on the Union blue, the war was as good as over for the Confederacy. As the Union ranks swelled with the two hundred thousand fugitives ready to take up arms against their former enslavers, the Confederate lines thinned, the plantations failed, and the planter class perished in a storm of fire and blood.

THE EMANCIPATION PROCLAMATION OF 1863 ARISES AS A CRUCIAL MOment in the Union winning the war. The fact that the war was then being framed as a fight against slavery made it politically impossible for European capitalists to recognize the Confederacy as a sovereign nation and support it in combat. Just as importantly, it opened up the Union Army ranks to Black soldiers and convinced Black people that the Union was a cause worth fighting for.

The Emancipation Proclamation did nothing to free the enslaved. It only declared slavery ended in the Confederacy, where the federal government had no actual power to enforce it, in effect only freeing those who had already freed themselves. Slavery was maintained in the border states of the Union, the states where Lincoln actually had the power to

---

*The romantic historical fictions of latter-day Confederate apologists and Union fantasists that see the war being won or lost by a brave stand on a little hill in Gettysburg, for example, or that imagine a better-organized Confederate attack winning the war are structurally racist fantasies that focus solely on the military context. But wars are social and political events, not merely armies meeting in combat, and much as the Russian army in World War I was defeated not by the Imperial German Army but by revolution at home, so the Confederacy was defeated not by the Union Army but by the revolution of the Black people it enslaved, who used the Union as their tool of liberation.

enforce emancipation. The proclamation affirmed and perhaps encouraged the general strike, but, as Lerone Bennett Jr. records:

> Secretary of State William H. Seward, who heaped scorn on the Emancipation Proclamation, [told] his friend Donn Piatt that "we have let off a puff of wind over an accomplished fact."
>
> "What do you mean, Mr. Seward?" Piatt asked.
>
> "I mean," he said, "that the Emancipation Proclamation was uttered in the first gun fired at Fort Sumter, and we have been the last to hear it."[32]

Lincoln did not want to be an emancipator, but the enslaved understood what his war meant, and they surged forward to freedom anyway. Lincoln—that rarest of things, an intelligent politician—still spent nearly two years in denial before recognizing the enslaved were the key to Union victory and changing war policy to reflect it. But the enslaved moved his hand. Theirs was the glory of the Jubilee, theirs the defeat of the Confederacy, theirs the collapse of the planters and the building of Reconstruction.

The general strike of the slaves was but one of the largest culminations in the long and continuing history of fugitive attacks on property and white supremacy in America. Indeed, "nowhere in history had so large a revolutionary seizure of property taken place."[33] When the British abolished slavery in the West Indies in 1833 (it remained legal in India), the Crown compensated all the enslavers for the value of their chattel, cash that constituted the seed money for many modern British corporations. But the Confederate planters received no such bailout. The value of human property in 1860 was $3 billion, which was equivalent to about two-thirds of the GDP. An equivalent percentage of the GDP today would be about $14 trillion. All of it abolished in the span of four years.

To get free, the enslaved had to steal themselves and, in so doing, abolish themselves as property. They had to loot themselves, entering a lawless relation to property and the state. The relationship between liberation and the stealing and destruction of property was never so obvious nor so clear cut as it was during the period.

An entire class of people, the planters, who had reigned aristocratic for two hundred years, was suddenly destroyed, submerged entirely into the general population. When Du Bois wrote *Black Reconstruction* in 1935, he was contesting a narrative by wealthy white Southerners and Ku Klux Klanners that they were the noble descendants of the slavocracy. But as he made clear:

> Of the names of prominent Southern families in Congress in 1860, only two appear in 1870, five in 1880. Of 90 prominent names in 1870, only four survived in 1880. Men talk today as though the upper class in the white South is descended from the slave-holders; yet we know by plain mathematics that the ancestors of most of the present Southerners never owned a slave nor had any real economic part in slavery. The disaster of war decimated the planters; the bitter disappointment and frustration led to a tremendous mortality after the war, and from 1870 on the planter class merged their blood so completely with the rising poor whites that they disappeared as a separate aristocracy.[34]

The fugitives and the ex-slaves, impoverished, illiterate, faced their freedom in a war-torn country that resented their very existence and tried to make a good life for themselves. As Frederick Douglass remarked at the time: "The work does not end with the abolition of slavery, but only begins." They built schools, hospitals, and cooperatives, organized mutual aid societies and democratic ordinances, petitioned the federal government for land and autonomy or simply took it for themselves: this is the period called Reconstruction. In the 1660s, they would have been able to make a claim for freedom dues for their servitude, but in 1865, as in 2020, they and their descendants were scorned for demanding reparations. Yet still they tried to build a better world on the salted grounds of slavery.

And even as the Southern planter class collapsed, ex-Confederates held onto their racial power through campaigns of vigilante terror, and Northern capitalists swooped in to win the spoils of war. The railroad men and the mine owners, the bankers, speculators, and merchants, the senators, governors, and judges watched the planters drown and vowed not to let it happen to themselves. They ensured that their property could not be so easily looted; neither would they ever allow its destruction to gain the moral righteousness and historical clarity of the struggle for emancipation.

The revolution was begun, but not completed, and, as all partial revolutions, it would eventually sink back down under a morass of repression, violence, and confusion, waiting for a future generation to lift it up out of the muck, study its tactics, its promises, and its visions, and finally complete the dream of Jubilee.

chapter three | **ALL COPS ARE BASTARDS**

WITHOUT THE PLANTERS AND THE CONFEDERACY, WITHOUT A HUGE class of enslaved people, how could the Southern economy, based on brutally exploitative agricultural labor, regain its footing after the war? How could the economy be rebuilt? Would it be? Though Northern capitalists had just financed a war that destroyed the slave system, they had no intention of truly developing or even transforming the South: the agricultural products produced by Black labor were essential for their profits, and they wanted the South to continue to contribute cheap cotton, tobacco, and other staple commodities.

But the formerly enslaved had no intention of returning to the bondage they had just destroyed. How could the country re-create the agricultural base its profits so relied on without being able to re-create the slave power that had been so thoroughly discredited and destroyed, and without being willing to empower the newly freed and organized Black communities, who had no intention of simply providing cheap labor? It was going to require politics, and it was going to require violence.

In that task, they found willing accomplices in the white Southern Democrats, who had just come through the humiliation of total defeat and were wanting revenge. Ex-Confederates formed gangs of vigilante terrorists, and police forces that had developed in the urban centers of the South were reinforced and re-empowered. The ad hoc combination of these forces—police, white terrorists, Southern Democrats, and Northern liberals—ultimately defeated the enslaved people, who had struck off their bonds, created a social revolution in the South, and won a war against their former masters. Anti-Black violence, carried out by the state and its volunteers, ensured that emancipation would not mean equality, freedom, and justice for all any more than the Constitution did. And this continuity of racial violence did not merely harm the emancipated people of the South.

As the United States followed its Manifest Destiny to the West Coast, it furthered its genocidal displacement, internment, and war on Indigenous Americans. With the conquer and occupation of large swaths of Mexico, the American border crossed lands inhabited by Chicanx people, who increasingly found themselves the targets of murderous white dispossession. So too did the Asian workers brought across the Pacific to build the cities, railroads, farms, and mines of the West. This violence was also turned against anarchists, communists, socialists, and radical labor, many of them newly arrived German and Italian immigrants who were not yet considered white.

It is well beyond this book to even begin to look at or analyze all the riots, lynchings, and police violence that occurred across America between Reconstruction and the Black Freedom movement of the sixties. What's notable, though, is that the police, alongside white collective punishments, played an increasingly central role in society and became a crucial factor in all of the transformations occurring throughout the country. Urbanization, industrialization, western expansion, Black internal migration, labor struggles, American imperialism, political machines, and "gilded age" financial and corporate concentration of wealth all relied on or responded to police and vigilante violence in their daily enactments.

Race riots and lynchings were a way of "stabilizing" white supremacist settler-colonial capitalist hegemony—by terrorizing and disorganizing the American proletariat, by transferring wealth and power to white capitalists—while the police served as a new tool for legitimizing and regulating this violence. The historical emergence of the police, and their relationship to fugitives, urban slave patrols, colonial administration, and crowd suppression, helps us analyze looting and rioting in the present.

The proposition that history does not primarily happen in parliaments or on battlefields but rather in workplaces, in homes, in theaters and schools, in factories, and in the streets refers not only to the history of resistance and revolution but also to its repression, deferral, and destruction. And in the United States, the forces doing that everyday work of repression, deferral, and destruction have tended to wear a blue cap or a white hood.

IF STANDARD AMERICAN HISTORY FORGETS, DOMESTICATES, DECONtextualizes, or de-radicalizes revolutionaries, the police are so embedded within the ideological reproduction of the present that they are hardly imagined to have a history at all. As historian of the police Kristian Williams writes, people "seem to imagine that the cop has always been there, in something like his present capacity, subject only to the periodic change of uniform or the occasional technological advance."[1] Luckily for those of us who think that there will be no justice without the total abolition of police forces, however, modern police departments are a relatively recent phenomenon, with even the oldest forces being just over two hundred years old.

As anyone who has followed their actions or battled against them in the streets knows, different local police forces in America have different tactics and different relations to their municipal governments and varying levels of power—though they share the same structural goals and behaviors. This is because they have different local histories, and so any unifying story of the police in America is necessarily generalized and will have exceptions. Still, tracing this outline not only helps us to denaturalize the police and thus imagine a world without them but also recognize the way that looting makes immediate sense as an antipolice tactic. To do so, we will follow the distinct but similar development of three of the earliest police forces: London's Metropolitan Police, the New York City Police Department, and the Charleston City Guard.

THE HISTORY OF THE POLICE IN AMERICA BEGINS WITH THEIR PREDE-cessors in England. For more than six hundred years, comprising the English Middle Ages up into the eighteenth century, policing functions in English towns and villages were distributed among a number of different people. In the main, the law was upheld by communal agreement among the heads of households. These literal patriarchs had jurisdiction over either groups of ten people (a "tything") or ten tythings together (a "hundred") into which the community was divided. Victims of a crime pled their own case before these patriarchs and pressed charges themselves. Other policing duties, such as tax collecting, enforcing royal decrees, or mustering a militia or a *posse comitatus* to capture fugitives, were spread out among a number of other officials, including various constables and a monarch-appointed sheriff.

The only force patrolling towns was the night watch. Night watchmen were unpaid, unarmed, save a lantern and a staff, and mostly functioned as a human alarm system, raising "the hue and cry" in case of crime or fire, with the intention of gathering other people to deal with the situation together. Watch duty was required of all male residents of a town, and was deeply resented. For the centuries that they were the main force of order, watchmen had a propensity to wander the streets blind drunk, and they hardly instilled fear in would-be criminals.

Across the eighteenth century, however, the London watchmen transformed to reflect rapid changes in the city. English cities grew rapidly through the early Industrial Revolution, beginning in this era. Urban growth was driven by the process of enclosure, in which the state and landlords privatized England's common grazing and agricultural land, rural land that had previously been free for all to use. Peasants who had for generations worked on these commons, who had subsisted on their own agricultural produce, found themselves unable to pay the new fees and rents suddenly required for use of the land they and their forebears had farmed for centuries. Without a place to farm, and thus without a way to grow food or subsist, peasants were made homeless and plunged into desperate poverty by these laws and land grabs.

Many left the countryside to find work in the towns, where they ended up living in densely packed slums. This new urban poor proved the crucial factor in growing the ranks of the rich and the merchant "middle classes," who could profit off paying these country bumpkins terrible wages for grueling work and charging them high rents for miserable hovels. Where once towns were small settlements where rich and poor often lived more or less side by side, as cities grew, classes also increasingly stratified in their daily lives, making for entirely different experiences of the city in completely separated neighborhoods.

This great mass of newly impoverished people tended to resent their bosses and landlords—who stole their lives week by week through rent and wage—and tried to live the best they could in spite of it all. They skipped out on work and contracts, didn't pay their debts, drank, caroused, gambled, and behaved in all sorts of "immoral" ways—the same leisure and economic activities practiced by the English aristocracy, of course, but suddenly immoral when practiced in public by former peasants. This "immorality," crucially, was not violent: violent crime actually dramatically decreased during the eighteenth and early nineteenth centuries. These people merely hadn't internalized or didn't respect the new economic and social relations developing in the period and had to be forced to recognize the "rational," "natural" ways of the new system of property, commodity, labor, and contract.

As one method of keeping these newly dispossessed in check, various London watch organizations took up modernizing experiments, most significantly paying watchmen, but also hiring more men, increasing hours of operation, granting pensions, and purchasing modern equipment and weapons. They also increasingly criminalized debt, unemployment, gambling, drinking, and public gathering: transforming people into criminals is one of the core methods of social control under capitalism. But, although the night watch and other early experimental police forces were capable of punishing individuals—public hangings

became an incredibly common spectacle in eighteenth-century London—they could do nothing to control the new proletariat when they
gathered and acted as crowds in the streets, increasingly riotous, in organized demonstrations, strikes, and the "disorderly" use of city streets
for socializing, informal business, and as living spaces. The government
found itself facing new, massive crowds with only one tool for suppression: the army.

But, as historian David Whitehouse notes, "there are really only two
things the army could do. . . . They could refuse to shoot, and the crowd
would get away with whatever it came to do. Or they could shoot into the
crowd and produce working-class martyrs."[2] What could the state do to
keep these people paying rent and going to work and not, say, recognizing
their own power, taking over society, and changing it in the interests of
all? How could it regulate repressive violence so that it maintained order
without producing conditions of outright civil war? Robert Peel, then the
home secretary, hit upon a solution in 1829 when he proposed Parliament
put into action a police force. His ideas transformed the various disparate
watches into the centralized, uniformed, twenty-four-hour-operating,
professionalized, citywide Metropolitan Police Force. These "bobbies,"
named after their founder, are widely (but inaccurately) considered the
first modern police force in the world.

Importantly, Peel did not introduce this innovation from thin air—in
previous years he had developed policing methods in a more openly brutal and violent context, using his proto-cops to suppress and control Irish
populations during his service as chief secretary of Ireland.* These colonial methods were, in turn, influenced by labor management techniques
developed in the West Indian slave colonies. English policing methods

---

*Robert Peel's infamy includes not only brutal management in Ireland and the inven-
tion of the English police but also the founding and reinvigoration of the modern Conservative Party and, as prime minister, exacerbation of the Great Famine in Ireland. For
two years, he denied its effects, doing nothing while hundreds of thousands died, then,
when the suffering became too great to ignore, in 1846 he cynically used the famine to
repeal the Corn Laws and advance his cause of free trade—the repeal represents a crucial governmental shift from supporting the landed aristocracy to supporting the bourgeoisie. But, lovely man that he was, Peel set up the repeal to go into place gradually,
rather than all at once, so that its effects would not help the Irish come out of the famine
for another three years.

were developed to maintain imperial domination in the colonies, then were applied to the newly developed striking, riotous poor and working classes back in the metropole. The English police represent the internalization of the empire's colonial relations. The methods that best work to stamp out colonial resistance also work to repress class conflict, allowing us to see that class relations and colonialism are not always easily distinguishable: class power is in many ways fundamentally colonial.

In the northern American colonies, the development of the police followed a similar trajectory. In eighteenth-century New York City, an involuntary, ineffective, and unpaid watch combined with constables—formal officers of the court who served warrants and summonses—to make up the apparatus of order. However, because slavery was still legal in New York, these watches were empowered to harass Black and Indigenous people—who were often under curfew—on the streets, demanding passes and detaining, beating, or murdering those without them. After the end of legal slavery in New York, the watch continued to enforce state laws specifically targeting nonwhite people.

In the early nineteenth century, as the city swelled with immigrants, particularly Irish ones (who were at this point still racialized and not considered white), an ideology emerged among the rich that referred to the "dangerous classes." As this ideology developed, poor and immigrant communities began to be regarded as officially alien groups with fundamentally different ethics and values. The drunkenness and "vagrancy" of these "dangerous classes" were not recognized as a product of their material conditions; instead, such behaviors were regarded as somehow biologically inherent to their being (the Irish reputation for being drunks has never gone away, but you might be harder pressed to find people who think all Catholics are a degenerate force of laziness and moral decay these days).

In other words, class was increasingly understood racially. The lifestyles of the dangerous classes were seen as a threat to social order, morals, and the regular and dependable work-readiness industrial capitalism required. The wealthy began to agitate for a more formal method of controlling these unruly people, just as they did in England, despite the fact that US cities saw a decrease in serious crime through the 1800s.

As in London, New York City crowds grew larger, more powerful, and more disruptive. As mentioned in the previous chapter, in the early decades of the 1800s Black New Yorkers rioted to prevent fugitives from being returned to the South, which often resulted in violent battles with the watch. During the same period, anti-Black race riots, instigated and led by both "native" New Yorkers and European immigrants alike, targeting Black churches, theaters, and businesses became increasingly common.* The city also saw the emergence of militant strikes, which often destroyed property and shut down entire neighborhoods. And finally, as David Whitehouse writes, at that time workers "began to engage in more and more 'run-of-the-mill' riots wherever crowds gathered. . . . In the opening decades of the century, there was one of these riots about four times a year, but in the period from 1825 to 1830, New Yorkers rioted at a rate of once per month."[3]

In response, the state legislature put into place a series of reforms that would result, by 1845, in a professionalized, specialized, centralized twenty-four-hour police force, just as Peel had done in London.

Whereas London's Metropolitan Police Force shaped itself on Irish colonial domination, the New York Police Department took many of its organizational cues from the slave patrols of the South, and one of its first major responsibilities was enforcing the Fugitive Slave Act of 1850.[4]

The NYPD as it exists today thus emerged to enforce the racial and class hierarchies essential to urban capitalist development. To keep things "orderly" meant, from its beginning, keeping the white and the rich on top by protecting their property and keeping the Black, Indigenous, immigrant, and poor in their place by limiting their organizing, street presence, and political power. The police are an apparatus designed to reinforce the white supremacist, bourgeois order. And that order finds many of its origins in the practices and techniques developed in the early days of settler colonialism.

---

*New York, with its bankers and merchants who managed business between the South/the Caribbean and the North and Europe, had the most staunchly pro-slavery, pro-Democrat, and actively anti-Black white population of any major city in the North.

THE CONSTANCY OF MAROONAGE, RESISTANCE, AND REBELLION IN slave colonies and societies meant that settlers tended to develop specialized policing forces earlier than the metropoles, such as London or New York, that grew off the profits from geographically distant plantations. Howard Zinn notes that "in the 1520s and 1530s, there were slave revolts in Hispaniola, Puerto Rico, Santa Marta, and what is now Panama. Shortly after those rebellions, the Spanish established a special police force for chasing fugitive slaves."[5] Spanish, French, and English colonies in sixteenth- and seventeenth-century Americas all saw the development of both semiregular slave patrols and professional slave catchers. In Barbados, English soldiers were stationed in plantations *exclusively* to surveil and control the enslaved, not to do any other work: a rare and noteworthy historical fact, considering how valuable manpower was and how few Englishmen were brought to the Caribbean colonies. These forces tended to lack some of the defining features of modern police departments but serve as forerunners.[6]

Indeed, the British colonists of the early continental South consciously studied and copied the Caribbean model. Across the seventeenth and early eighteenth centuries, Southern enslavers developed voluntary unwaged slave patrols, made up of plantation owners, their sons, brothers, overseers, and other "trustworthy" white people. These patrols rode a number of times a week, in the roads and fields between and within plantations. They patrolled on horseback and usually carried guns, whips, and rope. Though patrols varied from state to state, they were, like the forces in the Caribbean, formed initially to capture fugitives, but very quickly they evolved to also watch for and prevent slave uprisings.

As such, they harassed and captured any Black person found between plantations. Free or enslaved, Black people were required to carry a pass in order to travel alone. Being caught at a slave gathering or between plantations without a pass resulted in lashings or even life-threatening beatings. But a pass didn't protect Black people from the whims of the patrols any more than official ID protects Black people from the police today: random violence, sexual assault, and robbery were common.

The patrols were sent in to break up and disperse any large groups of Black people, whether groups formed as social gatherings, religious meetings, or family celebrations. They also searched slave quarters and homes for weapons, stolen goods, or any "signs" of rebellion. Police nowadays rely on the legal tool of civil asset forfeiture—and the pretense that they're investigating drug crimes—to take whatever cash and valuables they find in a car or a home they search. They seize items even if they don't find any guns or drugs, even if they search the wrong house, even if they have a faulty warrant or have illegally stopped a car. This is a direct policy descendant of the slave patrols, which could take anything they found of value, regardless of any "real" signs of insurrectionary plotting or actual stolen goods. While plantation owners benefited from the repression of revolt and rebellion, stealing possessions served as a main incentive for overseers and volunteers, who made up the bulk of the patrol, a significant supplement to their wages.

The slave patrols started off as informal groups set up by planters themselves rather than by local governments, and before American independence, they tended to be autonomous, technically part of the colonial militias but answering to no real official authority. As the slave colonies became slave states, they enacted legislation that empowered (and theoretically limited) the patrols as separate from militias. The huge increase in the number of enslaved people in the United States at the turn of the nineteenth century meant that these voluntary patrols proved insufficient to discover planned revolts or stem the tide of fugitives, so state governments often stepped in to fund patrols and make them stronger and more organized. For example, in 1819, in response to two failed slave revolts, a law was passed in South Carolina that required all white men between eighteen and forty-five years of age to serve in slave patrols without pay.[7]

But even in the predominantly rural and agricultural South, policing developed most quickly in the cities. Southern cities grew, and, though small in comparison to the metropolises of the North, they, too, produced their unruly crowds. As discussed in the previous chapter, Southern urban economies were built around the practice of enslavers "hiring out" laborers to other employers in town. These enslaved workers earned a wage from their bosses, most of which they would then turn over to their enslaver. These laborers most often lived together, usually at a remove from both their employer and their enslaver, and their daily lives outside work unfolded mostly in Black neighborhoods called slave quarters.

Slave quarters were spaces of relative autonomy for the enslaved, and as such were a cause of massive anxiety to the white residents of the cities, who feared the possibility of Black peoples' organization and righteous rebellion. The neighborhoods were frequently outside of white control, a place where maroons could organize and trade, where recent fugitives could hide out and Underground Railroad stations could form, where African, creole, and subversive Christian religious practices could flourish, and where white people weren't respected, deferred to, or welcomed.

Such communities presented an imminent threat to the slave order. So Southern cities developed "city guards," militarized forces of young white men whose large numbers and modern weaponry allowed them to patrol and control those quarters. Rather than evolving slowly out of the traditional and ineffectual night watch, as the police forces did in London and New York City, the urban guards of the South were adapted directly from rural slave patrols and put into place directly to replace the watch.[8]

The first of these slave-patrol-cum-police-forces was the Charleston, South Carolina, City Guard and Watch, incorporated in 1783. As Kristian Williams writes, this force "represented a significant advance in the development of policing."[9] Armed, professionalized, and uniformed, with the same officers working every day, the force patrolled Charleston in a company rather than as individuals. It was a modern police department, the first, perhaps, in the world. Similar "guards" popped up across the South in the following decades.

Though these guards were ostensibly formed to stop crime, they largely worked by instilling terror in the Black population. They raided Black people's homes, monitored and controlled their movement, enforced a curfew (for Black people only), and regularly mustered in full force to parade through the streets behind fife and drum, armed to the teeth, beating anyone they could catch, sending people fleeing ahead of them.

Unlike in the rural areas between the plantations, Southern cities required that the enslaved be able to move freely between their various jobs and home, so a patrol that stopped and harassed everyone moving through the streets was undesirable and unprofitable. The enslaved were still required to carry a pass from their employers, and failure to produce one could result in terrible violence, but unlike their rural counterparts, the guard didn't stop anyone and everyone they met. Thus, the Guard and Watch developed the essential police tactics of selective enforcement and random terror, which, alongside keeping Black people from certain places (e.g., bars and public parks), became the everyday job of the guard. As Williams writes, "This body was responsible for arresting vagrants and other suspicious persons, preventing felonies and disturbances, and warning of fires. But one guard described his job succinctly as 'keeping down the n***ers.'"[10] The police are one of the first "color-blind" institutions in American history: formal responsibility for urban safety and crime prevention is simply a cover for enforcement of white supremacy and anti-Blackness.

This emergence of a modern police force in the South was different from that in London, which was different, again, from that in New York City, but all three shared some clear tendencies. In all instances, the police developed as a formal governmental organization when the enslaver, colonizer, and/or capitalist could no longer sufficiently protect their property or control on their own the crowds of laborers they required. In all three instances, the state stepped in to take over a repressive function by forming an organization with a separate agenda from that of the army or the militia: an armed bureaucracy under the aegis of stopping crime. As we can see from the examples of London and New York City, the police did not evolve exclusively or simply in response to the chattel slavery relation. However, police evolved and modernized *earlier* in cities with slavery and appeared sooner in settler colonies than in their metropoles. Police forces in the colonial center always took tactical, organizational, and methodological cues from colonizing and enslaving police forces in the outposts. The slave catcher is thus embedded in the DNA of all modern police forces.

Many reactionaries confront abolitionists with the question: Well, then, what do you replace the police with? But that question implies that the police exist for generalized protection of the people. The police do not exist to protect citizens from crime, and they never have. As revolutionary labor organizer Lucy Parsons observed, already true more than a hundred years ago, "We have laws, jails, courts, armies, guns and armories enough to make saints of us all, if they were the true preventives of crime."[11] America currently has more police per capita than any nation in Europe, and the highest rates of imprisonment in the world, yet it continues to have higher rates of crime.

So, what do the police do? The police exist to enforce the rule of the powerful few over the weak and many. I do not see a need to replace or reproduce that function in a liberated society. As Mychal Denzel Smith puts it: "What do you do with an institution whose core function is the control and elimination of black people specifically, and people of color and the poor more broadly? You abolish it."[12]

THIS TRANSITION FROM SLAVE PATROL TO OFFICIAL POLICE FORCE IS mirrored by the similar transition of the object of police violence from slave to criminal. Following the collapse of the Confederacy, in the very first days of emancipation, Southern state governments attempted to rebuild the slave system in all but name by installing a series of new criminal laws, the infamous Black Codes, vagrancy and convict laws. The vagrancy laws are particularly telling. As Michelle Alexander writes,

> Nine Southern states adopted vagrancy laws—which essentially made it a criminal offense not to work and were applied selectively to blacks—and eight of those states enacted convict laws allowing for the hiring-out of county prisoners to plantation owners and private companies. Prisoners were forced to work for little or no pay. One vagrancy act specifically provided that "all free negroes and mulattoes over the age of eighteen" must have written proof of a job at the beginning of every year. Those found with no lawful employment were deemed vagrants and convicted. Clearly, the purpose of the black codes in general and the vagrancy laws in particular was to establish another system of forced labor.[13]

These laws were enacted *immediately* following the collapse of the Confederacy, most of them installed in 1865 and 1866. This means that the former rulers of the slavocracy understood that, although the legal category of *slave* had been abolished, they could use the category of *criminal*, and the enforcement mechanisms of the state, to return Black people to a state of bondage. The fact that this happened so quickly reflects the fact that state power was always already poised to serve this function.

Slavery in America did not occur in a legal vacuum or as an extralegal system: slavery was maintained under the purview of constitutional law. In the laws administering slavery, the Slave Codes, the equation of Blackness with criminality was already strongly established. As Saidiya Hartman writes, "The law's selective recognition of slave humanity nullified the captive's ability to give consent or act as agent and, at the same time, acknowledged the intentionality and agency of the slave but only as it assumed the form of criminality. The recognition and/or stipulation of agency as criminality served to identify personhood with punishment."[14] Under this legal regime, the courts did not recognize slaves as legal subjects—humans—unless they were accused of a crime. Black subjecthood could only be understood through punishment, a logic initiated in the slave ships but carried into the present through criminalization. Criminal law was thus a crucial part of producing and maintaining slavery, and it has always been a key way of producing race in America.

The police of Charleston and other Southern cities thus served a relatively continuous function across the event called emancipation. The name given to the object of their gaze and their violence shifts to become the "vagrant," but the vagrant of 1865 was the enslaved of 1860: the policeman and his target are still literally the same people.

It is rare to see principles so clearly delineated in history, but the Slave Codes' smooth transition into vagrancy laws and Black Codes is a perfect example of the notion that crime is not some transcendental fact of life against which the police nobly battle but is rather the thing identified by the state and the police as a post facto explanation for the repression they *already* carry out on behalf of society's rulers.

And this transition from slave to criminal was not merely a function of reactionary Southern governments: the Thirteenth Amendment, passed in 1865, abolishes slavery and involuntary servitude "except as a punishment for crime whereof the party shall have been duly convicted." To this day, the Constitution supports the enslavement of criminals: prison abolition activists in the Free Alabama Movement and behind the growing waves of prison strikes today insist that modern mass incarceration labor regimes are a direct, legal continuation of slavery. Though the vagrancy laws and Black Codes were struck down by the Fourteenth Amendment in 1868, alongside the Thirteenth Amendment, they formed a precedent for the segregation, convict leasing, sharecropping, and chain gangs of the Jim Crow era.

Convict leasing was a horrific regime. As Angela Davis writes: "Scholars who have studied the convict lease system point out that in many important respects, convict leasing was far worse than slavery. . . . Slave owners may have been concerned for the survival of individual slaves, who, after all, represented significant investments. Convicts, on the other hand, were leased not as individuals, but as a group, and they could be worked literally to death without affecting the profitability of a convict crew."[15]

The transitions from slave to criminal, from overseer to officer, are not always improvements for those caught within the system, although they are "reforms."

We might begin to understand the police and their prisons, then, as the most direct continued embodiments of the legacies of colonialism and slavery in our society. Their function, from the beginning, has been to maintain relations of colonialism, property, and slavery among races, classes, and genders. If we are serious about ending the domination and dispossession of white supremacy and settler colonialism, about making reparations for that vast historical crime, and healing, one of the most crucial steps must be to abolish the police. We cannot reform them. As Davis puts it, "The entire history of police, the entire history of prisons is a history of reform." Reforms merely make these institutions more palatable, more acceptable in their task of caging, torturing, murdering, and disappearing people. Anything less than the total abolition of the police and prisons means keeping the colonialist and enslaving violence, ideology, and control intact: that violence is what they are.

The self-looting fugitive was the spark for the genesis of the earliest policing forces—the slave patrols—and enforcing federal fugitive slave law was one of the earliest tasks of American police forces. Beyond the loss of property she represents, the fugitive anticipates and precipitates rebellion with her flight. The police have from the beginning existed to protect racialized property relations from the threat posed by the looter, the rebel, and the crowd. The looter is one of the historical nemeses of the police: it is no wonder that, during antipolice uprisings, she reappears again and again.

But if the looter reappears in uprisings against capital and the police, hardly all rioters and looters in American history have fought against the state, the police, or the regime of white supremacist property.

In the chaos of a collapsed economy and "way of life" in the wake of the Civil War, gangs of ex-Confederate soldiers wandered the South, using their soldierly skills to murder Black people and rob what little they had. One of these groups of Confederates formed the Ku Klux Klan, which would become America's most powerful fascist popular movement.

First organized as a social club for white supremacist "pranksters" in December 1865, the KKK's racial terror, irony-drenched "pranks" quickly transformed into lynchings, and the organization spread all across the South. Its branches terrorized freed slaves, attacking and killing Black leaders and occasionally the white activists who had come south to assist them, in an attempt to destroy nascent Black political power and re-enslave Black labor. They were joined in this task by other post-Confederate Southern paramilitary white terrorist organizations, such as the Red Shirts and the White Man's League, which focused their attacks around elections and taking out local Republican politicians and civil servants.

White people behaved in the former Confederacy like apocalypse survivors, using bare violence and terror to regain control of a South fundamentally shaken by social transformation. Polling places, then open to Black people, could be sites of unspeakable violence, as white terrorists attacked both Black voters and white people voting for the Republican Party. The plantation owners may have been defeated in war and in law, but they marshalled what power and wealth they had left to try to maintain the system that had deemed them masters. In most of the South, civil war continued at a lower level of violence for another decade, often taking on the form of open combat, and even expanding into statewide civil war in Mississippi and Arkansas.

Against these white terrorists stood the newly emancipated. A generation of Black people had realized their power through their great strike, their emancipation, and their participation in the Union Army. Having begun a radical transformation of society, they set about consolidating those gains and pushing them forward. In some places they won local and federal elections, built schools and businesses, and increased democratic participation; in others they carried on more militant insurrection, following the outlaw traditions of maroon and Indian communities, looting and expropriating planters and owners in order to live on their own land without bosses or work. This often took the form of outright armed rebellion against bosses and landowners, as in the Ogeechee Insurrection of 1868–1869, when hundreds of Black rice farmers in the Ogeechee Neck of Georgia, fed up with stalled negotiations with the bosses, armed themselves, rose up, kicked the owners and overseers off the farms, and occupied them, forming an autonomous commune.[16] The formerly enslaved people of the South became, briefly, the heralds of a different world. And they sometimes did so with the improbable support of the federal government and Northern capital.

Whereas a portion of the support from the North stemmed from solidarity with radical abolitionists, most of it came from capitalists and politicians who recognized that, in the power vacuum created by the Confederacy's collapse, they could finally crush the planter class, capturing and rationalizing the Southern economy and government toward the needs of industrial capital in the process. As a result, federal support tended to emphasize reforms that transformed the newly emancipated Black people of the South into wage workers, sharecroppers, and debtors. This worked against or deemphasized the radical autonomy and agrarian land reform—succinctly captured by the rallying cry of "forty acres and a mule," promised in General Sherman's Special Field Orders that redistributed land in the Sea Islands—that emancipated people across the South anticipated and had fought for.

Reconstruction is an incredibly important moment in American history. Some currents within it—those led by the newly emancipated—flowed toward a different trajectory for Black people in America, a trajectory marked by Black autonomy and sovereignty, by real social transformation. But another stream shows the power of liberal elements of the bourgeoisie to pacify liberation movements and repress revolutionary social change in favor of their own interests. The period also saw states and vigilantes develop methods of white supremacist retrenchment, empowerment, and violence that last to this day.

Some of the more formal political currents are well summarized in the Sojourner Truth Organization's *Introduction to the United States*:

> The Reconstruction acts passed by the radical-dominated Congress disenfranchised former Confederate officials and stationed federal troops in the South to protect the voting rights of the former slaves. Under these conditions, Reconstruction was carried to its furthest extent in South Carolina and Mississippi, the two former pillars of the Confederacy and the only states with a black majority. Of the delegates to a convention called in South Carolina for the purpose of writing a new state convention, almost half were former slaves and another fourth were so poor that they paid no taxes. Has the world ever seen a parliament of purer proletarian composition?[17]

The Reconstruction legislatures enacted a series of laws that brought the South the most extensive, and in some cases the only, social reform it has ever known. Child labor laws, free public education, women's property rights, credit structures to enable the poor to obtain land—these and other measures flowed out of the law-making bodies that the men of property, north and south, denounced as "parliaments of gorillas." And behind these legislatures stood the Black masses.[18]

But this Northern support, quite unified in the years immediately following the Civil War, fractured and dissolved along class lines. Once Northern capital had installed itself fully in the South, once planter power had been broken and Southern agriculture had been revived along lines of wage labor and sharecropping, the industrialists and politicians withdrew their support for Reconstruction. The capitalists didn't want Black and working-class autonomy any more than the white terrorists did: they had merely wanted those pesky Southern "gentlemen" out of their way and sufficient stabilization of the South to maintain access to cheap labor and raw materials.

While the reforms and work of Reconstruction in the South are often credited to Northern carpetbaggers, by both Southerners at the time and proud Northern liberals today, few are happy to talk about the extent to which the great white supremacist capitalists of the post-Reconstruction South also came from the North. We can't forget that after the plantation class disappeared almost entirely, it was not replaced by entrepreneurial Southern yeomen. Instead, Northern industrialists and bankers, many of whom saw an opportunity in the collapsed region, moved into the South in the years following the Civil War. The sharecropping, convict leasing, and segregation that so resembled re-enslavement were carried out on behalf of Northerners as much as for Southern white supremacists.

The liberals of the Republican Party were happy to grant the ex-Confederacy a states' rights (then as now, code words for white supremacist) basis for racial and social issues in return for swift reunion of a national free market and a more centralized federal executive regulating trade and commerce issues, most importantly railroad expansion. As Neal Shirley and Saralee Stafford put it, "Whatever the benevolent intentions of individual Radical Republicans may have been, Yankee-engineered Reconstruction was chiefly a step in forcefully reintegrating newly available populations of desperate and destitute former slaves into industrial and agricultural production."[19] The dozens of insurrections, communes, and maroon societies formed in the aftermath of the war were either crushed or slowly starved out by both white vigilantes and Northern backstabbing.

This all became finalized when, in 1876, the Republican Party fully betrayed and destroyed even the liberal parts of Reconstruction. In the "compromise of 1877," Republicans agreed to withdraw federal troops from the South, troops that had been the guarantors of Reconstruction, in exchange for the Democrats conceding the presidential race. White vigilantes, who had been violently fighting for the white supremacist order for the entire period, found their most powerful antagonists in the effort withdrawn, and in the years following 1877, white "redeemers" across the South purged Black officials—sometimes at gunpoint or amid rioting— and ushered Democrats back into office, then putting in place laws that foreshadowed or transformed into Jim Crow, halting and reversing the progressive gains of the Reconstruction period.

Those who argue that reform is "more practical" or "more realistic" than revolution forget how easily reforms are rolled back to leave the white supremacist, heteropatriarchal capitalist state in place. The gains made in the midst of a civil war that led to 750,000 deaths, won by the largest uprising in American history—the general strike of the enslaved— and consolidated in a decade of local and autonomous governance were traded away by politicians and leaders for the four-year presidential term of Rutherford B. Hayes, and the freedom movement was set back for decades to come.[20]

Of course, this betrayal is merely the most clear and dramatic political component of the ongoing nationwide process of white supremacist retrenchment, a process that would continue well into the twentieth century, a process of disenfranchisement, disempowerment, and work regimes resembling re-enslavement that ensured a continuation of slavery-like relations in America despite the technical end of slavery. And one of the main agents in this process was the white lyncher, rioter, and arsonist. The white supremacist looter.

chapter four **| WHITE RIOT**

I N STANDARD HISTORIES, JIM CROW IS LARGELY CONCEPTUALIZED AS a legal regime. This suits the "postracial" narrative that sees the civil rights movement, marked by legislative and legal victories, as the end of racial justice struggles, a narrative that imagines that the greatest achievements of the Black Freedom movement were the various civil rights bills of the mid-sixties. In this telling, Jim Crow was a series of Southern laws, protected and upheld by bigoted white Southerners, that kept Black people from achieving freedom: once struck down, the ultimate victory of racial equality was ensured. As a result, the thinking goes, we now live, finally, in an era of racial justice.

This absurd fantasy has largely been destroyed by the Movement for Black Lives. It is belied by the facts of the prison-industrial complex, of the anti-Black carceral state, by the surveillance, violence, and deportation wielded against Latinx and Muslim communities in the name of borders and antiterrorism, by the continued dispossession and genocide of Indigenous peoples whose reservations sit on top of gas fields and in the way of oil pipelines, by the election of Donald Trump.

But something fundamental *did* shift in the wake of the civil rights movement: white supremacy was increasingly upheld by the state, the police, and the prison-industrial complex rather than by a mix of state actors, volunteers, vigilantes, and rioters. As Naomi Murakawa points to in her seminal *The First Civil Right*, one of the things that liberal civil rights legislation ironically ended up doing was bringing the work of those volunteers under the official policy of the federal government. By framing the violence of extralegal white supremacist volunteers as a *crime* issue, and Jim Crow as a question of bad laws and individual racists in government, civil rights legislation under Truman and onward focused on producing race-neutral criminal law and centralizing political power in the federal government. These bills reined in *de jure* white supremacy and gave the federal government authority to intervene with white vigilante violence, but they also built the legal and political frameworks for a "color-blind" criminal policy that would become Black mass incarceration.[1]

It is not that these vigilantes ever disappeared, as Dylann Roof's murder of nine at the Emanuel African Methodist Episcopal (AME) Church in Charleston in 2015 shows. Indeed, vigilantism is again on the rise, with more or less direct encouragement from the Trump administration. But in the ninety years between the Civil War and the civil rights movement, lynchings, vigilante violence, and white riots occurred regularly, a form of oppression as common, daily, and universal in the lives of people of color as police violence and incarceration are today. The extent and spread of the violence can be hard to imagine, but, particularly in the decades immediately following the collapse of the Confederacy, constant terror was often the only thing keeping white supremacist state governments together.[2]

Less a formal legal regime to ensure water fountains remained segregated, Jim Crow, which emerged in the South in the 1870s and 1880s to be struck down only in the 1960s, was a reign of terror and violence, protected by law but enforced by upstanding white citizens whose three-piece suits hung cozily in their closets beside white robes.

And this great white supremacist terror was not contained in the South nor restricted to anti-Blackness. Anti-Asian and anti-Mexican riots were common occurrences in the cities of the American West, cities largely built by their labor, while the continued genocidal dispossession of Indigenous peoples and all-out war on the Plains Indians were mythologized as the romantic settling of the frontier. As European immigrants filled American cities, riots occasionally attacked national or ethnic minority communities—Greeks, Jews, Irish, Czechs, Germans, Italians, and others who, at various times, were not yet fully assimilated into whiteness—though these people might be the victims of a mob one year only to participate in aggressive mob violence the next. As revolutionary movements developed, the same terror techniques were deployed against leading activists and organizers—many communists, anarchists, and radical labor organizers were disappeared by the KKK or similar vigilantes. And anti-Black riots and lynchings occurred all across the North, in Chicago, New York, Pittsburgh, Detroit, and Philadelphia, from Mapleton, Maine, to Tacoma, Washington.[3]

So why, if we want to understand looting and rioting as essential tactics in fighting racial capitalism, is it vital that we see the role that riots played in enforcing the white supremacist order? For one, it is important to understand that rioting is a common political tool and, as such, can be used for many different political aims: rioting is powerful. More importantly, we can through this study tease out the differences between liberatory rioting and its opposite and see the ways in which property, violence, and race are organized differently in these separate riots. We have to stop thinking of a "riot," which can after all encompass so many different functions—from sports celebration to overthrow of a regime—as an easily grasped and unified concept. If we learn to pay attention to the content, tactics, and actions contained within them, we can learn not to dismiss, misunderstand, or reject moments of possibility for revolutionary change and start to think and strategize about how to move toward that horizon.

I have tried, for the most part, to avoid detailed description or graphic focus on violence against Black people and their bodies in this book, because I follow many theorists in finding these descriptions predominantly a way of reproducing prurient consumption and political profiting off of Black death. This danger is doubly likely if those descriptions are coming from a non-Black author, let alone a white one such as myself, and though I've worked very hard, it's likely I've reproduced some of those structures here through my own blind spots. Although I keep it to a minimum, some depictions of violence seemed necessary to trace the way lynching functioned in American political life. And the chapter describes in general, if mostly nongraphically, moments of suffering, cruelty, murder, and assault. If this is likely to be traumatic or difficult for you, I suggest you skip directly to the next chapter.

THE MYRIAD FORMS OF WHITE SUPREMACIST TERROR FIND THEIR MOST dramatic expression in two historically differentiated kinds of violence: lynching and white rioting. The former mostly but by no means only occurred in rural areas, the latter, mostly but not only in urban ones. Instances of both occurred across the entire time period between the start of the Civil War and the civil rights movement—with perhaps the largest race riots in American history the New York City Draft Riots of 1863 and the lynching of Emmett Till in 1955, one of the initiating events of the civil rights movement.

Broadly speaking, however, lynching was the predominant mode of terror in the immediate aftermath of Reconstruction and the latter decades of the nineteenth century, with the annual number of lynchings peaking in the 1890s; rioting became much more commonplace at the turn of the twentieth century, beginning in earnest in the 1880s and reaching a peak in the Red Summer of 1919, which saw dozens of race riots all across the country, after which point both forms of terror subsided some. The distinction between lynching and rioting is not always particularly meaningful: for example, many riots began when white people were prevented from carrying out a lynching, and torturous, spectacular, vigilante public murder—a decent basic definition of lynching—was one of the main events of the riots.

Nevertheless, a gradual shift toward rioting occurred across the post-Reconstruction era. This change partially reflects the continuous migrations of Black people out of the rural South—where conditions of sharecropping, convict leasing, and debt peonage were so similar to those under slavery that Frederick Douglass, after a tour of the South in 1888, called emancipation "a stupendous fraud"—into industrializing cities in the North and the West, as well as general and increasing urbanization across the country.

These migrations were political movements, or flights of freedom. The first major wave of migration, known as the Exoduster Movement, saw forty thousand Black people, disillusioned by the collapse of Reconstruction and by white supremacist violence, organize and migrate from the Mississippi valley to the Great Plains in 1879. Migrations continued throughout the period, in waves large and small. Migration north and west was not simply an aggregate of personal flights for safety but a political tactic against sharecropping, lynching, and oppression—it was a form of strike that had, after all, served effectively under slavery. Migration was famously advocated as such by the country's largest Black newspaper, the *Chicago Defender*, as well as by other antilynching publications and organizers.*

During high points of organization and agitation, or in the face of particularly intense labor injustice or white violence, the majority of a Southern town's Black population might pack up and migrate within days or weeks of each other, leaving white landlords with crops rotting in their fields. In one of the contradictions of action produced by white supremacy, racist vigilantes and police forces would ride out to try to *stop* trains from leaving for the North, to try to keep the Black people they hated in their towns and counties. This means that the concentration of Black people in Northern and midwestern cities already represents something of a form of protection and resistance against white terror, because it reflects both flight from the places where that terror was most concentrated and formation of communities capable of more ready self-defense. It is also why urban police forces become an increasingly important force in white supremacist domination.

The trend from lynching to riot thus also reflects resistance and organization among the Black community, whose struggles across this period are often skipped over in standard histories. These people, who had brought themselves out of slavery, who had struck the fetters from their

---

*Migration-as-direct-action continues today, with the migrant caravans from Central America that marched to the US border.

wrists, did not simply fall silent as Reconstruction collapsed, as the coffle was refashioned as the chain gang, the slave hut rechristened the share-cropper's hovel. Though they and their children's movements are less well remembered and often less spectacular or legible as "protest," these generations did not live submissively and unhappily under Jim Crow, doing little until tension and anger finally boiled over into the civil rights struggle in the fifties. A continuity of Black armed resistance, struggle, organizing, and self-defense against white supremacy runs through the period that is crucial to remember and learn from.[4]

However, that continuity of resistance faced an organized and thor-ough campaign of white supremacist terror. It is important to insist how consciously lynching was used as both a political weapon of oppression and a tool of white community consolidation, particularly because we are living through a second era of lynching: many more Black people have been murdered by police in each of the last few years than were lynched in 1892, the worst year of that terror, which saw 162 people killed.[5]*

Usually not chaotic, sudden, or disorganized bursts of violence, lynchings were instead prepared for days, even weeks in advance, called for and explained by community leaders, hyped and built up in local newspapers. Though some lynchings happened in the dead of night, many occurred in broad daylight and appeared as nothing so much as massive popular festivals. Free trains might be organized to bring white people from the surrounding rural counties to the town of the lynching, where crowds paraded the victim from jail to the site of the lynching: there white families might picnic before or after the murder, while enter-prising white entrepreneurs might sell popcorn and lemonade.

Though white people north and south usually claimed and believed that the regime of lynch law was a response to sexual violation of white women, Ida B. Wells's investigations showed that the actual proximate causes for lynching were various: "Of these thousands of men and women who have been put to death without judge or jury, less than one-third of them have been accused of criminal assault." Wells lists the reasons for

---

*However, because the Black population has increased four times since then, lynching was more common per capita, at least in 1892—though such morbid math completely misses the way this form of terrorism operates.

lynchings: for accusations of murder, robbery, arson, burglary, "race prejudice," "quarreled with white men," making threats, rioting, miscegena-
tion, and in many cases "no reasons were given, the victims were lynched
on general principle."[6] Such a varied list belies the claim that lynching
was in response to crime: the reproduction of white supremacy was its
reason and its cause, plain and simple. The modern-day regime of police
lynching has a similarly absurd list of instigating causes, including selling
CDs, playing in a playground, walking in the middle of the street, and
holding a toy gun in a Walmart.

But just as the arbitrary nature of the violence was crucial in enforcing
terror in the Black community, unifying claims around sexual violence
were crucial to justifying the violence to the white "community." Wells
demonstrates how this regime of lynching, validated as the "protection"
of white womanhood, functioned as a two-directional re-enforcement of
white supremacist patriarchal power. Hazel V. Carby summarizes Wells's
argument: "White men used their ownership of the body of the white
female as a terrain on which to lynch the Black male. White women felt
that their caste was their protection and that their interests lay with the
power that ultimately confined them."[7] Lynching solidified a politics that
used the Black male sexual threat to defend white violence—a thread
that still runs through many carceral white feminist projects that appeal
to the state and its police and prisons for protection.

Photographs of lynching victims' remains were taken and turned into
postcards, which participants sent to friends and loved ones, and white
people sometimes scrambled to take scraps of clothing or even pieces
of the victim's body as souvenirs. Though individuals might have, as a
group they felt no shame or confusion about what they were doing; on
the contrary, lynchings could be a major form of social gathering and
togetherness in rural white communities.

In the period, white people, more commonly but hardly exclusively
in the South, thought of lynchings the same way we are taught to think
of criminal trials today: as an integral part of American democracy and
society, as a crucial mode of criminal justice. The criminal courts and
their police agents today do the same work of white supremacist terror
and oppression as the lynch mobs of the nineteenth century, though

their exploits, rather than watched or participated in directly in the public square, are instead heroized through the news and through social and
popular media about courts, cops, and vigilantes.

AS PART OF THE SUPPRESSION OF BLACK POWER IN THE AFTERMATH
of Reconstruction, white supremacists, especially in the cities, used their
own forms of looting and rioting. If the tactics, on the surface level, are
the same as those defended in this book, the goals were fundamentally
different.

During the Ferguson uprising, a tongue-in-cheek political hashtag
sprang up on Twitter, #suspectedlooters, which was filled with images
of colonial Europeans, plantation owners, cowboys, and white cultural
appropriators. Similarly, many have pointed out that, had Africa not been
looted, there wouldn't even be any Black people in America. These are
powerful correctives to arguments around looting rioters, and the rhetorical point—when people of color loot a store, they are taking back a
miniscule portion of what has been historically stolen from them, from
their ancestral history and language to the basic safety of their children
on the street today—is absolutely essential. But purely for the purposes of
this argument—because I agree wholeheartedly with the political project
of these campaigns—what white settlers and enslavers did wasn't mere
looting.

It was genocide, theft, and cruelty of the lowest order. But part of how
slavery and colonialism functioned was to introduce new territories and
categories to the purview of ownership, of property. Not only did they
steal the land from native peoples, but they also produced a system under
which the land itself could be stolen, owned by legal fiat through force
of arms. Not only did they take away Africans' lives, history, culture, and
freedom, but they also transformed people into property and labor power
into a saleable commodity.

White supremacist rioting thus served to *strengthen* this everyday robbery known as the law, as property, as society. White rioters aim to keep
people of color from developing autonomous economic, political, or so-

cial power as much as possible, or to crush it where it has appeared. To do this, they produce submission, fear, and economic ruin in the people they attack. White supremacist race riots thus tend to feature significantly more personal violence than they do attacks on property, more property destruction than looting, and, when looting occurs, these white rioters tend to target people's homes and persons much more than these items are targeted during antipolice/anticapitalist uprisings, which tend to focus on stores and workplaces.*

We can see the extent to which looting is not a natural feature of the white supremacist riot, ironically, from one of the historical examples when it occurred to a significant degree. The Elaine, Arkansas, riot of 1919, the final and bloodiest event of the infamous Red Summer, is one of the most violent and horrible incidents in American history. Over sixty-some hours, white rioters killed an unknown number of Black sharecroppers and their families, then looted a valuable cotton crop those sharecroppers had grown and picked. At least 150 people were killed, but some estimates put the numbers as high as 850 people murdered.

This attack—if the latter number is correct, the deadliest race riot in American history—took place not because of some supposed crime or outrage but because the sharecroppers had organized. Refusing to continue purchasing overpriced farming supplies through their white employers or selling their crops for a tenth of what they were worth, the sharecroppers of Elaine instead formed a union and hired a lawyer to guarantee that they would be paid market price for the year's bumper cotton crop.† As Ida B. Wells, whose activism and journalism are essential to understanding the social production of lynchings and race riots,

---

*This is not to make a moral distinction between looting and property destruction or to imagine that property destruction is "worse" or more white supremacist than looting. Property destruction has been just as much a significant part of liberatory uprisings as looting. It is merely a historical fact that the system already guarantees that most of the products of people of color's labor goes to white people. When it did occur, looting often reflected the mixed class composition of white supremacist riots: lynch mobs and rioting masses were often led by the respectable heads of communities, but working-class white people took part, too, and used them as occasions to literalize the wages of whiteness.

†Massacres and white riots were a common method of repressing Black worker organization—in Thibodaux, Louisiana, in 1887, thirty-two Black sugar plantation workers on strike, including Black union leaders, were massacred by a white mob.

pointed out, while general strikes by white labor unions were shutting down whole cities in the North without facing mass murder, merely organizing a union and demanding the most basic economic rights proved to be deadly for Black sharecroppers.*

The riot began when whites from Elaine and nearby counties surrounded the Hoop Spur church, three miles north of Elaine, where the sharecroppers' union was having a general meeting, a gathering that included children and old folks, full families. At a certain point, perhaps once all the vigilantes had arrived, the white landlords, sheriffs, and farmers who encircled the church fired guns indiscriminately into the building. Though a couple of Black organizers had come armed and, guarding the doors, fired back—killing one white man, though it's also possible he was shot in the back by his white compatriots—the Black sharecroppers were significantly outgunned, and unknown numbers died in the church. After those who could flee escaped into the surrounding countryside, the white rioters burned the church to the ground without removing the bodies of their victims. As so often is the case with Black people murdered by America, the number of dead is unknown.

The next day saw a full-out murderous rampage. As Wells describes it: "Hundreds of . . . white men were chasing and murdering every Negro they could find, driving them from their homes and stalking them in the woods and fields as men hunt wild beasts. They were finishing up the job from the night before."[8] The Black residents who survived did so by fleeing the town and hiding in the woods for days. Late the second day, after nearly forty-eight hours of this violence, federal soldiers were sent in; their arrival forced white rioters to return to their homes. These soldiers promptly rounded up and arrested any Black person they found on charges of inciting the riot, putting them in stockades. They also murdered a handful of Black people who had survived the initial mobs.

Later, Elaine's white population would claim that the death of the one white man at the church (and another killed the next day) was the

---

*Indeed, it would be over a decade, and only in the depths of the Great Depression, before a sharecropper's union would actually spread across the South and gain real material power. And that union, too, would be harried by intimidation, evictions, riots, and lynchings.

reason the riot happened in the first place. For these two white men killed, twelve Black men, some of them labor organizers, were sentenced to death for the riot. Black people were the only ones arrested or prosecuted for the events in Elaine.

One survivor Wells interviewed returned to her home for the first time four weeks after these events to pack up her belongings and claim the money owed for the cotton she and her husband had picked. Discovering her house completely empty, she went to the white landlord's house to ask for the money owed her. The landlord told her she would receive nothing and threatened to kill her and "burn her up" if she didn't leave immediately. During this ignoble exchange, she noticed her family's furniture and clothing in his house. As though that wasn't enough, after leaving with nothing but the clothes on her back, she was then arrested in town by another landlord and put into forced labor for eight days at the Elaine jail.[9]

The white people of Elaine rioted to prevent Black people from successfully organizing, to keep them indebted to white landlords and trapped in the system of neo-slavery known as sharecropping. Tactically, the difference between how and when the looting happened is instructive: the looting that did occur didn't appear to actually happen *during the riot* but rather in its aftermath, after federal soldiers had restored order. White people taking Black people's things is what happens under the conditions of *order*, not the conditions of *riot*. The most common relation to property in white riots is the simple destruction of Black people's personal property rather than any organized looting of private businesses or commercial goods. For example, in the East St. Louis Massacre, in 1917, white rioters entered homes Black people had fled, gathered all their things into piles, and burned them.

Anti-Chinese rioting in the West, meanwhile, was driven by rioters' desire to steal jobs, not property. In these rarely mentioned atrocities, white settlers—many of them working-class European immigrants— rioted to take over industries largely built by Chinese laborers. Violent assaults on Chinese immigrants had been occurring with shocking regularity since the Gold Rush of 1848–1855, at which time non-Indigenous people began settling California en masse. European Americans and

Chinese people made up the vast majority of this new population. The extreme and common violence of the "Wild West" was real, but its victims were much more likely to be Chinese, Chicanx, or Indigenous laborers than the white outlaws and their white sheriff nemeses mythologized in westerns.

Chinese workers did the mining, construction, and, crucially, the laying of the westernmost leg of the transcontinental railroad—a task almost entirely done by "coolie" labor—transforming access to California from a months-long journey into and through wilderness into a quick and simple fact of life for people in the eastern United States. But this task's completion in 1869 was a disaster for Chinese communities, because the suddenly easy journey west meant a flood of European immigrants from the East. Those Europeans, with their dreams of "finding gold boulders lying in the streams" dashed, "demanded the jobs that Chinese labor had created."[10] They were supported in these demands by capitalists and labor unions alike.

Chinese people were marched out of towns at gunpoint, lynched in the streets, their businesses and homes looted and burned down, and, eventually, they were literally outlawed with the federal Chinese Exclusion Act of 1882. This bipartisan law, supported strongly by organized labor, stopped all Chinese immigration and made reentry incredibly difficult (meaning anyone who had arrived but had left family or friends behind in China had to decide to return to China permanently or give up ever seeing their loved ones again).* Similar to Dred Scott before it, this act held that Chinese people could not be and never had been citizens of the United States.

Much as the Minutemen and other militia groups voluntarily patrol the borders of Mexico today, in the new towns of the West it fell to white rioters and vigilantes to enforce this act. And, much as anti-immigrant sentiments today hold that immigrants are at fault for low wages, organized labor of the American West argued that the mere presence of Chinese laborers depressed wages. Three decades earlier, their union

---

*President Trump's Muslim Ban is no innovation, it is merely a return to previous American immigration policies.

counterparts, who had been against emancipation, believing free Black labor would be bad for white earnings, shared this racist ideology.

Organized labor therefore supported and perpetuated, both electorally and through industrial action, violence against Chinese workers. The Knights of Labor (K of L) was the preeminent labor organization in America in the 1880s and one of the largest in American history, with at one point over 20 percent of all American industrial workers as members. The K of L had Black locals that participated in inspiring struggles in the South, but its national and western offices were famously and openly supportive of the Chinese Exclusion Act.[†]

In the 1880s and 1890s, a genocidal push was made to entirely remove Chinese people from California and the West, one legalized and encouraged from above but driven by popular vigilante action from below. A K of L local branch was behind the infamous 1885 expulsion of Chinese residents from Tacoma, Washington, a major town with a population 10 percent Chinese up until that point. The most notorious of these ethnic cleansing actions was the 1885 massacre in Rock Springs, Wyoming, led by K of L miners, "where over 20 Chinese miners were killed by a storm of rifle-fire as European miners enforced their take-over of all mining." As J. Sakai writes, "Similar events happened all over the West. In 1886 some 35 California towns reported that they had totally eliminated their Chinese populations." [11‡]

As the twentieth century turned, this violence was continued and replicated against the increasing numbers of Japanese, Filipino, and other Asian immigrants. Filipino immigration was a direct result of US imperial war on and colonization of the Philippines: settlers continued the

---

[†]This was in part to do with the largely decentralized and contradictory nature of the K of L. Whereas the official leaders of the K of L—most importantly, its head, Terence Powderly—were reactionary, racist, and totally opposed to radical industrial action, including even simple strikes, K of L locals took action into their own hands. Thus, while the K of L pushed Chinese exclusion in the West, radical workers in the South organized under the banner of the K of L to pursue revolutionary agitation.

[‡]The cross-class, effective, and organized expulsion of Indigenous, Asian, and other nonwhite peoples from the Pacific Northwest left a sinister political legacy: the modern American neo-Nazi movement has its roots in Oregon, and other white nationalist currents have emerged from the now overwhelmingly white Oregon and Washington.

state's colonial violence through a number of major anti-Filipino riots in California in the twenties. FDR's internment in 1942 of 120,000 Japanese Americans, most of them from the West Coast and most of them citizens, in concentration camps—which of course "opened up" thousands of jobs for white people and "cleared" the land the Japanese workers had been farming—is only the most well-remembered instance of the organized dispossession and domination of Asians in America.

The argument of this book is that when looting appears in an anti-police uprising, it is a radical and powerful tactic for getting to the roots of the system the movement fights against. The argument is not that all instances of looting increase freedom, are righteous or politically anti-propertarian. Rioting, property destruction, and looting are all tactics, and though they may be more favorable to certain forms of struggle, they can be and have been used to further differential and opposing political goals and agendas.

Indeed, in the last ten years we've witnessed the right-wing and even fascist appropriation of liberatory tactics that exploded onto the scene in the revolts and revolutions of 2011. Winter 2013–2014 in Ukraine saw an "occupation of the squares" co-opted by Far Right nationalists, while in Thailand a right-wing middle-class mass movement calling itself "Occupy Bangkok" tried to abolish parliament and install a military dictatorship run by the king. Spring of 2016 saw a right-wing "soft" coup in Brazil that was legitimized by a predominantly white, middle-class street movement, which eventually led to the rise of fascist president Jair Bolsonaro. That movement stole its tactics from the 2013 working-class uprisings against public transit fare hikes and the gentrification, evictions, and corruption of the World Cup and Olympics.[12] And in Turkey in July 2016, a failed coup against president Recep Tayyip Erdoğan ended with him calling people into the streets and into Taksim Square to "protect democracy" (i.e., his regime), despite the fact that he had been brutally persecuting, imprisoning, and murdering people involved in the democratic uprisings of 2013 against him that were first centered in Taksim. Indeed, Erdoğan used the coup attempt to push through the redevelopment of Taksim that had sparked the 2013 uprising in the first place.

When a Donald Trump supporter said that "riots aren't necessarily a bad thing" in March 2016, she wasn't thinking of Ferguson or Baltimore. It's Elaine or Rock Springs whose legacy she was evoking. And Trump and his Far Right cohort's intent focus on the media (both through attacking "fake news" and turning Fox News and the like into de facto policy organs) reflects a similar desire to return to the legacy of turn-of-the-century media, which directly encouraged, supported, and even caused white mob violence.

THE DOMINANT MEDIA IS A TOOL OF WHITE SUPREMACY AND STEADfast ally of the police. It repeats the lines the police deliver nearly verbatim and uncritically, even when the police story changes upward of nine times, as it did in the murders of Mike Brown, Tyrone West, and Sandra Bland. The media uses phrases like "officer-involved shooting" and switches to passive voice when a white vigilante or a police officer shoots a Black person ("shots were fired"). Journalists claim that "you have to hear both sides" in order to privilege the obfuscating reports of the state over the clear voices and testimony of an entire community, members of which witnessed the police murder a teenager in cold blood.* The media is more respectful of white serial killers and mass murderers than of unarmed Black victims of murder.

This media collusion with white supremacy and the police is not new. In fact, its modern form is incredibly subtle and crafty compared to its turn-of-the-century manifestations. In the late nineteenth and early twentieth centuries, the relationship was more intimate, local, and direct. And few writers or thinkers traced this relationship between white supremacist violence and the media as clearly and carefully as Ida B. Wells.

Quite frankly, many lynchings and white riots were directly instigated, encouraged, and even produced by the media, which was, after

---

*"You gotta hear both sides" is a century-old white supremacist obfuscation. As Ida B. Wells wrote in 1899: "The Southern press champions burning men alive and says: 'Consider the Facts.'"

all, owned by the men who most benefited from the white supremacist power structure. The main form of media in the period was the local newspaper, and these papers were not bastions of democratic truth nor some noble fourth estate of society any more than Fox News or MSNBC are today. Owned and operated by the richest and most "respectable" men in their communities, these newspapers directly incited lynchings, riots, and racial violence. The infamous Tulsa Race Riot of 1921, discussed more below, was instigated by front-page headlines that read TO LYNCH NEGRO TONIGHT.

The Atlanta riot of 1906 was similarly prompted by a series of misleading and outright false headlines about Black men assaulting white women. A month before the riot, a man had been lynched in an Atlanta suburb for an alleged sexual attack, and violent tension had been building all summer. But it didn't boil over into a massacre until the media got involved. On the night of September 22, the *Atlanta Evening News* released *three* extra editions, separated from one another by only an hour, with headlines proclaiming an attempted assault, then a "second" and "third assault," the latter perpetrated by a "fiendish negro" who attacked a white woman in her backyard. As the newspapermen knew well, these repeated extra editions meant that newsboys on every street corner would be shouting out the news of black-on-white assaults all evening. As white men got off work, some ten thousand of them formed into mobs that terrorized Atlanta for seventy-two hours.[13]

The Wilmington, North Carolina, riot of 1898, a coup d'état in which two days of rioting brought down a mixed-race Republican government, installed a white Democratic one in its place, killed dozens, and drove thousands of Black residents permanently out of Wilmington, was largely made possible and given ideological force by the media. Historians recognize the Wilmington coup as a key moment in consolidating post-Reconstruction white supremacy, because it saw a white mob overturn a legitimate election result, drive Black officials out of office, disenfranchise all Black voters, and establish an officially white supremacist local government. The coup was reported nationally, and the fact that the federal government witnessed these events and did nothing to

stop or overturn them demonstrated to the entire country that white violence and supremacy—not law or elections—formed the real basis of
American governance.

White Democrat newspapers unrelentingly slandering Black public officials in their editorials laid the groundwork for the coup in the
months leading up to the 1898 elections. The day after Republicans (and
an aligned party called the Fusionists) again won the majority in the elections, a group of Democrats rallied a white mob to overthrow the election result. The mob's first act was burning down the offices of the *Daily
Record*. The *Record*, the local Black newspaper, had been running antilynching editorials, some arguing, factually, that sexual assault on white
women was not in fact the cause of lynchings. The white papers reported
on these editorials incessantly in the days before the coup, claiming absurdly that such words were encouraging sexual violence and that "white
womanhood" needed to be protected from Black Republican power as
embodied in these editorials. Creating white victimization and grievance
via willful misinterpretation of reality is one of the oldest tricks in the
settler-colonial book. The mob posed for photos in front of the burning
newspaper office, photos that would be published in Democratic papers
across the country.

The following year, the April 1899 lynching of Samuel Hose "was
suggested, encouraged, and made possible by the daily press of Atlanta."[14]
Hose had killed his white boss in self-defense. When Hose had the au-
dacity to ask for months of owed back wages to help pay for his grievously
ill mother's medical care, his boss, rather than draw out his wallet, drew
his gun and told Hose he was going to kill him. Hose, who had been
chopping wood, threw his ax at his boss, killing him, and fled. The newspapers reported it as a cold-blooded, unprovoked, premeditated murder.

Every day for a week, the *Atlanta Constitution* published double-
columned headlines about Hose "predicting" that he would be captured and lynched, in particular focusing on the detail that he would be
burned to death. Pretending that it was merely reflecting and reporting
on the mood of the public, day after day the paper beat the drum for his
immolation, making it a near certainty. When Hose was finally captured,

two thousand white people gathered and burned him alive. The next day, the paper published a gruesomely detailed blow-by-blow account of the lynching.

Today many in the current movement claim that the widespread sharing and distribution of videos of police violence against Black people represent a step toward justice—with some activists calling for body cameras on police—but in fact, the widespread sharing of images of white supremacist violence and Black death was an essential part of lynch law. Not only did newspapers write moment-by-moment accounts of lynchings and riots, but also photographs of lynching victims circulated the country in prints and postcards, while cartoons and illustrations of lynchings were a common sight in papers and political propaganda. Despite the lack of televisual mass media or internet technology, images of Black death proliferated—though the images were also sometimes used by activists to produce moral outrage against lynch law.[15] But more often than not, the media's deployment of lynching images served to normalize white supremacist violence, narrativizing it into a digestible and socially acceptable form.

The media didn't merely precipitate and incite racial violence, it also defended the police and their role therein. The July 1900 race riots in New Orleans, in which white mobs roamed the streets for a week murdering any Black people they could find, erupted when policemen attempted to arrest two local organizers, Robert Charles and Leonard Pierce, for the crime of sitting on a stoop while Black. When Charles and Pierce objected to being arrested, the officers drew guns, one putting his to Pierce's temple. Charles, who was armed, drew to defend himself, and a gunfight ensued in which Charles and one cop were wounded; the cop died of his wounds the next day.

Reporting on this in the next morning's news, the two main papers in New Orleans proclaimed the cops' innocence and righteousness. Lacking the instantaneous communications technologies and advanced police–media apparatus of today, they failed to get their stories straight, telling completely different tales of the gunfight. Nevertheless, just like they do when police lynch people today, the media focused on smearing the two Black men who had been assaulted by the police and defending the policemen's actions. The *Times-Picayune* wrote Charles and Pierce were "desperate men" who will "no doubt be proven to be burglars" and that the neighborhood they were attacked in "has been troubled by bad negros." As a result of these inflammatory reports and insinuations, white mobs formed and engaged in a week of mob violence and collective punishment as they hunted for Charles.

Not satisfied with instigating the riot, in the days that followed the New Orleans police stopped Black people they found in the street—when they didn't simply arrest them—in order to disarm them, turning their weapons over to rioters and leaving them defenseless against the white mob. After outright participation and mass-arresting Black victims, this disarming was the most common function carried out by the police during race riots in the period.

The police didn't intercept rioters or try to calm down white crowds in Atlanta in 1906, Philadelphia in 1918, Chicago in 1919, or Tulsa in 1921: they merely arrested or disarmed the Black people. Sometimes uniformed police straight up joined in the rioting, though their relationship to the action was frequently a little more subtle. Off-duty officers joined white mobs, while on-duty police gladly gave prisoners up to white mobs, though they would later claim, with unquestioning support from the media, that they were outnumbered and unable to do anything. Sometimes this ruse was quite elaborate: police would secretly inform Klansmen and rioters when and where they would be transporting their prisoners, making it appear that the mobs had intercepted and overwhelmed them, allowing them to look "innocent" and separate from the lynchings in official accounts. Journalists and newspaper owners, themselves often members of lynch mobs, would then dutifully repeat these stories of the noble police being overpowered, thus clearing the state of responsibility for vigilante violence and masking the deep interconnections of the vigilantes, the media, and the police.

The dominant media and the police have long been mutually supportive organizations, working together to maintain white supremacy and police domination over society. The media washes the police's hands of wrongdoing, and the police give the media "access," special treatment in the street, direct reports, and dramatic stories that sell papers. The media is a necessary part of the state apparatus in a liberal democracy, and though it might very occasionally "speak truth to power," it usually just speaks power's truth. Marginalized activists, researchers, and reporters, like Ida B. Wells, must use their skills not only to "speak truth" but also to use truth to organize and encourage action. But Wells's reception by mainstream history shows how revolutionary activism gets reduced into speech.

Much as popular history domesticates Harriet Tubman, transforming her from a revolutionary waging war against patriarchy, property, and state into "a role model for leadership and participation in our democracy," as Obama's Treasury secretary Jack Lew put it, so has liberal history disarmed and deradicalized Ida B. Wells. Search for mainstream articles and historical accounts of Wells and you will learn that she was a journalist-crusader against lynching who focused national and international attention on the facts of white terrorism and was one of the most prominent writers, thinkers, and activists of her day. You'll also probably learn that she cofounded the National Association for the Advancement of Colored People (NAACP) and spent her later life campaigning for women's suffrage.

So you would be forgiven for thinking that her antilynching activism was largely liberal, pointed outward from the Black community toward "raising awareness" among powerful white people or bringing legal action from the federal government. But that wasn't so. Her popularity and reach arose not only because she brought attention to and preserved empirical evidence on the horrors of lynching but also because she proposed and argued vociferously for more immediate solutions to lynch law: she urged Black people in the South to migrate north, boycott white businesses, and arm themselves and get organized on the basis of self-defense. As she wrote in 1892, "A Winchester rifle should have a place of honor in every black home, and it should be used for that protection which the law refuses to give."*

---

*The context surrounding Wells's declaration is this: "Of the many inhuman outrages of this present year, the only case where the proposed lynching did *not* occur, was where the men armed themselves in Jacksonville, Fla., and Paducah, Ky., and prevented it. The only time an Afro-American who was assaulted got away has been when he had a

Schools don't teach the fact that W. E. B. Du Bois was a staunch advocate of armed self-defense, let alone the fact that, as soon as news reached him of the 1906 anti-Black riots breaking out in Atlanta, he raced home from his research in Alabama to stand guard with his wife, where they protected their home with a shotgun. They don't tell you that A. Philip Randolph, ally of Bayard Rustin and MLK, organizer of the Pullman Porters and honorary lead marcher in the 1963 March on Washington, spent his early career as founding editor of the radical Black socialist magazine *The Messenger* calling for armed self-defense against lynching.

Although the Black Panthers and the Black Liberation Army are the most famous advocates of Black armed self-defense, the tactic's high-water mark might well have been in the years immediately following World War I, particularly during the height of the Red Summer of 1919. Most of the major antilynching activists and intellectuals of the period—Du Bois, Randolph, Wells, Lucy Parsons, Robert Abbott, and many more—agreed on the centrality of armed self-defense. Even many within the more reformist leadership supported it. In 1919, a gathering of Black Methodist bishops, repeatedly pressed, refused to denounce violence used to resist white terrorism. Marcus Garvey's Universal Negro Improvement Association (UNIA) advocated self-defense against racist oppression in 1920.[16] And, indeed, many of these Black activists had been trained in armed action as veterans of World War I.

WAR HAS ALWAYS BEEN A FUNDAMENTAL FACTOR IN CAPITALIST EXPANsion and growth, a major tool of capitalist societies to increase and rationalize production, spur innovation, capture resources, open new markets, capture foreign labor forces, keep profits from stagnating, and centralize political power. But wars built around mass mobilization can also be dangerous to capitalists, because they can produce social instabil-

gun and used it in self-defense. The lesson this teaches and which every Afro-American should ponder well, is that a Winchester rifle should have a place of honor in every black home, and it should be used for that protection which the law refuses to give" (Wells, *Southern Horror*).

ity and chaos. Mass mobilization and generational war trauma can overturn traditional hierarchies and, as in the American South in 1861, Paris
in 1871, and Russia in 1917, create the conditions for social revolution.

In the run-up to US entry into the Great War, particularly from 1916
to 1917, the sudden increase in lynchings was no doubt linked to the
incredibly jingoistic propaganda that built the popular case for war—US
patriotism is always deadly to nonwhite people the world over. But, as
five million US soldiers demobilized at the end of World War I, white
vigilante violence made an even more dramatic upsurge. This spike in
violence reflects an attempt to reconstitute cisheteropatriarchal white supremacist capitalism in the face of numerous threats to its dominance
empowered and made visible during the war.

During the eighteen months of US mobilization, women had come
to play a major role in economic life and society in the absence of men,
doing men's labor and learning "male" trades—by the end of the war,
women made up 20 percent of the industrial workforce, with much
higher numbers in health care and agricultural sectors. This empowerment came on the heels of the suffrage movement's massive growth
and popularization in 1916–1917, as women were organizing politically
as women and publicly pushing for change. On the front lines, meanwhile, many soldiers, perhaps pining for suffragette fiancées back in
America, found comfort in each other's arms: gay sex was commonplace
in the trenches, if deeply repressed, punished, and denied by military
hierarchies. No doubt many fiancées found the same queer comforts at
home. And masses of soldiers returned disabled, mentally or physically,
to reckon with and struggle against an ableist society that required neu-
rotypical able bodies to earn a living, a society that denied veterans and
people with disabilities sufficient benefits and care.*

At the same time, the revolutionary labor movement, enflamed by
the Russian Revolution and a seemingly imminent revolution in Ger-

---

*This group of veterans and their families would eventually form a massive protest move-
ment during the Depression. Called the Bonus Army, in 1932 they marched from all
across the country into DC and occupied the Mall in a tent city, sending out marches
and petitions and rioting against police. The movement was stopped only when Hoover
sent in federal troops, led by six tanks, to evict them in a bloody battle.

many, enlarged by a huge wave of radical immigrants, grew increasingly powerful and militant: strike activity increased dramatically from 1914 through 1919. War production brought employment almost up to 100 percent, which meant bosses couldn't easily find replacements for strikers, and so labor action became more effective. And increased war production meant hundreds of thousands of Black migrants from the South found work in Northern industrial centers and entered industries once dominated by white labor. The Great Migration of Black people out of the South had one of its peak years in 1916. Black veterans, trained in combat, who experienced greater freedom and power overseas, were radicalized in large numbers after serving and gaining respect abroad in a war they were ostensibly fighting for democracy, only to return to a racist and oppressive society.

A generation of young white men, both empowered and traumatized by their experience of war, felt enraged to return to an American society struggling against their power on all fronts. Studies show that incidence of domestic violence increases appreciably after sports matches and increase much more dramatically among the fans whose team has *won* the game. Victory is an emboldening experience for violent patriarchs—part of why both war and victory are such highly valued principles in fascist movements. In the same way, victory in World War I may well have further inflamed the white men of America in their repressive activity.

The government saw the threats to the system clearly and initiated what would eventually be known as the First Red Scare, which saw an upsurge in both government repression and collective vigilante violence against anarchists, communists, and labor organizers.

Simultaneously, the white people of America engaged in the biggest wave of anti-Black collective punishments and riots in American history.[†] White veterans' groups and patriotic associations most frequently formed the core of the angry mobs that participated in this violence.

But Black people fought back. The 1919 riots in Omaha, Nebraska (one of the white riots that featured extensive looting, as rioters attacked

---

[†] Some of these riots took the form of white organized labor, on strike, attacking Black strikebreakers brought in by the bosses.

a well-established Black business district), Knoxville, Tennessee, Wilmington, Delaware, and Dublin, Georgia, began when armed resistance prevented a white mob from lynching a Black man. In Bisbee, Arizona, a white serviceman harassed and attacked members of a Black cavalry detachment: when the Black soldiers reported it to the police, the cops just tried to disarm and arrest the Black cavalrymen who had been attacked. But the Black soldiers did not relinquish their arms, and a gunfight ensued that ended only when the Black cavalrymen were fully surrounded and arrested.

In Chicago, the Black community rose up after a group of white teens killed a boy by throwing rocks at him and his friends because they were swimming too close to the white beach.* A crowd gathered, demonstrating and demanding justice from the police, who had refused to arrest any of the boys throwing rocks. The police merely arrested several of the protesters. Mobs of white men, emboldened by police (in)action and gathering in response to the Black uprising, attacked the protesters—some of whom were armed, and most of whom fought back—and as news of the fighting spread, so did the fighting itself.

Mobs Black and white gathered across Chicago, and skirmishes occurred citywide, though violence was largely centered in the Black Southside. According to Harry Haywood, a Black veteran of the war, his neighborhood appeared "like a besieged city. Whole sections of it were in ruins. Buildings burned and the air was heavy with smoke, reminiscent of the holocaust from which I had recently returned." But these white gangs were just as often driven out of the Southside in gun battles or killed in ambushes set up by Black workers and veterans. As Haywood, who would go on to become a leader of the Communist Party, put it, "Had race prejudice in the U.S. lessened? I knew better. Conditions in the States had not changed, but we Blacks had. We were determined not to take it anymore."[17] These were the "New Negroes," a movement of Black people who expressed racial pride, who refused to submit to racist

---

*This is a classic example of the violence maintaining Northern segregation. Though there were no Jim Crow laws, kids, adults, and police all violently maintained the de facto distinctions between "Black" and "white" beaches, neighborhoods, and businesses, even if, legally speaking, there was no distinction.

violence, and who would play crucial roles in Marcus Garvey's Back to Africa movement, the Harlem Renaissance, the Communist Party, and the labor movement.

These race riots reflect a much more complicated and conflictual history than the tales of Black victimization and helplessness they often come to stand for. Whereas some, like the Elaine Massacre, were direct and successful attacks on Black autonomy—pogroms—others involved extensive Black resistance and uprising that changed their meaning and their effects.

The perfect example of this is the Tulsa riot of 1921. This riot has recently been brought back into public consciousness by the important work of activists and writers, and it is remembered now largely as the moment when "Black Wall Street" was destroyed. The Tulsa riot saw the Greenwood district, also called Little Africa, the wealthiest Black neighborhood in America, burned to the ground in about sixteen hours of intense fighting. Sometimes a partial history of this event is deployed to argue that white people rioted predominantly because of that Black wealth. This segues into the argument that such success—Black achievement of the American Dream—should be the main goal for the Black community. These analyses tend to exaggerate the actual economic power Greenwood represented and downplay the role of Black self-defense in the riot.[†]

If the riot in Tulsa saw the tragic destruction of a symbol and community of Black power, why did many Black Tulsans who lived through it look back on it with pride?[18] And if it was an emboldening victory for white supremacy, why, after the riot, was there never another lynching in Tulsa County, when lynchings continued for years in the surrounding counties?

The Tulsa riot, like many of those discussed above, erupted after a white lynch mob was thwarted in its murderous purpose. In this instance,

---

[†]"Whites owned a large portion of the land in the district. Furthermore, black Tulsa's service-oriented businesses were geared toward catering to a wage-earning population. Few of them employed more than a handful of people. Economically, black Tulsa was dependent upon the wages paid to black workers by white employers" (Scott Ellsworth, *Death in a Promised Land: The Tulsa Race Riot of 1921* [Baton Rouge: Louisiana State University Press, 1992], 16).

the mob's target was Dick Rowland, a shoeshine falsely accused of attempting to rape a white elevator operator, which he allegedly did in her elevator, in a public building, during business hours. The mob turned riotous when armed residents of Tulsa, led by members of the African Blood Brotherhood (ABB), intercepted and stopped the attempted lynching.

The ABB, a clandestine pan-African all-Black Marxist revolutionary organization, formed in direct response to the Red Summer of 1919. It arose as a self-defense organization to empower and protect Black communities from lynchings, collective punishment, and race riots. Though it was founded in New York City, branches spread across the Midwest and the South. A predecessor of the Black Panther Party, the ABB advocated and agitated for armed self-defense, with a long-term goal of armed insurrection and, ultimately, socialist revolution led by Black workers. A chapter operated in Tulsa almost from the ABB's inception.

Outside of the North, the ABB was an insurrectionary secret society—being an out Black Communist in the Jim Crow South would have been a death sentence—with an internationalist bent, working to foment revolution while supporting and spreading information about the Russian Revolution and anticolonial struggles in Africa and the Middle East. It did so through local organization and its newspaper, *The Crusader*. Rumors of an imminent Black uprising or insurrection frequently factor in to the buildup of white riots and lynchings—a direct legacy of lynch mobs' slave patrol predecessors. Such rumors were particularly strong in white Tulsa in the months leading up to the riot and may reflect increased radicalization and on-the-ground organizing in the Tulsa chapter of the ABB.

In any case, when, the day after Rowland's arrest, his lynching was announced and planned in the local newspaper (as mentioned above, the May 31, 1921, Tulsa *Tribune* afternoon edition headline read TO LYNCH NEGRO TONIGHT), the ABB pledged to resist the lynching, and organizers spread throughout Greenwood, urging residents to gather their arms and head to the jail to protect Rowland.

At the jail that evening, some two thousand white people dutifully gathered into a lynch mob. After two rounds of negotiations in which the sheriff refused to hand over Rowland, the mob prepared to storm the jail by force. Some hundred or so Black men, some of them ABB organizers, arrived at the jail with rifles, pistols, and shotguns and offered the sheriff assistance in protecting Rowland. As the groups faced off in front of the jail, someone—it is not known on which side—fired a shot, and a shootout began. The initial wave of gunfire lasted only a few moments, but when the dust settled ten white mob members lay dead in the street. The Black group, who had lost two of their number in the skirmish, retreated to Greenwood. Rowland had been successfully defended and would survive the night in the jail.

From there a rolling gun battle unfolded across Tulsa deep into the night, with white rioters trying to enter Greenwood but being repulsed by Black snipers at the railroad track bordering the neighborhood. The white rioters kept pushing, however, and on the morning of June 1, their attack intensified as they deployed military machine guns and some even flew decommissioned WWI biplanes over Greenwood, sniping and dropping firebombs. This assault eventually succeeded in pushing the defenders deeper into Greenwood and then out of the city, when white rioters then turned to the expediency of arson. They set Black businesses and buildings aflame, destroying much of the commercial main street and surrounding residential district, looting and burning houses and stores alike. The police, of course, worked through the night and the morning to disarm, round up, and jail any and all Black people they could find, incarcerating between four thousand and five thousand Black residents for days. The arrival of federal soldiers meant the end of the rioting by noon on June 1.

It had lasted less than twenty-four hours, but some fourteen hundred buildings had been destroyed. Reports about the number of dead vary, with some estimates claiming seventy-five dead, while others put the number nearer three hundred. All accounts suggest that some significant number—a third to half of those killed, in the case of the lower total estimates—were white rioters. Although the numbers and proportions will never be accurately known, many in Tulsa believed the true casualty numbers were covered up because they would have become a source of shame for the white community. It's certainly true that the legacy of the riot in Tulsa favors Black power: "during the 1950s and 1960s black civil rights leaders used the threat of 'bringing up' the riot as leverage in negotiations with white leaders" and, though white papers in Tulsa never mentioned the riot thereafter, Black papers spoke of it openly and often.[19]

The vast property destruction in Greenwood, however, proved to be a massive loss for the white rioters as well, because most of the Black residents and business owners rented their properties: some two-thirds of the real value destroyed in the riot belonged to white folks. In the aftermath, Greenwood was rebuilt and flourished again. The white community lived in fear of another riot, which it remembered with shame and humiliation. Meanwhile, "for many Black Tulsans, the riot, and particularly the rebuilding of their community, is an issue of pride."[20]

Was it only the legacy of Black Wall Street that Black Tulsans were proud of, or was it also their armed resistance against white rioters? In the months after the Tulsa riot, the ABB's newspaper, *The Crusader*, used the event as a point of nationwide recruitment. "What other organization can claim that brave record?" the editors wrote about the action in Tulsa. After the riot, there wasn't another lynching in Tulsa County for seven decades; only in the current era of police lynching has public white supremacist murder returned to Tulsa, and Greenwood was only truly destroyed by a recent wave of gentrification.

This is not to deny that day in 1921 was tragic. The destruction and loss of every Black life in that riot must be both mourned and avenged. (I count every white rioter killed a victory.) It is a travesty of justice that reparations committees, bills, and lawsuits failed through the nineties and early aughts to give Black survivors recompense. But what happens when we tell narratives of white oppression without including the stories of brave, violent, and partially successful resistance to it?

There are thus two versions of the events in Tulsa: one that tells of a white town destroying the Black American Dream, and another that recognizes Black armed organizers saving a man from lynching and fighting back against a murderous white lynch mob. The former narrative emphasizes the Black community as eternally suffering peaceful victims of white supremacist violence; the other, as an oppressed people organizing and defending themselves, fighting for their lives. It is no coincidence that the narrative of total innocence and victimhood also foregrounds peaceful economic advancement—Black Wall Street—as the real form and goal of racial justice.

But this fantasy comes up against the fact that, under the white supremacist imaginary, Black people are never and can never be innocent—even a Black president is liable to be treated as though he has suspicious national origins and ascended to the presidency illegally. Indeed, notions of criminality and guilt are synonymous with Blackness in America. This racial logic of criminality produces a trap for antiracist organizing.

As Jackie Wang argues in "Against Innocence," antiracist organizing in America often forms around raising up individual victims of police or vigilante violence. In order to do so, the victim is made to appear pure and innocent. Because the "Black criminal" is legally stripped of subjecthood and ideologically stripped of humanity, only total innocence—like the youth and clean record of Trayvon Martin or Tamir Rice or Mike Brown[21]—can make the victim legible as human, adequate for empathy, and a legitimate subject of political action.

The press and right wing's most frequent method to counter these movements, therefore, is to deny the innocence of the victims. Mike Brown was slandered as a thief, and the completely irrelevant fact that an autopsy revealed marijuana in his system was widely reported. Similarly, the media reported a rash of burglaries by Black men had occurred in the surrounding neighborhood in the months before George Zimmerman lynched Trayvon Martin, and the right-wing press widely circulated a photograph of Martin with his middle fingers up. Cleveland police claimed twelve-year-old Tamir Rice pointed his toy gun at officers, a story that was repeated and spread widely *even after* video was released proving he did no such thing. This technique is more than a century old: in the New Orleans riot of 1900, the press claimed Robert Charles and Leonard Pierce would "no doubt" prove to be burglars and reported that the neighborhood where they fought with the police was troubled by Black crime.

But part of the reason that this right-wing tactic works in the first place is because the terrain of "innocence" is one that already forecloses a truly radical resistance to white supremacy. Though the method works as a movement-initiating logic, by raising up and stressing the innocence of particular victims of violence, Wang argues, these movements foreground purity and noncriminality as the traits that signify people are worth defending from violence. This may make a powerful argument for a particular victim, but it reproduces the division between subjects deserving of empathy and "Black criminals" who, as Sylvia Wynter shows us, are not seen as human at all. This is precisely the structure of racialized criminalization that produces and protects police lynching in the first place, making it legible and possible.[22]

This logic of innocence animates the desire to describe the Tulsa riot as a moment of pure victimhood rather than as a messy, violent, partial victory for the Black community of Tulsa. It feels strange, even frightening to refer to the riot in Tulsa as anything other than a tragedy. It is certainly not the romantic stuff of revolutionary fantasy: it is desperate, bleak, neither clearly "political" nor ethically simple. Its history is confused, bloody, and obscure; it does not fit neatly into liberal or progressive narratives of overcoming, of movement and protest, of consciousness changed and political accommodations won. But it is, perhaps, one form that victory might take when a small, outgunned, and overpowered group, one deemed disposable, stands up and faces down a foe backed by all the technology, force, state power, and ideology of their times.

When we treat the riot as a straightforward moment of victorious oppression, we not only ignore and disrespect the Black Tulsans who fought back, but we fail to see that white supremacy is always lethal. To paraphrase Martin Luther King Jr.: the absence of a riot doesn't mean that there is peace.*

There is no such thing as peace under current conditions. Social peace is just the condition under which patriarchal white supremacist violence is acting most fluidly and most thoroughly and is distributed most invisibly. When white supremacist violence appears in the streets,

---

*"I have almost reached the regrettable conclusion that the Negro's great stumbling block in his stride toward freedom is not the White Citizen's Councilor or the Ku Klux Klanner, but the white moderate, who is more devoted to 'order' than to justice; who prefers a negative peace which is the absence of tension to a positive peace which is the presence of justice" (Martin Luther King Jr., *Letter from a Birmingham Jail*).

it is not an aberration or a dramatic change of direction: it is a continuation of the world as it is in more direct, open terms. If we want a new world, we have to learn to see in the policeman's crisp blue uniform, in the grinning politician's handshake, in the banker's penthouse suite the whole howling violence of the white rioters and lynch mobs that helped create them. Only when we find such "peace" intolerable will we be able to envision what real peace might look like, and what it might take to get there.

| LOOTED BREAD, STOLEN LABOR

REVOLUTIONARIES LOVE ORGANIZATION. ORGANIZATION, SIMILAR TO *community* and *democracy*, is sometimes a carefully conceived concept, but, more often than not, it is just a floating signifier, a moral value. Organization is, in theory, the thing that keeps people activated, that makes them capable of forming a movement powerful enough to counter the work of the bosses, the ruling classes, and the state. Organization is a good thing, a revolutionary thing. More of it makes a movement better, less of it makes a movement more likely to fail. How do you know whether a movement is sufficiently organized? Because the movement wins! It is a tautological structure of faith. Like obscenity in the eyes of the Supreme Court, the revolutionary knows it when they see it.

Perhaps that's why so many otherwise self-proclaimed revolutionaries oppose looting in social movements. The history of looting, and the riots in which it occurs, is also often a history of "disorganization"—despite the fact that rioters usually coordinate in complex ways. When looting appears, it is not always as part of clearly demarcated political action or as a part of organization-led movements fighting for social justice, although it can both give rise to or emerge out of more formal movements.

This organization-ist tendency becomes particularly pronounced in histories that inform our understanding of the labor movement in America, which focus heavily on the formation of national trade unions capable of winning demands through coordinated action. If we equate organization, in particular the formation of unions, political groups, and parties, with revolutionary activity, then we don't see much looting at all: when it appears, it does so as "opportunism" or mistake, before or after the real action.

Indeed, the more "organized" a movement is, the less likely is there looting. Massive looting occurred in the great strikes of 1877, which, despite—or more likely because of—the lack of strong union leadership, was the largest wave of industrial action in America in the nineteenth century. After the general strike of the enslaved, the strikes of 1877 were the century's largest insurrectionary movement. Meanwhile, during the highly organized Seattle General Strike of 1919, a central council literally mandated that dairies and food stores stay open and continue delivering for the duration of the strike, forestalling any necessity of looting.*

But the history of looting in the labor movement tells another story, one in which the unemployed, immigrant, internal migrant, and non-white masses take direct, decentralized action to usher in a more livable world. These movements are largely forgotten and poorly documented, but fragments of the history remain, and in them we can see another way of imagining workers' struggles. We see anarchist women at the heads of thousands of unemployed marchers, urging them to rob bakeries to feed themselves, and hungry coal miners descending on state capitols to take whatever they can carry away. Instead of the orderly formation of dues-paying union members and party cadre, we see how often leftists "organize" working-class folks already taking their lives and their power into their own hands. We also see how often those unions and parties,

---

*Two of the biggest years of industrial action in American history—1877 and 1919—are also two of the worst years of white supremacist retrenchment and violence in that history: the end of Reconstruction and the Red Summer. I don't know quite what to make of this—a number of contradictory explanations offer themselves—but it seems significant and of serious interest for further study.

once established, immediately begin to repress the "unproductive" "anti-social" activity that gave birth to them, and in the process often cripple the power of the people they claim to fight for.

By tracing looting and rioting through the Progressive Era and the Great Depression, therefore, we arrive at a necessarily harsh critique of unionism and reformism in America. Again and again, the movements of workers and unemployed persons, immigrants, and internal migrants were betrayed by trade unions and party organizations. These betrayals are made more bitter by the fact that the workers themselves demanded, fought for, and built these organizations and unions to help them usher in a better world.[1]

The classical labor movement, framed by two moments featuring extensive looting, can reorient our concepts of organization, work, and struggle: the Great Unrest of 1877 and the unemployed people's movement during the Great Depression. These two movements existed largely outside the sweep of "unionism" but are also inextricably linked to the development of the trade union movement and its historical understanding.

Looking outside the mainstream union movement is also important for any history that centers the foundational nature of white supremacy and heteropatriarchy. For the entirety of the nineteenth century and much of the twentieth, the vast majority of unions were "whites-only." And, despite the massive presence of women in the industrial workforce, particularly in textiles—although dramatic and inspiring exceptions exist—most of these parties and unions were staffed and led exclusively by men. "Disorganized" looting and rioting, however, tended to more prominently feature immigrants, people of color, and women, both in the makeup of the crowds and in "leadership" positions.

Furthermore, the last five years has seen the largest upsurge in strikes, union organization, and other forms of industrial action in the United States in decades. Though this strike wave has been inspiring, it has also led to a consensus among parts of the US Left that union organization (and its accompanying electoralism) is the only significant way forward for the movement. These narratives already downplay or even erase the role of the most significant social struggles of the last decade, the Black insurrections against the police and Standing Rock and Indigenous land defense, as they attempt to funnel energy into the sphere of workplace organization and electoral political gains.

To tell the stories of unions, of "organization" as *the* story of worker resistance, therefore, is to leave out the movements, tactics, and goals of millions of working people, often the most radical, oppressed, and marginalized of them. The history of looting decenters these working men without erasing the historical importance of the struggles they fought in.* If we tell the story of the unruly, riotous masses, and their often overlapping, sometimes conflictual and contradictory relationship to "the labor movement" proper, we get a clearer picture of how we might act in the present to honor and recapture that power without falling into the same traps that doomed US American working-class movements to liberal accommodation and repression.

LOOTING ENTERS THE AMERICAN ENGLISH LEXICON FOR THE FIRST time during the struggles of the post-Reconstruction era, when it became a more present and viable tactic of resistance to the forms of social organization and economic power of the period. The transformations of the half century from the end of Reconstruction through the Great Depression shaped daily life in America into a form we can recognize today. The ongoing transition from a largely rural, agrarian society to a more urban, industrial one accelerated dramatically. The Jeffersonian ideal of a nation of small farmer–landowners and self-made men—an ideal always based in slavery, patriarchy, and colonialism—began to unravel, even for the white male American citizens it was designed for.

---

*It is also the case that the history of the labor movement, even that history critiqued here, goes largely untold in American curriculums, ignored by culture both popular and elite. Most Americans have a big blank in their historical consciousness regarding the years between the closing of the Civil War and the opening of World War I, a period of both massive US imperial expansion and great social upheaval. Hopefully, this critique will drive people to investigate this incredibly important social era, one that, in the organization of economic power under increasingly plutocratic monopoly, quite often reflects our own.

The economy, instead, was increasingly dominated by massive banks and corporations, with both economic and political power concentrated in the hands of monopolists and businessmen. The increasing numbers of European American workers, then, owned nothing but their own labor power. The policeman on the beat emerges in force and becomes a major figure both in the formation of urban political power and in the control and repression of proletarian life in the period. Urban governance, meanwhile, changed from being dominated by more visibly corrupt political machines based in patronage, neighborhood gangs, and cash handouts to a form more centralized, bureaucratic, and structurally corrupt. This last transition had as much to do with the formation of the police as with progressive governmental reform.[†]

At the same time, an urban middle class emerged, and with it an economy based on consumerism. *Consumerism* here means a system in which the economy, the market, and the worker are all driven by expanding access to goods and services. We tend to think of this change as occurring in the mid-twentieth century, but treatises on consumerism and conspicuous consumption appear for the first time in America in the 1890s. The availability of mass-produced commodities takes off in this period.

Production of those commodities was powered by exploitation of Latin America through imperialist treaty, the growth of American colonies in the Caribbean and East Asia, and an expanding base of cheap laborers within the country's borders. Massive imperial expansion, mass immigration from Europe and Asia, and concerted internal migration of white settlers to the West and Black people out of the South all meant growing, diverse populations of urban poor crowded into industrial centers, whose geography in this period was shaped largely by the growth of the railroad and its hubs.

The increase in industrial goods and the stores in which they were sold, alongside the concentration of impoverished proletarians in city centers, meant that daily life began to feature the humiliation of wealth and luxury taunting poor folks from behind a plane of plate glass.

[†]As Kristian Williams shows, the centralizing, bureaucratizing transition largely follows the development of police forces, which are in most cases the first citywide centralized bureaucracies on which other departments of urban governance are then based.

Though the differences between the poor and the rich have always been an experience lived more immediately by the poor, the rise of the middle classes and the appearance of consumer goods and mass-manufactured commodities gave these differences a new material content and visibility on city streets. Looting became an immediately sensible response to this novel state of affairs.

However, if the presence of these industrial goods to loot was new, looting as a tactic was already well established in its classical form: the bread riot. This kind of riot, aimed at stealing the food the people needed, lowering the price of food in the market through direct action, or forcing official distribution or policy change, is an ancient practice. Bread riots occurred repeatedly in ancient Rome. They usually worked by rioters attacking the officials who controlled food policy—during the Roman republic these were senators and various other wealthy elites, but later crowds jeered and harassed emperors and other imperial officials—rather than by looting, though the houses of Roman merchants and landlords were occasionally ransacked in these movements.

The bread riot was a particularly common feature of early modern Europe. But the cause of these riots is often treated as a simple correlation: food prices go up, people get hungry, and they then "instinctively" riot and take whatever food they need to live. Indeed, some economists explained the uprisings of 2011 as a result of global grain price increase. As labor historian E. P. Thompson argues, this mechanical view of the masses simply responding to stimuli, this "crass economic reductionism," does not bear out in the record of food rioters' self-explanation or in the history of emergent food riots.[2]*

The rate and occurrence of bread riots exploded in the early days of capitalism, which aimed to drive down the price of bread. As theorist Joshua Clover argues, this price was reduced literally to zero in the imme-

---

*Nor, indeed, do such explanations hold in Roman bread riots, which, as Paul Erdkamp argues, often responded to and were organized against perceived injustices, such as hoarding corn to artificially raise prices or personal political squabbles in which certain state actors stopped distributing or importing grain (Paul Erdkamp, "A Starving Mob Has No Respect: Urban Markets and Food Riots in the Roman World, 100 BC–400 AD," in *Transformation of Economic Life under the Roman Empire*, ed. J. Rich and L. De Blois [Amsterdam: Gieben, 2002], 93–115).

diate case of looting, but rioters also frequently worked to control prices in other ways. They would riot to stop ships laden with grain, salt, or meat from leaving port, because they understood that growing and selling for export drove the domestic price of food up. Clover calls these "export riots." Rather than inchoate expressions of material necessity, bread riots were often directed political acts, focused on particular villains of the market, particular modes of price gouging or food quality adulteration.[3]

Though bread riots became less frequent as the nineteenth century progressed, they hardly disappeared. An oft-overlooked event in the Civil War was the rash of two dozen or so food riots, largely carried out in the cities of the Confederacy, in the spring of 1863.

Unable to afford the price of food, which increased exponentially both from the terrible inflation of the Confederate dollar and the massive supply problems facing both army and civilian organization, thousands of Southern women rose up and looted the stores of Richmond, Atlanta, Salisbury, and many smaller cities and towns. Groups of men formed to watch the action, sometimes egging the women on, but rarely joining in. The looting spread from city to city, where war widows, refugees, and indigent "camp followers"—polite nineteenth-century language encompassing both soldiers' wives and children and the sex workers who could also be hired to clean and cook for soldiers on the march—found themselves increasingly impoverished by the slaveowner's war. Much as CNN would today, the Confederate press blamed the riots on outside agitators, foreigners, and career criminals, though they also called these rioters Yankees and prostitutes, adding, for extra spice, that these female rioters were all ugly. Like the draft riots a few months later would be to the Union, the bread riots of 1863 were both a part and a sign of the collapse of morale on the Confederacy's home front.[4]

As industrial production shifted to occupy a more central role in the American economy, however, the bread riot receded and the industrial workplace became an increasingly central site of struggle. The goods produced there, and the modes of their production and distribution, became the new objects and scenes of conflict: of strike, riot, and looting.

In the late nineteenth century, these new technologies had a particular apogee: an industry employing over seven hundred thousand, making products fundamentally central to American society, psychology, and ideology. Much as the internet does today, in the latter decades of the nineteenth century "the railroad stood for technology in popular rhetoric, and Americans endowed technology with qualities they imagined to be uniquely American: prosperity, mobility and democracy."[5]* The Great Unrest of 1877, which saw more than a hundred people killed in combat with the police and the army, and millions of dollars of value looted and destroyed, which even briefly saw a Paris Commune–inspired council take over St. Louis, was sparked by a strike on the railroad.

IN MOST NARRATIVES, THE AMERICAN LABOR MOVEMENT BEGINS WITH the events of the Great Unrest of 1877, a series of strikes and riots that shook the country to its foundations. Starting here, of course, already misses the largest struggle against work in American history—the general strike of the enslaved—as well as the massive battles of Reconstruction. This myopia emerges from the labor movement itself: "New York in 1871 witnessed a march of 20,000, demonstrating solidarity with the workers of Paris, 20,000 radicals who were able to look across the ocean to the Paris Commune but were unable to look five hundred miles to the South to the South Carolina commune!"[6] From the very beginning white organizers tended to distance themselves from the projects of emancipation and Reconstruction, while simultaneously evoking "wage slavery" as the name of their oppression. This refusal of solidarity and alliance constantly enfeebled the labor movement and saw labor "radicals" betray Black people and their struggles again and again.†

---

*You could replace *nineteenth* with *twenty-first* and *railroad* with *internet* and the sentence still makes the same sense. The ways in which society is fundamentally *unchanged* over the last hundred and fifty years—particularly in meta-narratives of progress, history, technology, and change—are as numerous and significant as the ways in which it has changed.

†It does not escape my attention that, by having labor struggles in a separate chapter here, I do some of that same dividing. My hope is to tell this story of the labor movement in such a way as to reduce that division.

This failure emerged in part, no doubt, from the directly white supremacist nature of organized labor up to the moment. Even the most pro-union histories shy away from the first decades of trade unionism in America, ignoble years when most organized labor actively positioned itself against emancipation and agitated in favor of genocidal colonizing of the West. Through the 1880s, unions were tiny and weak. Wage laborers made up a small percentage of the population; organized laborers, a small percentage of them.

The Great Unrest, then, a massive, disorganized, multiracial series of strikes, riots, and uprisings, represented as much a break with the previous labor movement as a continuation. But its historical size and relevance are usually downplayed, even by historians of labor. A common position sees the strike of 1877 as "significant primarily because it gave workingmen a class consciousness on a national scale."[7] This perspective makes sense only if we value organization and worker identity as the fundamental precepts of revolutionary struggle, and it lets us see how thinking of struggle in those terms blinded previous laborers and even revolutionaries to the mass movements happening all around them. But viewed in tandem with the general strike of the enslaved and with Reconstruction, the Great Unrest looks just as much like an ending: the ending of a period of revolutionary struggle against wage labor itself and the final victory of reactionary Northern capital in organizing American society around industrial production.

The Great Unrest began on July 16, 1877, when the Baltimore and Ohio Railroad (B&O) cut wages by 10 percent, the second such wage cut in eight months. As workers gathered in frustration in the Martinsburg, West Virginia, railyard, the crew of a cattle train struck, abandoning their train and refusing to move it until the pay cut was rescinded. Traffic on the line was stopped, and other workers refused to replace them.

The next day the state militia arrived and, filling the cattle train with armed men, tried again to drive it through the yard. A workman named William Vandergriff ran up to derail the train at a switch, and when the militia pilot jumped down to oppose him, Vandergriff shot the scab. Vandergriff was in turn shot and fatally wounded. But the train crew fled, and another could not be gathered. With news of this victory, striking spread across West Virginia, and across the entire B&O.

Freight traffic was completely stopped, "while the workers continued to run passenger and mail cars with no interference."[8] More than that, sympathetic workers from other industries went out in support of the strikers, and talk of a general strike began to spread through the state. Desperate, the governor of West Virginia and the president of B&O begged President Rutherford B. Hayes for federal troops to suppress what they were already calling an "insurrection."

Hayes obliged, but, though the three hundred heavily armed soldiers he sent managed to finally get trains out of the Martinsburg yard on July 19, four days into the insurrection, it was a Pyrrhic victory. Because in town after town crowds of railroad men, unemployed workers, sympathy strikers, and huge groups of women derailed, attacked, and otherwise sabotaged the scab trains. Where trains from Martinsburg went, strikes and riots followed, and soon all of neighboring Maryland's railroads and much of its industry were also on strike.

One of the most common tactics used in this insurrection was to overturn, loot, and then burn the freight cars. This had three immediately powerful effects for the movement: it blocked the lines and the yards, making them impassable for scab trains; gathered goods and food to sustain strikers; and cut into the railroad's bottom line. This tactic reappeared in the United States in September 2016, when protesters in Charlotte fighting for justice for Keith Lamont Scott overturned and looted semi-trucks, turning some of the goods into burning barricades that blocked the interstate.

Back in 1877, in response to the chaos spreading, the governor of Maryland called out the National Guard. But the residents of Baltimore, where the guard was stationed, rioted, attacking the guardsmen with stones and brickbats and preventing them from boarding trains to go to break the strike. Exasperated, the governor begged for a full federal intervention. It was at this moment that Pittsburgh and St. Louis exploded into insurrection.

How did strikes, rioting, and looting spread so widely and so quickly? After all, barely any of these workers were organized into a national union. In fact, as labor historian Jeremy Brecher argues, the Great Unrest occurred in the wake of unionism's repeated failures to win change. The Panic of 1873, one of the most severe depressions in American history, saw unemployment skyrocket. As ever, capitalists used the downturn as grounds to cut wages and enforce speedups. But the organizations that existed, the various "Brotherhoods" (of firemen, engineers, and conductors), had been bought off, out-politicked, or frightened out of striking. They agreed, against the rank and file's wishes, to speedups and pay cuts. Their membership plummeted and many of the unions ceased to exist except on paper.

In the wake of their failure, a clandestine insurrectionary organization formed, the Trainsmen's Union, and spread quickly across the country. But the Trainsmen's Union was just as quickly infiltrated by feds, police, and Pinkerton thugs—the infamous private police force that spied on and sabotaged the labor movement and that was often called in to violently break strikes—such that in the buildup to any actions mass firings of radicals and organizers would lead to confusion and disunity within the movement. Soon the TU collapsed as well. Union membership was at a decades-long low when things kicked off in Martinsburg. Furthermore, for one of the last times in American labor history, forming or protecting a union would *not* be a major demand of the struggle.[9]

The rioters of 1877 had a different political precedent and goal in mind: the Paris Commune of 1871. As Nell Irvin Painter shows in her seminal *Standing at Armageddon*, the Commune was a common point of reference for rioters, and their critics, across the country. US workers fought to take control of their daily lives, their local and workplace governance in much the same way that the Communards had for seventy-one glorious days in 1871. And conservatives and liberals alike feared that French revolt and class war had finally crossed the Atlantic.

In St. Louis, during one week, a strike that started against wage cuts in the railyards generalized and eventually completely shut down the city. Political power moved into the hands of a commune made up of . . . whoever showed up. It was run, like the Paris Commune, on genuinely radical antihierarchical principles. "Nobody ever knew who that executive committee really was; it seems to have been a rather loose body composed of whomsoever chanced to come in and take part in its deliberations."[10] This "disorganized" assembly managed commerce in the city, halted all railroad traffic, and requisitioned food for strikers — whose numbers encompassed more than a dozen professions outside of the rails, constituting an almost total general strike. But after eight days, three thousand federal troops and five thousand deputized police officers descended on the city, killed more than two dozen people, and shut down the commune.

This lack of official organization and union leadership also meant that Black workers were widely involved in the Great Upheaval. In the border states, Black and white workers banded together to shut down roads and coal mines. A Black worker, his name unknown to history, made one of the crucial speeches opening the St. Louis General Strike with a demand to white laborers to support Black steamboat and levee workers. "Will you stand behind us regardless of color?!" Black workers ran the movements in the South, leading particularly massive strikes in Galveston and Marshall, Texas. Black sewer workers in Louisville, Kentucky, marched through the sewers and then the city, beginning a three-day-long general strike that brought all industry in Louisville to a halt.

The response was more than just immediate violent repression on the parts of the guard and the police: the national media built a narrative of a menacing and dangerous working class. Although there wasn't a full-blown Red Scare, 1877 was one of the first times American papers and capitalists talked about and feared communists. Of particular portent was the insurrectionary rioting in Pittsburgh.

The rioting in the industrial city in western Pennsylvania followed a couple of days of striking on the railroad. Sent in to repress the strike, local national guardsmen instead fraternized with strikers, and police were unable to break the strike, which left thousands of full boxcars sitting idle in the Pittsburgh yards. The railroads, panicked by the thought of all that property and profit languishing, brought in national guardsmen from Philadelphia, knowing they wouldn't hesitate to fire on the working men. These outside agitators promptly did their bosses' bidding, massacring twenty strikers. They even brought a Gatling gun to mow down rioters.

But the massacre backfired. Though the company technically retook the yards, no one, not even those workers who hadn't originally gone on strike, would drive trains captured in such blood. The entire Pittsburgh guard switched allegiance to the side of the workers, giving over their weapons to the workers, and in response to the capture of the rail depot "the entire city mobilized." A massive crowd formed and attacked the yards, forcing the Philadelphia National Guard to flee. Having driven away the guard, the crowd broke into and looted all of the freight cars left in the yard. Then they burned them, alongside all railroad property, letting the fire devour huge swaths of railroad and capitalist property, but organizing fire breaks to prevent the conflagration from spreading to nearby residential areas. This tactic of controlled arson would return in the major urban riots of the sixties and in LA in 1992.

By the time the various riots, strikes, and insurrections had been quelled by repression, over a hundred lay dead and millions of dollars in property had been looted and destroyed. In some cities and workplaces, demands were met; in many they were not. But the looting and property destruction terrified owners and government officials alike. Led by Pennsylvania Railroad president Thomas A. Scott, who had lost tremendous wealth in Pittsburgh, a movement grew among capitalists to reinforce urban defenses against their new working-class enemies and the revolution their mass riots pointed toward. And so it was in response to the property destruction, looting, armed rebellion, and general strikes of 1877 that almost every city in America built a huge armory to garrison weapons and guardsmen—buildings that remain to this day, massive monuments to anticommunal politics and glaring symbols of the bosses' power over daily life. And though these armories are now mostly decommissioned, when riots get too powerful for police to handle, it is still the National Guard, armed to the teeth, that is called in to face down rebels.*

---

*Painter compares these armories to the Haussmannization of Paris in which the French government ripped up neighborhoods of small, winding streets and replaced them with massive boulevards that ran through the heart of Paris, enabling French troops to move unencumbered and making barricades and rioters less effective.

FROM HERE, LABOR HISTORIES LEAPFROG THROUGH THE DECADES from major flash point to flash point, tracing the ebb and flow of union membership and class consciousness, as the labor movement marches toward its supposed apotheosis in the sit-down strikes of the thirties, the Congress of Industrial Organizations (CIO), and the New Deal.

These histories trace how the tradition of craft unions gives way, slowly and painfully, to industrial unionism.* There's the eight-hour movement, bursting onto the scene in a furious wave of strike and organizing activity in 1885–1886, culminating in a general strike in Chicago and ending in infamy with the Haymarket bombing, the execution of four anarchists for a bombing they did not commit, and the creation of May Day. This movement is often told in tandem with the story of the Knights of Labor, a cautious and conservative organization that, as a fluke of a strike victory in 1885 by a radical local over notoriously antilabor steel baron Jay Gould, suddenly became the largest mass worker organization in American history. Its effectiveness emerges largely from the fact that it was necessarily decentralized, having grown too large too fast for its antistrike, antiaction "Grand Master Workman" Terrence Powderly to handle, despite literal attempts on his part to stop and to sabotage the strike wave, to have effective repressive control.

But in the aftermath, the K of L faded, as the AFL, the American Federation of Labor, took its place at the center of the labor story. The AFL, organized on craft principles and run by the hardnosed, racist, antistrike

---

*Craft unionism is a model that emerged from the nineteenth-century conditions of labor, organizing workers on the basis of their particular job in the shop (so that one railroad workforce might split into fifteen different unions based on their job and level of skill) and negotiating separately with the bosses for craft-based wage scales and hours. Craft unions often represented a conservative or reactionary brake on the movement, because the highest paid and highest skilled workers' unions could often be bought out by getting a good contract from the boss, getting workers back to work, and effectively breaking a strike. This played right into the hands of capital as industrialization increasingly deskilled the workforce, leaving tiny pools of well-paid conservative skilled workers—sometimes referred to as the "aristocracy of labor." As immigration increased, craft unions overwhelmingly became nativist white organizations of labor aristocrats, often explicitly racist and anti-immigrant, more allied with the foremen and bosses than the general laborers. Industrial unionism is the basis of organization by industry so that everyone who works on the railroad or in steel can join the same union, and it has become the dominant mode of unionism since the thirties.

Samuel Gompers, dominated official labor politics until the 1930s, and everywhere militancy and insurrection appeared, the AFL attempted to tamp it down. Still, AFL locals were often at the heart of strikes throughout the period: the AFL was, often, the only game in town, much to the detriment of the strikes and struggles it came to represent. In 1892, the bitter lockout at the Carnegie-owned, Jay Gould–managed Homestead Steel Works in Pennsylvania would see AFL-affiliated mill workers engage in and win a gun battle with a barge full of Pinkertons, who had sailed up the Monongahela River to break the workers' siege on the mill. In 1892, a multiracial general strike also shut down New Orleans.

An even more violent and drastic struggle broke out in 1894, as more-or-less military conflicts raged between strikers and strikebreakers and militias in the coal mines, with strike action reaching from Pennsylvania all the way to Colorado. Miners, who lived in utterly desperate poverty in isolated rural communities owned and managed by the coal conglomerates, banded together not just to fight but also to loot company stores and groceries to keep the strike going, as they would again in West Virginia during the infamous mine wars of 1912–1921.

The year 1894 was also when the famous Pullman Strike, a mass boycott-cum-strike on the railroads led by Eugene Debs's American Railway Union (ARU), "rapidly came to be understood as a general struggle between all workers and corporations as a whole."[11] The ARU exploded in membership and power, and the strike spread across the rail lines that Pullman cars traveled. US president Grover Cleveland sent federal troops into Chicago, the heart of the strike, to break it, but this backfired disastrously, as mobs of working-class people, most not strikers, formed to fight off federal troops, loot, riot, and burn. This conflict turned the movement into a massive upheaval that spread even more broadly across the country, as rail traffic almost completely collapsed, particularly west of the Appalachians. The working class was ready to fight.

But here again the leadership failed the workers. First, the associated AFL unions, meeting in an emergency conference, rejected the demand of the rank and file to call an official sympathetic general strike and instead ordered workers back into their shops. Then, with the ARU isolated by their compatriots and the militia, the leadership balked.

When the troops came in, making legal success impossible, workers throughout the country responded with mass direct action. But for the ARU to adopt such a policy would have meant a challenge to the entire social order—a step from which it recoiled. Thus we are presented with the spectacle of Eugene Victor Debs, perhaps the greatest example of a courageous, radical and incorruptible trade union official in American history, trying to end the strike to prevent it from becoming an insurrection.[12]

Thus, even in this moment of mass action, with the most radical available leader at the helm, the union failed its membership and folded. If the required next step is generalizing and socializing the revolt, and therefore, giving up control, legitimacy, or negotiating powers, a union will always choose to abandon a fight, even if the fight, and the revolt it emerged from or helped create, is the very basis of the union and its power. The logic of formal organizational power, no matter how noble or radical the organizations' goals, will in crisis lead it to preserve itself for "the next fight" rather than abandon it all for this one.

But the organization that is preserved is one that, at the height of the people's power, turned its back on them, and the people do not forget these betrayals. The organization will never again achieve the leverage it had during the conflict—in other words, the organization doomed itself all the same to collapse and crisis, though a slower, more protracted, and ambiguous one.

LABOR STRUGGLES CONTINUED THROUGHOUT THE PERIOD. ONE OF their greatest heights during the first decade of the 1900s came when the Industrial Workers of the World (IWW), or Wobblies, the syndicalist union that organized across gender and racial lines to join all the working class into "one big union" for revolutionary social transformation, won strikes, fights for free speech and freedom of assembly, and other battles across the country. Much as Antifa has become the modern-day reactionary boogeyman, for decades during the early twentieth century no insult was worse than being called a Wobbly (or sometimes "an IWW"), and for many being a Wob led to arrest, torture, tarring and feathering, and even lynching.

But it wasn't just violent repression that held back workers. The gathering storm of world war complicated the trajectory of the labor movement. Although US antiwar sentiment prevailed for the first year of the interimperial European conflict, war fever was growing, and gradually socialists, trade unionists, and liberals alike unified to support the allied fight "over there." The continued outspoken and principled antimilitarism of the Wobblies and anarchists, which was a common enough position in 1914–1915, led to their marginalization and even criminalization as traitors.

Still, as war production ramped up in 1916 and with the young men of the working class vacuumed into the war machine via enlistment, big transformations took place in the makeup of the industrial workforce as women moved into men's industries and Black Southerners came into Northern industrial centers as part of the Great Migration. Labor agitation again increased.

News of the Russian Revolution lent a new vigor to the radical movement, and the October victory of the Bolsheviks meant the Wobbly and the anarchist were joined and soon replaced in the fevered minds of the foaming-mouthed patriots by the Red, the bolshie, the communist. And with the German Revolution of 1918, it seemed the victory of radical labor was inexorable.

In the immediate aftermath of the war, in the year 1919, a huge strike wave spread across the country, the largest since 1877, including a general strike that completely shut down Seattle. But the year also saw the country's first bona fide "Red Scare," as anarchists, labor organizers, communists, and socialists of all stripes were rounded up, imprisoned, and deported by federal Attorney General Palmer and his goons. Reactionary mobs of veterans rioted to attack socialist demonstrations; destroy union and Wobbly halls, presses, and infrastructure; and beat, maim, or murder organizers. The conservatives in the AFL, meanwhile, used the Red Scare to purge what socialists and militants remained in their ranks.

As we've seen above, 1919 also featured the highest number of anti-Black riots in American history, and the early twenties was a time of dramatic reactionary retrenchment as anticommunism and anti-Black sentiments merged into a molten stew of violence and hatred, embodied in the dramatic return of the KKK.

But despite the turmoil in the early years of the century, the twenties were widely seen as a time of social and industrial peace and prosperity—though that prosperity was being bought on credit, and the working class would soon be paying the bill. As ever, "social peace" just means the rich were winning the class war without much fight back, exploiting the workers in new, disruptive, innovative ways.

After fifty years of relatively constant social and class struggle, a new affluence seemed to have finally solved the "labor question," and businessmen and union heads alike celebrated a "New Unionism" free of strikes in which union bosses hashed out contracts with owners over Chamber of Commerce luncheons. As part of this union conservatism and "respectability," unions leaned into their role as the official arbiters of the color line in Northern labor. The Black workers who had moved north during war production were once again violently relegated, by boss and union alike, to an enforced status as unskilled, disposable labor.

The Roaring Twenties are associated with profligate wealth and consumption—and indeed, consumer goods spread rapidly, although, much like ownership of smartphones or flatscreens today, this did not reflect actual wealth or power. Wages stagnated through the decade and poverty deepened for millions alongside this increased access to consumer goods.* The twenties are also famous for their organized crime syndicates of bootleggers fighting the G-Men of Prohibition. Less well remembered is that those criminal syndicates built their model and got "organized" as part of labor "rackets" that used violence—"slugging," fire bombing, even assassination—to enforce control of a local employment space.

Though these hired criminals began as off-the-books employees of the union, as unions increasingly followed the AFL lead and shied away from collective action, striking, and industrial unionism, they lost all leverage beyond this professional violence. Unions came to rely on it

---

*Indeed, the invention of consumer debt through purchase by installment and (usually disastrous) popular entry into stock and bond speculation kept the party going for a while.

more and more. Gangsters quickly realized they were the true political power: they were running labor in whole industries, even whole cities—with the unions paying them and at their mercy—and from that position of organization and power, they extended into "protection" and other of their more infamous criminal activities.[13]

THE NEW DEAL IS CELEBRATED BY LIBERALS AND PROGRESSIVES AS the pinnacle of good governance, held up as the model for large-scale, government-backed actions in response to crises, from health care to climate change. But the New Deal was in fact one of the greatest innovations in counterrevolutionary statecraft in American history. A response to the threat of communism and Black revolt, it funneled the anger and activity of a massive movement into charity, unionism, work, and electoral politics, fully embedding racist divisions of welfare and public action in federal relief structures. FDR quite possibly staved off the formation of a real revolutionary rupture and set the terms of liberal domination of the poor for the next fifty years—particularly by structuring federal relief in fundamentally anti-Black but technically "color-blind" ways—all, crucially, without significantly improving the conditions on the ground.

Because when the bottom fell out, it fell very far. Within twelve months of the Black Tuesday crash of October 1929, the official count of the unemployed went from around five hundred thousand to eight million people (though these numbers themselves are probably low, because the unemployment count was one of the demands won by the movement, so unemployed persons weren't reliably counted until after 1929). The unemployed in America faced a crisis exacerbated by an American ideology that rejected and minimized social services, pushing most relief onto churches and other private charities; an utterly unprepared and fundamentally unsympathetic federal government; and a plutocratic gang of billionaire monopolists who uttered patriotic pieties and predictions of imminent economic recovery while laying off tens of thousands of workers. The people were, as ever, on their own.

One of the first things that occurred, spontaneously and across the country, was looting. Numerous contemporaneous accounts agree that mass looting was commonplace around the nation, but its extent will never be known. Mauritz Hallgren's *Seeds of Revolt*, published in 1933, describes the pattern in Detroit, in 1932, and explains why it is so little remembered by history:

> Windows of small retail shops were smashed at night and relieved of their goods. Children from the poorer districts were frequently observed snatching bundles from customers coming out of grocery stores. They ran off to barren homes with their booty or ate it themselves in out-of-the-way alleys. More frequently, grown men, usually in twos and threes, entered chain stores, ordered all the food they could possibly carry, and then walked quietly out without paying. Every newspaper in the city knew of this practice and knew it was spreading, but none mentioned it to print. The press excused itself on the ground that these occurrences were not a matter of public record. And the chain-store managers refused to report such incidents to the police lest the practice be encouraged by the resultant publicity.[14]

In New York, "bands of thirty or forty men regularly descended upon markets."[15] The scope of this organized, spontaneous looting has largely, therefore, been lost to history. However, we must imagine that looting kept not a few people alive during these tragic years. And it wasn't only grocery stores. "In a few cities . . . there were spontaneous raids on restaurants."[16] This looting was not always done in small groups.

The unemployed movement took shape in a recognizably national form around the March 6, 1930, "International Employment Day" demonstrations. These demonstrations shocked even their Communist Party organizers in their size and ferocity, with the CP claiming 1.25 million people protested across the country on the sixth. Immediate, mass, violent repression sprang up: hundreds of policemen charged into the crowd, viciously beating dozens and shattering the demonstration in New York City's Union Square.

But the repression did not break the back of the movement. Huge marches and riots of unemployed workers became a regular occurrence across the country. They demanded work, relief, and bread; just as often, they took it. "In March, 1,100 men waiting on a Salvation Army bread line in New York City mobbed two trucks delivering baked goods to a nearby hotel." Although riots and marches like these were more common in the large cities of the North where workers were concentrated, they were not limited to them. "In Henryetta, Oklahoma, 300 jobless marched on storekeepers to demand food, insisting they were not begging and threatening to use force if necessary."[17] Hallgren describes a scene in West Virginia:

> Fifteen hundred miners, together with their wives and children, marched upon Charleston . . . in May 1931. They came from the Ward district to demand help from the government. Governor Conley met them at the edge of the city, explained that the state could do nothing for them, and gave them ten dollars out of his own pocket—ten dollars to be divided among fifteen hundred hungry people. Frank Keeney, the leader of the protesting miners, flared up in anger . . . to his followers, as they marched on into the city, [Keeney] said: "All that stands between you hungry people and food are a few plate glass windows; no state has a right to call you criminal if you take what you must have to live."[18]

The logic of property, in the face of starvation and mass unemployment, was breaking down, perhaps not as easily as a pane of plate glass, but surely and steadily. And as the logic of property breaks down, so too must the logic of race. After five decades of labor struggles that quite often reinforced rather than challenged the white supremacist order of the workplace, the unemployed movement was openly multiracial, led by and often made up of Black militants and, in most places, opposed by and to the anticommunist and racial terror politics that had resurfaced so openly in the twenties. Many of the Unemployed Councils that sprang up were interracial and often were the first interracial organizations to appear in their areas.[19] Where property teeters, so too does white supremacy.

This spread to the question of housing, as rent and anti-eviction riots became one of the most common forms of resistance to Depression
conditions. Groups of unemployed people, usually Black activists, often
Communists, formed anti-eviction flying squadrons.[20] These squadrons,
sometimes called "black bugs," would march through poor neighborhoods gathering crowds, then arrive at the eviction, often thousands
strong, replace furniture inside the house and forcibly keep the marshal
from carrying out the eviction. "Sometimes the flying squadrons arrived
before the police, and directed the family and bystanders to sit on the
furniture to prevent its removal. An old spiritual 'I shall not be moved'
became the theme song of resistance."[21]

This movement was widespread, and wildly successful. The unemployed movement stopped or reversed literally one-third of the evictions
in New York—seventy-seven thousand households!—during the early
thirties. When a rent riot in Chicago ended with three Black people
killed by police, the fierce, combative funeral march the following day
saw unified crowds of Black and white protesters, which terrified the city
government. "If it had been an out-and-out race riot it would have been
understandable, but here was something new: Negroes and whites *together* rioting against the forces of law and order."[22] Chicago City Hall
declared a moratorium on evictions. By 1931, the movement had more or
less ceased evictions in Detroit as well.

These tactics soon broadened to demanding relief and welfare, as
thousands of poor and unemployed people would descend on city halls
and state houses, relief agencies, charities, and anywhere else demands
could be leveraged. Often, these marchers then stationed themselves inside the offices, refusing to leave until relief was given and further plans
made. They won radical expansions of relief, and, where they couldn't,
they often just looted what they needed.

One of the great strengths of the early unemployed movement was
the energy and dedication of Communist Party organizers. In most urban
centers, Communist militants formed the backbone of the early movement, with the party-organized "Unemployed Councils" the nuclei of
the movement wherever they popped up. The organizers that remained
in the CP by 1930, who had survived splits, purges, and Red Scares, were

a hardened and experienced cohort. Shortly to be mobilizing in the defense of the Scottsboro Boys, the CP of 1930 was a multiracial and strongly antiracist party. Whereas movements in the twenties had distanced themselves from Communist organizers, in the misery of the Depression, communism didn't seem so scary, and evictions were often met with cries to "call the reds!" In the early years of the movement, Communist militants were invaluable champions of the fight, supporting neighborhood demands and politicizing the need for relief.

But the energetic and hard work of Communist militants on the ground often conflicted with the demands of the Party and the Communist International. "Few unemployed saw the connection between their immediate need for relief and demonstrations against the 'Imperialist war danger,' slogans about defense of the Chinese Soviets, or even electoral campaigns for CP candidates. Nor was it clear . . . why Socialists and Musteites were regularly labeled 'social fascists' and 'tools of the bosses.' . . . [This posturing] seriously handicapped efforts to recruit the jobless into the radical movement."[23]

This alienating propaganda, however, was less disastrous for the unemployed than were the organizational imperatives of the Communist Party. Sharp changes of strategic direction from above often left local movements whiplashed and reeling. For example, the decision that organizing mutual aid charity was an "open right-wing opportunist deviation" in mid-1931 cut the legs out from a few local groups. And the spontaneous and uncontrollable looting and rioting, unresponsive to party discipline or strategy, quickly became anathema to the CP. Although early on councils participated in this rioting, once the party developed an official position in 1931, many of its organizers worked hard to stop this tactic. "Unemployed Council leader Herbert Benjamin recalls that 'those of us who were more politically responsible' continually advised against food riots, and he believes that more such rioting would have occurred without the Unemployed Councils. 'It seems probable,' conclude two academic writers unsympathetic to the Left, 'that the Communist Party exercised an important influence in restricting the amount of violence against persons and property during the depression.'"[24]

This is the kind of achievement that only an organizer could love, because it demonstrates nothing so much as their gaining social power against and over the spontaneous needs and desires of the people. It certainly didn't help strengthen the movement.

Such repression of local mutual aid and direct action, in fact, played right into the hands of the liberals of the new Roosevelt administration. Elected in the largest landslide since Abraham Lincoln's reelection in 1864, FDR came in promising jobs and relief, a New Deal, and set about doing . . . a little bit. The jobs and relief programs that came from the federal government were far too little to stem the economic crisis, but they were hardly too late. Indeed, they were right on time to disorient the movement—the money and relief programs the New Deal distributed were not only too small but also left to states and localities to distribute. Without strong federal enforcement mechanisms, organizers and the needy quickly found themselves locked into protracted battles with local bureaucracies over money and jobs that were anyway inadequate to the size of the problem.

The same thing was happening to those lucky enough to be employed, who, with the official legalization of collective bargaining through the National Recovery Administration (NRA), flocked into unions at an astonishing rate. Those unions were mostly affiliated with the AFL, and these workers quickly found that the law meant little if the boss had more power than the workers. By 1935, workers were referring to the NRA as the "National Run-Around," and the explosion of union membership did little but inflate the wallets of conservative union bosses and funnel subversive energy into official bureaucratic channels. It would take another round of massive upheaval, this one against both the bosses and the will of the union leadership—the wildcat Sit-Down Strike wave of 1936–1937—to truly bring change to industrial conditions.*

---

*And here, too, the new unions formed, organized into the CIO, and were co-opted, legalized, and negotiated with by FDR and his New Deal. Whereas many of the gains made by the sit-down wave would last longer than those made by the unemployment movement, both times worker power was undercut as energy funneled into official movement organs.

It is precisely this sort of mass liberal co-option and diversion of energy that organizers, as politicized "strategists," are meant to be best positioned to resist. But the unemployed organizers were busy trying to unify and form a national council that could wield "real power." Frustrated with the "looseness" of the early councils, they wanted stronger organizations. Organizers of all socialist tendencies "shared the view that the victories won by the unemployed in the early Depression were mere handouts. A significant political movement capable of winning major victories depended, they thought, on firmly structured local and state organizations knit together in a national body and with a national program."[25]

This shared perspective, that real power flows from unified organizations, helped the organizers destroy the very power they wanted to expand.

> While the leaders of the unemployed groups had been concentrating on forming a national organization complete with a constitution and a bureaucratic structure, the local groups across the country were declining. They were declining largely as a result of the Roosevelt Administration's more liberal relief machinery, which diverted local groups from disruptive tactics and absorbed local leaders in bureaucratic roles. And once the movement weakened, and the instability of which it was one expression subsided, relief was cut back. That this happened speaks mainly to the resiliency of the American political system. That it happened so quickly, however, and at so cheap a price, speaks to the role played by leaders of the unemployed themselves.[26]

Organizers' visions of what an actual political organization looked like played straight into the hands of liberal recuperation, and what temporary gains the movement achieved with direct action were misunderstood by organizers as the sign to form a "real" movement. In doing so, they repressed the direct actions, leaving those gains vulnerable to immediate cut back as local power collapsed. They also left the historical narrative in the hands of FDR and his New Deal, which did nothing more than strangle a revolutionary movement in its cradle but which is now remembered as having saved the poor of the Great Depression. We can't afford to repeat those mistakes.

BY CENTERING LOOTING, AND SEEING ITS FREQUENT SIDELINING, RE-jection, or even repression by the organizers, historians, and bureaucrats of the labor movement, I hope we can begin to shake loose certain conceptions of what revolutionary activity can and must look like to succeed.

Meeting the needs and desires of the proletarian, the worker, the unemployed, and the downtrodden through direct struggle is not a mistake or a deviation from the real fight. It is not a failure that must be corrected by a militant, nor an opportunity to be seized by an organizer. It is the thing itself, the new world opening up, however briefly, in all its chaotic frenzy. It is uncontrollable, and as long as those who fight for freedom fear that uncontrollability, as long as they measure their success by their ability to direct, to dictate, to marshal, and to focus, they will never be able to achieve the liberation they seek. They must allow the real movement to change them, or they can only live to see themselves become its enemy.

chapter six | NO SUCH THING AS NONVIOLENCE

I N THE FOUR HUNDRED YEARS OF BARBARIC, WHITE SUPREMACIST, CO-lonial, and genocidal history known as the United States, the civil rights movement stands out as a bright, beautiful, all-too-brief moment of hope and struggle. We still live in the shadow of the leaders, theory, and images that emerged from those years, and any struggle in America that overlooks the work (both philosophical and organizational) produced in those decades does so at its own peril. However, why is it drilled into our heads, from grade school onward, in every single venue, by presidents, professors, and police chiefs alike, that the civil rights movement was victorious because it was nonviolent? Surely, we should be suspicious of any narrative that the entire white establishment agrees is of the utmost importance.

It is an appealingly simple narrative: in the fifties and sixties there was the good, successful, nonviolent civil rights movement in the South, which in the late sixties and early seventies gave way to a misguided, violent northern Black Power aftermath. This myth shapes not only our understanding of that period but also our perspectives on modern social movement activity in America. The division between nonviolence and militancy—the former moral, normative, and widely supported, embodied by Martin Luther King Jr. and the March on Washington, the latter unpopular, macho, and adventurist, represented by Malcolm X and the Black Panthers—did not exist until that period, but it has been used to attack and divide every movement since.

When police and politicians claim that it is nonviolent protesters that they listen to and protect, they are using this myth against our movements. It is why liberals, in the face of looting and rioting, share memes about what protesting used to look like featuring picket lines of civil rights activists, claiming that they would support *that* kind of protest. (At the time, of course, even that kind of protest was unpopular among white liberals, and Martin Luther King Jr. called out the white moderate as the "great stumbling block" to freedom.)

Though this myth is based on selective historical truths, the broader narrative is entirely false. To start with, there was no straightforwardly nonviolent civil rights movement. Nonviolence was a tactic designed at the time to appeal to Northern white liberals for funding and support. Nonviolence proved itself effective in desegregating certain public facilities, particularly with the student lunch counter sit-ins that spread across the South in 1960. Throughout the fifties and sixties, however, away from the cameras, demonstrators and organizers armed themselves. Idealistic, nonviolence-trained Freedom Riders were guarded where they worked, lived, and slept by local people with guns, sometimes over their objections. One of the most significant struggles in the whole nonviolent pantheon, the Birmingham, Alabama, desegregation movement, went from disciplined nonviolence to decidedly not-nonviolent rioting, with local teens throwing rocks and attacking property and police in its final victorious days. The very image of disciplined, philosophical nonviolence, Martin Luther King Jr. traveled with a heavily armed entourage. His home was protected by armed guards, and one visitor described the inside as "an arsenal." Guns were a crucial part of the freedom movement.

But what exactly was that movement? Although we learn about it in school as the series of struggles that achieved mass recognition—the Montgomery bus boycott, Little Rock, student sit-ins, Freedom Rides, Birmingham, the March on Washington, the Mississippi Freedom Democratic Party, Selma—the civil rights movement is better understood as the culmination of hundreds of local struggles against white supremacy, struggles large and small, across the entire country, unfolding across decades. These local movements shared some infrastructure, ideology, and tactics but had different histories, strategies (including rioting), goals, and results.

Nor was the Black Freedom movement predominantly driven by changes in federal law—*Brown v. Board*, the Civil Rights Act, and so forth—or by male ministers at the helms of a series of acronymned national civil rights organizations. Organizational histories, legal narratives, and leadership biographies are easier to write, to research, and to tell than the real, messy, grassroots history of social movements: they leave a paper trail and a clear subject to focus on. Rather than the resulting action of following orders from on high, however, social movements were usually organized through direct democratic mass meetings, enabling the grass roots to keep or wrench power from the big-name leaders. Those national leaders generally brought more media attention and fundraising opportunities than actual organizational strength. The majority of movement work was done by local people, joined in struggle and facilitated by young, idealistic student activists and experienced Black women organizers like Septima Clark, Ella Baker, and Jo Ann Robinson.[1]

Also, there is no clean historical break between the civil rights era and the era of Black Power. People practiced armed self-defense, organized around economic autonomy, and fought for Black community control—perhaps the core tenets of Black Power—throughout the years when nonviolent direct action was at its height of renown.

Similarly, Black Power and militant resistance cannot be simply reduced to Malcolm X, the Student Non-Violent Coordinating Committee, and the Black Panther Party, important though they all are. As Jeanne Theoharis and Komozi Woodard argue, the ideologies of self-defense, pan-Africanism, socialism, and independent Black political action all emerged from grassroots struggles. The leaders did not invent the rhetoric, ideology, and tactics of Black Power but merely gave effective expression to them, as police and government commissions consistently discovered when they tried to find the instigators and conspirators behind urban uprisings. Hardly limited to the urban North, Black Power also

wasn't predominantly a nationalist movement: it had an avowedly anticolonial and internationalist perspective, connecting its actions in solidarity
and direct alliance with Third World liberation movements.

Black Power, in other words, was a popular grassroots movement
built in both small-scale local organizing and massive rebellions. The
riots in Watts (1965) and Newark and Detroit (1967) are the most famous
uprisings, but such urban rebellions by no means only occurred in the
North; they spread across the entire country in dozens of major riots and
hundreds of smaller ones. Between 1964 and 1971, 750 Black riots and
rebellions took place in the United States. Rioting and looting were not
accidental offshoots of the Black Freedom movement, not some "oppor-
tunistic" or "tragic" consequence of civil rights struggle. Instead, they
formed a central part of the movement's power and effectiveness and a
core experience of the movement for many of those who rose up against
white supremacy.

And finally, and most tragically, is the myth that the civil rights movement succeeded. It is often told that the fall of Jim Crow, the granting
of the vote, and the destruction of openly racist laws via federal action,
through the Civil Rights Act of 1964, Voting Rights Act of 1965, and
the Fair Housing Act of 1968, achieved the core goals of the civil rights
movement.

From the start, the civil rights movement was about much more than
the right to vote and the end of segregation—it always centered economic
justice, freedom from violence, and communal autonomy. The movement's spark wasn't the Montgomery bus boycott against segregation in
December 1955 but the national reaction to the lynching of Emmett Till
that August: safety from white violence preceded integration as a concern
of the movement.

As Robin D. G. Kelley argues, this radical and broadly focused movement was "defeated on the shoals of race and property by liberals and
neoliberals" who co-opted and redefined the struggle into terms that did
not threaten their class position.[2] Even as it was unfolding, the media,
the government, moderate organizations, and white supporters worked
to make it appear that desegregation and voting rights were the only de-

mands of the movement, just as they worked to make nonviolence seem like the only viable tactic.

Furthermore, the end of segregation laws did not mean the end of segregation. American public schools—perhaps the most important terrain of integration struggles—are *more* segregated now than they were in the 1970s. Cities are slightly less segregated racially, but class-based urban segregation is more intense now than it has ever been, a circumstance that can perhaps be explained by the postmovement admittance of a small, nonwhite wing to the middle and upper classes. And the overturning of key parts of the Voting Rights Act, the disenfranchisement of felons, mass incarceration, gerrymandering, and the various other forms of voter suppression have meant that even that most basic victory—voting rights for all—may have been achieved in law but has remained sufficiently nonexistent in practice to put Donald Trump in the White House. Just as suppression of Black voters kept the Democrats empowered in the post-Reconstruction South, so does it keep the Republicans viable today.

The history of the Black Freedom struggle, alongside the histories of the associated and sometimes overlapping feminist, American Indian, Chicanx, Asian American, Puerto Rican, disability, queer liberation, and antiwar movements, has been mythologized and mystified. This mystification serves in the present day to divide us in our movements. It keeps those willing to follow the credo "by any means necessary" isolated and marginal; props up nonthreatening forms of resistance while attacking those who take the biggest risks and the biggest leaps to get free.

There is an increasingly clear historical consensus that there was never a purely nonviolent civil rights movement. The majority of those who worked within the nonviolent tradition treated nonviolence as an effective tactic, not a moral philosophy. Furthermore, to the degree that nonviolence was an effective tactic, it was so only because of a historical combination of national and international dynamics—chiefly Northern disdain for Southern backwardness and Cold War competition for influence over newly formed postcolonial governments in the Global South—that allowed Northern liberals to side with Southern Black activists to force the federal government to care about its moral image in the world. And still, *even under those circumstances*, nonviolent campaigners were often protected by force of arms, and many campaigns "devolved" into decidedly not-nonviolent rioting and direct action.

To understand riots and social movements today, tactically, strategically, and historically, many of us must transform our image of the Black Freedom movement. We cannot afford to think of the Black Freedom movement as made up of simple divisions between nonviolence and militancy, civil rights and Black Power, South and North, leaders and masses. Those historical and conceptual divisions were used then and are used now to appease white liberals and to enforce the white supremacist strategy of divide and conquer. The rioter and the looter were as fundamental to the movement as the Freedom Rider and the bus boycotter. They are deserving of just as much honor, gratitude, and study.

THE BLACK FREEDOM MOVEMENT WAS AT ITS MOST POWERFUL AND its most visible during the years 1955–1975. But the struggle did not begin suddenly in 1955, when Rosa Parks refused to give up her bus seat to a white passenger in Montgomery, Alabama. Intense civil rights struggles ensued throughout the forties. By 1955, however, these movements had been decimated by a massive wave of political and social repression organized under the banner of anticommunism. When the civil rights movement finally blossomed into national prominence, it grew from the ashes of a radical social justice movement dismantled by McCarthyism.

As France fell to Hitler's blitzkrieging armies in 1940, the United States embarked on an incredible expansion of defense spending and industrialization as it prepared to enter the war in Europe. It was this massive wave of military production that finally ended the Great Depression. The US government also began a military draft, which kicked into overdrive as the United States officially entered the war in December 1941. By the end of the war, nineteen million men had been drafted into the US Army.

War production created a lot of jobs, and more still were vacated by drafted young men. Most of these jobs were in heavy industry. Up until the war, this type of job had largely been the exclusive domain of white men, protected and maintained as such by racist union organizing and management hiring policy. But war destabilizes such traditions, and Black, Asian, and Chicanx men and women, as well as white women, were suddenly hired to fill the need for rapid production.

To get these jobs, and to escape the white supremacist violence of segregationists, millions of Black people migrated out of the South in what historians call the Second Great Migration, the largest internal migration in American history.* They left sharecropping and domestic servitude behind, hopefully forever, for the promise of higher-waged jobs and less discrimination in industrial urban centers. As one woman who worked in a factory during the war sardonically put it, "Lincoln may have freed the slaves, but Hitler was the one that got us out of the white folks' kitchen."[3]†

But the needs of war production did not suddenly turn American capitalists into champions of racial equity and justice. Black workers still did the worst jobs in the plants, and at lower pay than white people in the same positions. Black migrants ended up in redlined neighborhoods and faced terrible treatment at the hand of Northern whites, particularly landlords, police, and bosses.

---

*This migration was most pronounced on the West Coast, where Black populations grew exponentially in San Diego, Oakland, LA, Richmond, and other cities with naval production centers, but many laborers also went to Detroit, Chicago, the Twin Cities, and St. Louis, as well as Baltimore, Philadelphia, New York, and Boston. The migration continued for two decades after the war, though at a slower rate. Many of those who stayed in the South moved out of the fields and took jobs in cities like Charlotte, Memphis, or Atlanta. The Second Great Migration can also be understood as a movement of Black urbanization—by its completion, 80 percent of the American Black population lived in cities. The period also saw massive numbers of Latinx workers and families migrate to the same production centers. Much of the racial makeup of American cities was determined in these years, although migration from Southeast Asia, China, Central America, and Mexico post-1970, much of it in response to the Vietnam War and other US imperialist violence, would further transform the West, while Caribbean migration changed the Gulf states and migration from Brazil, North Africa, and the Middle East transformed the Midwest and East Coast. White flight and then gentrification have caused white populations to fluctuate dramatically in contested urban cores to this day.

†Jokes about Hitler and Tojo doing more to emancipate Black workers than FDR and Lincoln were common in the war years (Dan Georgakas and Marvin Surkin, Detroit, I Do Mind Dying: A Study in Urban Revolution [Cambridge, MA: South End Press, 1999]).

As a result of all these factors, World War II was a period of intense racial conflict and social movement on the home front. Riots occurred across the country, especially during the summer of 1943. The most infamous incident is the June 1943 Zoot Suit Riot, which saw gangs of white servicemen attack Mexican and Black teenagers in Los Angeles for wearing oversized, baggy zoot suits, a subversive, countercultural, and, in the face of wartime wool rationing, antimilitarist fashion. A few weeks later a white versus Black brawl turned into a massive riot in Detroit, one of the largest race riots of the twentieth century, in which thirty-four people were killed in sixty hours of combat that was only quelled when federal troops intervened. But rioting was not the only form of social conflict in the period.

In 1941, A. Philip Randolph—leader of the Brotherhood of Sleeping Car Porters—planned what would become known as the first March on Washington to protest segregation in the armed forces and the defense industries. As it became clear, a week before the march, that he had organized more than a hundred thousand people to move on DC, President Roosevelt panicked. Via executive order FDR banned segregation in the war effort and created the Fair Employment Practices Committee. As a result of this victory, Randolph called off the march but kept the organizational infrastructure in place, turning it into the March on Washington Movement (MOWM).

The Fair Employment Practices Committee proved to be another of FDR's canny concessions—it lacked enforcement mechanisms sufficient to create real integration. Still, MOWM could claim victory, and it gave agitators a framework for action. Alongside the National Association for the Advancement of Colored People (NAACP)—which, with the brilliant Ella Baker as new director of branches, would see its membership grow ten times during the war—Congress of Racial Equality (CORE), and other activist groups, MOWM continued to fight against defense industry segregation, successfully forcing more federal action in 1943. MOWM took a militant and radical approach, with an all-Black membership, a reliance on direct action, and open support for armed self-defense and "fighting the war against racism" at home. Local movements for work and housing justice also spread throughout the country, with pickets, boycotts, and marches among the most common tactics.[4]

As America fought a war in Europe against fascism, American leaders were forced to publicly denounce the racist logic that animated it. Black people called out the hypocrisy, pointing to racial discrimination in the United States and demanding a "double V"—victory over fascism at home and abroad. And the US allyship with the USSR meant the government had to stop promoting anticommunism, which since 1919 had been a potent force of social control. Indeed, propaganda and political pronouncements of the time praised the Soviet Union.

As a result, communists and radicals of all stripes, whose movement had ebbed dramatically from their revolutionary heights in the mid-thirties, were able to organize more openly. The Communist Party USA (CPUSA), with a large Black membership, reached seventy-five thousand strong in 1939, although much of the party's working-class base had left the party, and it was increasingly made up of professionals and the middle classes. Unions that had been whites-only opened up with the influx of Black workers into their industries and as emboldened radical voices took center stage in the labor movement. And so a social justice movement, involving Black Communists, reformers, and activists, unified with radical segments of labor, grew around demands for better housing, economic justice, and an end to Jim Crow and police violence.[5]

Meanwhile, within the armed forces, resistance grew in the ranks of Black soldiers. It is not stressed in heroic remembrances of the war, but the US military was segregated. The irony of a Jim Crow army fighting in the name of antifascism was not lost on Black soldiers. As Japanese citizens were shipped off to FDR's concentration camps, the vast majority of Black soldiers were shipped around the world as laborers, not combatants. Something like 90 percent of the Black men who went through basic training spent their service in work crews behind the lines, often doing hard, dirty work under miserable labor conditions, sometimes under white army officers/overseers pulled straight out of the sharecropping South. The Black regiments that did face battle, meanwhile, were deployed into continuous action on the front lines for much longer stretches than white regiments, which also received more rest and lived in better conditions in camp.[6]

This ill treatment of militarily trained young Black men had serious repercussions. As historian Timothy Tyson writes, "The War Department reported in 1943 [that] there was 'general unrest' among black troops all over the country and the imminent danger of revolt; 'most Negro soldiers have secreted ammunition,' one War Department memo stated."[7] Fights and riots broke out on bases and at training sites across the country as Black servicemen fought with white supremacist police, officers, and locals.

The full revolt never materialized, however, and the soldiers would not win their double V.* Nevertheless, like their World War I predecessors, Black veterans returned from fighting a "war for Democracy" abroad to a racist social system at home. Trained in armed combat, these veterans would become "the shock troops of the modern civil rights movement."[8]

When the war ended, many of the gains and concessions won by Black activists were lost. As war production spun down, Black workers were laid off in massive numbers—Black workers in America have always been last hired, first fired—turning already cramped and underserved Black neighborhoods into impoverished ghettos rife with unemployment. As white soldiers demobilized, white vigilante violence spiked. Bosses stoked racial conflict to keep labor divided.

Still, the wartime movement, which combined labor and communist radicalism with national Black civil rights struggle, might have survived this and sparked a radical, even revolutionary civil rights movement ten years earlier. In the immediate aftermath of World War II, the United States, projecting itself as the victorious champion of democracy as it occupied Japan and much of Europe, had to counterpoise these claims

---

*The armed forces wouldn't be desegregated until the movement and considerable international embarrassment forced Truman's hand in 1948. And after World War II, as the US Army occupied what would become West Germany, Black soldiers experienced better freedom of movement and action and more respect in post-Nazi Germany than they ever had in the Southern United States, an experience they would bring back with them into the freedom struggle (Maria Höhn, "'We Will Never Go Back to the Old Way Again': Germany in the African-American Debate on Civil Rights," *Central European History* 41, no. 4 [2008], 605–637).

with the bombing of Hiroshima and Nagasaki, a postwar increase in racial violence and lynching, and the army's segregation. As global attention turned to the war's victors, more than just Black Americans recognized Jim Crow for the fascism it clearly was. Black Communists such as Paul Robeson, W. E. B. Du Bois, and Claudia Jones advanced as leading national figures of the period, touring the country, writing, organizing, performing, and speaking on racial injustice and fascism at home.

For the white power structure, then, the Cold War provided a perfect opportunity to change the conversation and unleash a wave of repression. As US foreign policy turned from fighting fascism to solidifying US imperialism, in the form of market and political influence over the (soon-to-be-deemed) Third World, the Soviet Union transformed into enemy number one. And as a crucial domestic component of the Cold War, a paranoid, fear-mongering Far Right movement, spawned in the offices of FBI director J. Edgar Hoover, seeped out from the federal government to pervade the entire United States, with disastrous consequences.

In the name of "anticommunism," thousands upon thousands of Americans lost their jobs, their careers, their freedom, and sometimes even their lives. The second Red Scare, more often referred to as Mc-Carthyism, is most famous for two particular moments: Senator Joe McCarthy accusing hundreds of government employees of Communist subversion and artists, intellectuals, and Hollywood stars testifying in front of the House Un-American Activities Committee (HUAC) and the ensuing Hollywood blacklist. But it was much more.

At its height, from 1947 to 1957, the Red Scare, carried out by a network of intelligence agents, cops, federal employees, informants, and businessmen, argued that Communists had infiltrated the United States and all of its institutions. These Communists had to be mercilessly named, shamed, and taken out of positions of power to protect national interests and national defense.

The scare saw hundreds of political prosecutions, deportations of accused Communists, and even two people, Ethel and Julius Rosenberg, sent to the electric chair.[9] But its most widespread tactics were economic coercion, blacklists, and a generalized atmosphere of fear and suspicion. Thousands of rank-and-file workers in all industries, a huge number of them Black, most of them union, were fired and blacklisted, making earning a livelihood impossible. Workers were fired for associating with radical labor, leftist political organizations, and CPUSA front groups, for expressing left-of-mainstream opinions, or simply for being accused of any of the above. Radical academics, journalists, lawyers, and other professionals lost their jobs, and often their careers, as did many Hollywood writers, actors, and producers. The CPUSA, which had already largely been abandoned by working-class white people bought off by the New Deal, basically collapsed. Claudia Jones was imprisoned and deported; Robeson and Du Bois had their passports revoked.

The Red Scare, like all anticommunist and anti-Left repressions historically, included a significant uptick in oppression along other axes. A massive outing and purge of gay men and lesbian women in the federal government occurred, sometimes referred to as the Lavender Scare. Civil rights organizations such as the NAACP were accused of Communist infiltration and collaboration, and, shamefully, they too barred Communists from their organization and participated in purges of their ranks. As Keeanga-Yamahtta Taylor writes, "Socialists and communists were so identified with the antiracist movement that antiracist organizing was automatically assumed to be the work of communists."[10]

The final transformation of major labor unions into predominantly reactionary organizations was achieved in the period. Liberals and right wingers within unions, insisting on their patriotism, used the Red Scare to eliminate their political opponents on the left, while anticommunist unions used the scare to smash radical ones and take over their shops and industries. The CIO, little more than a decade removed from its heroic sit-down strikes, led the way, publicly and patriotically declaring the barring of Communists and the purging of leftists. The fact that these radicals and their unions were often the strongest and most dedicated organizers meant the labor movement would never again achieve the strength it had before the scare.*

---

*Of course, there were moments when labor seemed to be reviving in strength, particularly the powerful antiracist labor upsurge that lasted from 1969 to 1973. We are seeing a similar upsurge as of this writing, in 2020, with three years of increased labor activity building into the coronavirus-19 wildcats that are tearing through the country at the

Along with the disciplining of the labor movement and the near total collapse of the CPUSA came a general atmosphere of antiradicalism. Being accused of Communist sympathies could cost you everything: "These sanctions—or more commonly the fear of them—were sufficient to keep people from joining the Left or advocating unpopular positions in public."[11]

This atmosphere destroyed the momentum of Black organizing built during the war years. For one example, a powerful movement called the Black Popular Front had emerged in New York City in the late 1940s. As historian Brian Purnell writes, the Black Popular Front "brought together many different organizations and activists—labor unions, religious institutions, fraternal organizations, women's groups, Democratic and third-party politicians, Communists, Socialists, and others—and pushed an antiracist agenda into mainstream municipal and state policy debates."[12] But these alliances collapsed under the pressure of anticommunist accusations, smears, and paranoia. Thus, social movements and organizations not only kicked out radicals within their own ranks but also drifted away from one another. The cross-racial, cross-issue alliances built during the war died.

Gerald Horne has argued that the Red Scare, which disempowered Black radicals and led to an absence of radical labor and Communist organizers in Black communities, was one key factor in separatist Black nationalism—rather than a more anticapitalist politics—becoming the spontaneous worldview for many who rose up in the Black Freedom movement of the sixties.[13] Whatever the case, the Red Scare meant that when Rosa Parks did sit down on that bus in Montgomery, on December 1, 1955, she did so in a country that had swung far to the right on questions of economic and social justice, a country where potential allies were largely disorganized and demoralized.

---

time of this writing. But radical labor would never again be the leader of a general and nationwide movement for liberation in the United States, as it would be in Europe and Latin America in the 1960s and 1970s.

When Rosa Parks was arrested for refusing to give up her seat on that fateful morning, her local activist network saw it as the perfect "test case" they had been waiting for to challenge Montgomery segregation. Parks would go to trial the following Monday, December 5. The Women's Political Council—a local advocacy organization run by Black women—organized a bus boycott against segregation for the day of Parks's trial, hand printing thousands of leaflets overnight and distributing them over the weekend. The NAACP and a group of Montgomery ministers helped the Women's Political Council get the word out and joined them in supporting the boycott.

Almost no Black people rode the buses on the fifth; the boycott was a success beyond the organizers' anticipations. The boycott was meant to last only the one day, but at a mass meeting that night—a boisterous, joyous meeting that featured the inspiring oratory of a young preacher recently moved to Montgomery, Martin Luther King Jr.—the crowd unanimously voted to extend the boycott indefinitely.

The boycott lasted an entire year. Demonstrating the possibilities of grassroots organization in practice, the people of Montgomery and the Montgomery Improvement Association maintained the boycott by organizing and dispatching caravans of cars that brought thirty thousand working people to and from their jobs in white homes and businesses in downtown Montgomery *every day*.* As Rosa Parks describes it, "Quite a sophisticated system was developed. There were twenty private cars and fourteen station wagons. There were thirty-two pickup and transfer sites, and scheduled service from five-thirty in the morning until twelve-thirty at night."[14] It was an incredible achievement: the entire community organized and mobilized for a full year, overcoming police harassment and waves of arrest, intimidation, and bargaining. Their inspiring struggle

---

*Founded on December 4, the Montgomery Improvement Association was an autonomous local organization headed by Dr. King. It was formed to lead the boycott so as to avoid national interference from the NAACP, of which many of the MIA leaders, including Parks and King, were also members. They feared that the NAACP might either negotiate away the movement to declare an early victory or try to dominate the movement to follow in its image.

and eventual victory made headlines worldwide. King and Parks, in particular, were brought to national prominence during the boycott.

Even at the time, the incredible, women-led feat of people power was beginning to be mythologized and transformed into a story of individual heroics on the part of King and Parks. The myth that Parks had sparked the movement because of the singular bravery and novelty of her action was already growing. Though incredibly brave, she was not the first person to be arrested standing up to bus segregation in Montgomery. Nine months previously, Claudette Colvin had been arrested on the same charge for the same action. But Black organizers had decided that Colvin would not be their test case: Colvin was fifteen, impoverished, and pregnant out of wedlock from an affair with a married man. She was described as "feisty" and "mouthy." Her father had been in prison. She did not have the dignified, middle-class life or manners of Parks. Colvin's resistance, they reasoned, would have taken a backseat to a trial of her character.[15]

But even in portraying Parks as the definition of nonviolent, respectable femininity, as a quiet, demure seamstress who one day changed the world, the narrative clouds history to deradicalize its protagonists. Parks and Colvin were hardly alone: though theirs would become the most famous instigating moment, dozens of direct action movements were under way across the South in 1955. And Parks herself had been organizing for more than a decade already when she sat down on that bus. Though she was a proponent of organized nonviolent protest, she also believed in and practiced armed self-defense. Parks was a supporter of Robert F. Williams and would later call Malcolm X her personal hero. She spent her entire life a militant activist against segregation, sexual violence, and the justice system; on a few occasions she resisted white racists with threats of violence.[16] To reduce this radical lifelong activist to a single quiet act of protest serves as a good metonym for reducing the extensive spread of cultural, political, and social movements for Black liberation to a handful of nonviolent campaigns, protests, and sit-ins.

The choice to organize around Parks rather than Colvin was a tactical one made by a small organization that could have had no idea of its decision's success, let alone its national or historical impact. But still, from its very first moments of national recognition, the Southern civil rights struggle was stage-managed to appear respectable.

This strategy emerged from the antiradical movement atmosphere of post-McCarthyite America. Though it would win some allies and assist in some struggles, the political logic of nonviolence, propriety, media-focused-activism, organizational hierarchy, and internal antiradicalism placed a massive limit on possibilities that the movement would have to overcome. The strategy benefited middle-class leaders and middle-class concerns at the expense of true revolutionary change. Appeals to the movement's image and the moral imperative of nonviolence were used to silence and control poor Black people in their struggles, and they have been used in the intervening years to erase the vision and contributions of these people.

FOR MANY IN THE CIVIL RIGHTS STRUGGLE, THE CONTRADICTION EM-bodied by Rosa Parks—believing in the efficacy of the tactic of nonvio-lence and the moral righteousness of protecting yourself with guns—was solved rather simply. When white terrorists attacked the home of Hartman Turnbow, a Black farmer in Holmes County, Mississippi, he "pushed his family out the back door and grabbed the rifle off the wall and started shooting. And his explanation was simply that 'I was not being . . . non-nonviolent, I was protecting my wife and family.'"[17] In the face of white supremacist terror, shooting back was not a moral question, it was a necessity.

As the title of Charles Cobb's book about his experience in the move-ment put it, many in the South believed that *This Nonviolent Stuff'll Get You Killed*. The South in the 1950s was a place of constant state and vigilante violence. As Cobb writes, mass public "spectacle lynching" had largely disappeared. Instead, in the 1940s and 1950s "antiblack violence began to take on a more covert character: assassination, kidnapping, bombings."[18] The most common image of white supremacist terror was no longer the lynch mob or the white rioter but the night rider. The night rider gets his name from his most famous activity: driving through Black neighborhoods under cover of darkness, firing guns, throwing firebombs, kidnapping people, and making noise to intimidate. The night rider was no less common than his predecessors, but he did not always operate with the safety in numbers of the popular mobs of the prewar era, making him more vulnerable to a blast of buckshot.

The night rider gained national attention during the very first years of the civil rights struggle as the tactic spread across the South in response to Supreme Court decisions that pushed back against Jim Crow. In 1954 the Supreme Court ruled, in *Brown v. Board of Education*, that segregated schools were unconstitutional. As James Baldwin noted, many Black people at the time understood that "this immense concession would [never] have been made if it had not been for the competition of the Cold War, and the fact that Africa was clearly liberating herself and therefore had, for political reasons, to be wooed by the descendants of her former masters."* Throughout the era, the importance of America's global image in securing the allegiance of newly postcolonial African nations was paramount in national civil rights legislation, while links with anticolonial struggles in Africa inspired Black activists to greater and greater militancy.

Brown v. Board applied no mode of enforcement, no road map for integration. Nevertheless, it was a landmark decision. It provided a legal basis for change, allowing activists to bring lawsuits that resulted in court decisions outlawing local school segregation. But it would have remained a mere political gesture were it not for movements enforcing its decision.

The first to move were not the forces of integration, however, but of reaction. Immediately after the decision, Virginia senator Harry Byrd described it as an unprecedented threat to "states' rights"—a phrase that always has and always will mean white power. He got to work organizing politicians around what he would famously call "massive resistance" in which Southern state governments fought integration by all available methods.

---

*The quotation continues: "Had it been a matter of love or justice, the 1954 decision would surely have occurred sooner; were it not for the realities of power in this difficult era, it might very well not have occurred yet" (James Baldwin, *Fire Next Time* [New York: Random House, 1993], 75).

Massive resistance intensified segregation and its associated violence dramatically. In response to desegregation of school systems by local courts, whites-only private schools opened across the South. Some local school systems literally shut down, refusing to educate even their own white children rather than integrate. But massive resistance also meant a dramatic uptick in night riding, assassination, firebombing, and public harassment. The White Citizen Councils and the KKK dramatically increased their memberships, their presence, and their rates of action. They targeted politically active residents and community leaders in an effort to destroy local civil rights infrastructure.

Even so, dozens and dozens of struggles, large and small, north and south, desegregation campaigns, and organized self-defense were waged in the period between Montgomery's boycott of 1956 and the student sit-ins of 1960. But the outcomes of these struggles were often frustrating or inconclusive.

The most famous, the integration of Central High School in Little Rock, Arkansas, in 1957, demonstrates the ambivalence of the period's victories. Nine Black students, the so-called Little Rock Nine, enrolled, with the help of the NAACP, at all-white Central High in the summer of 1957. When they showed up for the first week of school, they were blocked by a racist mob. They were eventually admitted to the school at bayonet point when scenes of the mob ballooned into a national scandal and President Eisenhower sent in the National Guard. Even with the guard, the students faced white mobs lining their path, with harassment and threats of violence hurled at them every day. They suffered physical attacks and abuse in the school itself. The governor of Arkansas, Orval Faubus, shut down the entire Little Rock school system for academic year 1958–1959 rather than follow a court order to integrate further. When school resumed in the fall of 1959, so did the mobs. Though the impossibly brave Little Rock Nine continued to attend Central High, they hardly received a good public education, and they were not immediately followed by other Black students.

Thus, massive resistance, supported by state and vigilante alike, proved to be an effective block to nonviolent integration struggles. Of course, vigilantes were not particularly far removed from the state. Night riders and KKK processions were often escorted and led by police cars in the name of "public safety," and police turned over prisoners to Klansmen for savage beatings and lynchings.[19] It has been revealed that Birmingham, Alabama, public safety commissioner Bull Connor and local police coordinated the KKK attacks on Freedom Riders in 1961 and again on protesters in 1963, all with the knowledge and implicit consent of the FBI. But this kind of cooperation happened behind closed doors. Most often just enough room was left between government and assassins to provide plausible deniability.

Another major way the state supported night riders, white rapists, and lynchers was by not prosecuting them. In the rare instances when charges were brought—as in the case of Emmett Till—white juries just never found lynchers guilty. The police today have inherited not only their predecessors' campaign of terror and violence but also their judicial immunity. With no recourse to the courts or the police, and with the ever-present threat of the Klansman and the night riders, Black folks in the South did what they had been doing since the Civil War: they armed themselves.

chapter seven | # USING GUNS NONVIOLENTLY

I N 1959, ROBERT F. WILLIAMS, PRESIDENT OF THE MONROE, NORTH
Carolina, branch of the NAACP, caused a national scandal when he declared to reporters, after the acquittal of a white rapist who had attacked
a woman in broad daylight and in front of witnesses, that it was "time to
meet violence with violence." Though largely forgotten now, Williams
was nearly as important and famous a figure for the Black Power movement as Malcolm X.

Robert F. Williams was not, however, some visionary individually
pushing militancy forward. His comments that day had been wrenched
out of him by the women of Monroe, who were absolutely furious with
him. Just before he spoke, the women had been admonishing Williams
for convincing them not to attack the rapist's house and get justice on
their own terms, as they had planned. Williams had insisted that they
should wait for the courts, that they would find justice there. The analysis
by Williams, who would go on to advocate armed struggle and become
an internationally known proponent of Black Power and socialist revolution, was on that day trailing far behind that of the women. This internationalist revolutionary was the product of his local movement, whose
core activist base was poor Black women.

The struggle in Monroe had begun in earnest in the summer of 1957, when a Black boy drowned in a swimming hole outside of town. Monroe had a swimming pool, but it was whites-only, and so Black children beat the summer heat in unsupervised and often dangerous swimming holes in the countryside. As a result, drownings were a regular occurrence: pool segregation was lethal. So Robert Williams and local chapter vice president Dr. Albert Perry gathered a group of local young folks and went to "stand-in" at the pool.

The NAACP is hardly renowned for militant direct action—it was predominantly a respectable, middle-class organization focused on hiring lawyers to pursue legal challenges to segregation. But in many towns in the South, it was the only Black political organization around. In the period, its local branches were often more radical and less middle class than its central office and national image.

The Monroe chapter was particularly working class. Williams had inherited an almost entirely inactive branch and had directly focused on recruiting from pool halls, beauty parlors, and other places working-class folks were found. This makeup of the Monroe movement no doubt helped it set aside respectability politics as the summer and the struggle over the pool heated up. The town refused to integrate the pool and refused a number of other compromises Williams and the NAACP offered. And so activists would go down to the pool to try to get in, and officials would close the pool while Williams and others picketed outside.

But Williams hadn't merely revived the Monroe NAACP, he had also chartered a National Rifle Association (NRA) chapter. Many Black folks in Monroe who didn't already have guns acquired some, and men and women learned to shoot straighter as members of a gun club Williams organized.

These guns reflected the fact that Monroe was also one of the main centers of KKK activity in North Carolina. As the summer wore on, white crowds outside the pool and Klan night riders intensified their attacks. Rumor spread that the KKK was going to attack Dr. Perry's home. Activists reinforced his house with sandbags and stationed an armed guard there. The rumors were right: one night, the Klan showed up to shoot up the place, but the Monroe movement was prepared and the house was full of activists, who fired back. Surprised, the Klan fled. It appears that the defenders killed a Klansman in the fight, but the white folks covered it up so as not to let the news get out too widely that armed Black people had defeated the Klan.

This gunfight largely ended white violence in Monroe, both against demonstrators and from night riders. In Williams's analysis, white fascists are cowards: believing their lives to be more valuable than those of whom they oppress, they are rarely willing to risk death for their goals. Though the Klan continued to occasionally harass and threaten Williams and other leaders, it never regained the upper hand. As Williams would write five years later, "Our sit-ins proved that self-defense and nonviolence could be successfully combined. There was less violence in the Monroe sit-ins than in any other sit-ins in the South. In other communities there were Negroes who had their skulls fractured, but not a single demonstrator was even spat upon during our sit-ins. We had less violence because we had shown the willingness and readiness to fight and defend ourselves."[1]

When, in 1959, Williams declared it was time to "meet violence with violence," he wasn't espousing a macho creed, he was reflecting the learned wisdom of the Monroe movement.* And, as his wife, Mabel

---

*Williams's remarks were published widely in the national press, which claimed that an NAACP leader was calling for race war. After the controversy, the NAACP national office sanctioned Williams and stripped him of his presidency. But the local people organized around and protected Williams and kept him in a leadership position—where he would help the movement in its successful desegregation of Monroe civic services such as the pool and the public library. After a series of inspiring struggles in Monroe, tensions built to the point when a full-on insurrection seemed in the offing. To head it off, Williams was framed for kidnapping a white couple and chased out of the county, and then the country, and then off the continent. Williams would go on to organize and agitate from Cuba, where he wrote an autobiography, Negroes with Guns, a monthly radical newsletter, The Crusader, and a radio show, Radio Free Dixie, with which he sent increasingly militant propaganda into the South. He encouraged people to form gun clubs and to organize around self-defense, critiqued nonviolence as a moral philosophy, and presciently predicted and analyzed the riots of the mid-1960s. His journal gave instructions in guerilla and urban warfare and taught people how to make Molotov cocktails and explosives. But despite being hosted by Cuba and then, later, Mao's China, he resisted joining their official Communist Parties, maintaining an independent position as a Black radical and becoming leader in exile of the Revolutionary Action Movement (RAM) and then the Republic of New Afrika. For more on the incredible life of Robert F. Williams, read his autobiography, Negroes with Guns, and read Timothy B. Tyson's Radio Free Dixie.

Williams, remarked that same year, "Women are pushing harder than the men. . . . That is where our drive is coming from." In one of the first major moments in the campaign, before even the assault on his house, Dr. Perry had been arrested and was in danger of being lynched, so a group of women had gathered rifles and stormed the jail, freeing him.

Monroe's vision of an armed, self-defensive civil rights movement— though it was officially opposed by the NAACP, CORE, and the newly formed Southern Christian Leadership Conference (SCLC) centered around Martin Luther King and the other charismatic Southern preachers of the movement—had supporters across the country, including SCLC-aligned Rosa Parks and Ella Baker. It would go on to be the inspiration for many movements across the South, culminating most visibly in the Deacons for Defense and Justice, a group that formed in 1964 to provide armed escorts to marches in Louisiana and Mississippi.[2] But the inspiration of the events in Monroe largely remained unofficial and in the shadows because, in 1960, the students of Greensboro, North Carolina, spectacularly and bravely demonstrated the power of nonviolence, and nonviolence became the "official" tactic and philosophy of the movement.

THE EVENTS OF 1960–1963 ARE THE MOST FAMOUS AND MYTHOLO-gized of the entire civil rights era and among the most famous of the twentieth century in America. On February 1, 1960, four students from North Carolina A&T University sat down at a whites-only lunch counter in the Greensboro Woolworth, where they were refused service. They stayed until closing time. The next day twenty students showed up. The following, sixty. The day after that, three hundred protesters. Within a few weeks, sit-ins had spread all across North Carolina and to Nashville, Tennessee, Lexington, Kentucky, and Richmond, Virginia. By the spring, almost all the cities of the South were experiencing nonviolent sit-in movements in their downtowns. Dozens of lunch counters, hotels, and restaurants were desegregated, although some weathered the storm and remained whites-only.

Images of students being beaten, spat upon, and arrested for sitting on a stool spread nationwide and did exactly what nonviolence tactics are meant to do: galvanize anger, support, resistance, and pity. It was an important, radicalizing moment. To capture the energy unleashed by the student movement, Ella Baker, frustrated with the misogyny, hierarchy, and cult of personality dominating the SCLC she had just left, set up a meeting in Raleigh, North Carolina, in April that would give birth to the Student Non-Violent Coordinating Committee (SNCC).

The organization was infused with Baker's organizational style, which was structured around a simple, antihierarchical principle: "strong people don't need strong leaders." In the same vein, she would never be its official head, leaving that position to the students, though she would remain its philosophical and organizational lodestone. The SNCC adopted her grassroots approach that focused on cultivating local organizers, with the goal that an organizer eventually made herself unnecessary as the local movement took on its own momentum. This was coupled with internal democracy that made the organization capable of shifting dynamically to reflect the changing opinions of its membership.[3] This bottom-up approach, opposed to the paper-membership, media-spectacle, mass-demonstration style that has been passed down to us as MLK's legacy, made SNCC perhaps the most vital force in the Southern movement.

Nonviolent tactics again proved effective in the next massive campaign, the Freedom Rides of 1961. Modeled on the 1947 Journey for Reconciliation, in which CORE activists had attempted to test a 1946 Supreme Court ruling outlawing segregation on interstate travel, CORE again organized white and Black activists to ride together on buses into the Deep South, to test that and another Supreme Court ruling, from 1960, that desegregated restaurants and seating areas in stations.

The Freedom Riders traveled through the upper South in relative peace, but in Alabama and Mississippi they faced terrible violence, with a few activists beaten nearly to death. After a ferocious attack by the Klan in Birmingham, Alabama—coordinated with local police and with FBI knowledge—CORE withdrew its organizers. SNCC, led by Diane Nash, was convinced such a defeat at the hands of mob violence would be a disaster and sent replacement activists to continue the rides. Massive mobs met buses at stations; segregationists lit one bus on fire while Freedom Riders were still on board. The violence shocked the country, and the rides lasted throughout the summer of 1961, eventually forcing President Kennedy to end bus segregation on interstate travel.

The Freedom Rides were incredibly inspiring events, putting the whole country on notice of the seriousness of the movement. They both proved SNCC's effectiveness and inspired local movements wherever Freedom Riders went in the South. Ironically, however, the Freedom Rides, which cemented nonviolence as the definitive tactic of the movement, would also be the last major success of the tactic.

As struggles blossomed all over the South, the philosophy of nonviolence met the reality of Black life under Jim Crow and the truth of night riders, the KKK, and fascist police. Many Black people in the rural South were already armed as a result of subsistence hunting combined with a history of effective Black self-defense and a generalized Southern gun culture: many Northern workers who went south acquired guns as well. Even the Freedom Riders had been protected, while they stayed with Black supporters overnight, by armed guards.

As many recent historical studies have demonstrated, although the major organizations—SNCC, CORE, NAACP, SCLC—all declared themselves officially nonviolent, guns kept their activists safe in the South while they carried out agitation, organization, and movement.* Akinyele Omowale Umoja argues that Robert F. Williams was an exception because he advocated armed tactics publicly, not because he used those tactics—most of the movements and activists in the South had recourse to guns during their struggle. As professor and SNCC member Charles Cobb wrote, "Willingness to engage in armed self-defense played an important role in the southern Freedom Movement, for without it, terrorists would have killed far more people in the movement." Rather than the stark distinction polemically laid out by Malcolm X, that it was either

---

*There is now an exciting group of books about this subject. For this study I've used Charles Cobb's *This Nonviolent Stuff'll Get You Killed*, Lance Hill's *Deacons for Defense*, Akinyele Omowale Umoja's *We Will Shoot Back*, and Timothy Tyson's *Radio Free Dixie*, but more and more book-length histories of this trend continue to be published.

the ballot or the bullet, Kwame Jeffries writes that for most in the Black Freedom movement, "the relationship between ballots and bullets was both/and."[4]

The advocates of nonviolence were, of course, well aware of this dynamic. Charles Cobb writes, "For most activists . . . nonviolence was simply a useful tactic, one that did not preclude self-defense whenever it was considered necessary and possible. Even King . . . acknowledged the legitimacy of self-defense and sometimes blurred the line between nonviolence and self-defense."[5] It wasn't just MLK. As Lance Hill records: "James Lawson, the movement's foremost spokesperson for Gandhian nonviolence, admitted later that there 'never has been an acceptance of the nonviolent approach' in the South and the idea that blacks had initially accepted nonviolence and then became disillusioned was 'nonsense.'"[6]

But if none of that was the historical case, how has it become such a unified narrative? As ever, history has been written by the victors. The Northern media and white liberals were eager to support the end of Jim Crow, as it tainted the image of the United States in the Cold War and, no less significantly, offered a massive potential bloc of Black voters to the party that could end it. But, just like their Republican and union predecessors a hundred years previously, they were unwilling to accept any fundamental challenges to the system, let alone any tactics that might threaten their own white supremacist hegemony in the West and the North, and so "nonviolence" became the happy and celebrated compromise.

The tactic of nonviolence was critiqued and ultimately disproven in the streets, but, after the movement was defeated in the early 1970s, a huge media, academic, and governmental project of falsification via co-optation of MLK, Parks, and the movement took place, unfolding over decades and slowly defanging and mystifying the actual way the movement moved. And the falsification involved in proving the efficacy of nonviolence is nowhere clearer than in the history of Birmingham.

IT WAS THE STRUGGLE IN BIRMINGHAM, ALABAMA, THAT WOULD LEAD
to the creation of the first Civil Rights Act. The Birmingham desegregation fight in 1963 shook the world, with televised images of Black children
being blasted with fire hoses and attacked by public safety commissioner
Eugene "Bull" Connor's police dogs. The harrowing images brought
MLK and the SCLC, leaders of the Birmingham struggle, back into the
national spotlight after a disastrous previous campaign.

From 1961 to 1962 in Albany, Georgia, King and fellow activists had
been utterly defeated by chief of police Laurie Pritchett, who took careful
advantage of nonviolence's tactical weaknesses. Disciplining his police
force to never engage in violent arrests, and dispersing arrested activists to
jails outside of and around Albany—thus destroying the core nonviolent
tactic of "filling the jails" that creates logistical crises for the police—
Pritchett completely removed nonviolence's main forms of leverage. The
Albany movement, despite a very large activist base and almost fully mobilized community, ended in bitter defeat.

But, though the Birmingham campaign started much the same way
as Albany had, it faced a much less peaceful and disciplined police force
and was itself less insistent on nonviolence. King had much less control, and this lack of top-down control was to the movement's benefit.
As activist-historian Lorenzo Raymond writes: "King wasn't able to get
consistent media coverage until after protests became, as Taylor Branch
put it, 'a duel of rocks and fire hoses.' One of King's aides, Vincent Hard-
ing, later acknowledged that the black youth who came to dominate the
campaign's street action were 'the children of Malcom X' and that their
escalation to 'a burning, car-smashing, police-battling response' marked
Birmingham as 'the first of the period's urban rebellions.'"[7]

Rioters took over and held the downtown for days, smashing store-
fronts and successfully beating back the police. This rioting not only defined the campaign but also proved crucial to its historical effects and
relevance. It was this riot and the fear of it spreading to other cities—
combined with international relations problems caused by images of Birmingham police violence—that forced Kennedy into giving his famous
speech calling for civil rights legislation and compelled his administration to draft what would become the Civil Rights Act of 1964. The rioting

wouldn't have happened without the organizing, marches, and rallies of the movement, and that effort, as in Albany, wouldn't have won without the rioting.

But in the wake of Birmingham, national civil rights leaders downplayed the violence. The official text of the moment became MLK's *Letter from a Birmingham Jail*, while the images that broke through the national consciousness (and remain to this day) are dogs snapping and firehoses blasting Black children—images of Black victimization—not images of those children getting up and throwing rocks at the police. MLK distanced himself from the rioters to promote a narrative of a unified and nonviolent philosophy of the movement, and he immediately pivoted toward organizing the March on Washington.

If so many of the movements were driven by not-nonviolent methods, and so many of the activists remained alive by force of arms, why did they so widely spread the myth of their own nonviolence?*

NONVIOLENCE GAVE THE EARLY CIVIL RIGHTS MOVEMENT THE LEGIT-imacy it required to receive support from Northern liberals. Money from liberals kept organizers in the field, while white media coverage kept national attention on the struggle. Nonviolence gave Black folks moral room to maneuver in a country that always a priori viewed them as criminal and immoral—no small achievement. And it won widespread sympathy and demonstrated that the violence of police and (Southern) white people was unprovoked and thus inherent to their power.

---

*I use the rather clunky phrase *not-nonviolent* purposely. For some nonviolence ideologues, breaking windows, lighting trash on fire, or even building barricades in the street is "violent." I once witnessed a group of Black teens chanting "Fuck the Police" get shouted at for "being violent" by a white protester. Though there are more forms of violence than just literal physical blows to a human body, I don't believe a conception of "violence" that encompasses both throwing trash in the street and the murder of Michael Brown is remotely helpful. Calling breaking a window "violent" reproduces this useless definition and places the whole argument within the rhetorical structure of nonviolence ideology. *Not-nonviolent*, then, becomes the more useful term. I first encountered the term in the work of Lorenzo Raymond.

But nonviolence suffered from strategic weaknesses, too, namely, overestimating the power of the white liberal. The strategy of nonviolence hinged on Southern racist violence producing sympathy among liberals and thus leading them to fight for structural change in state and federal governments. As C. E. Wilson wrote in 1964, "The extent of white liberal influence with the power structure had been totally overestimated and its direction misunderstood. The Southern white liberal was only a celebrity in the North and the Northern white liberal was more interested in the South. In his own back yard the white liberal was virtually powerless or isolated and attacked by other hostile whites."[8]

But there is a more fundamental problem with nonviolence: when it is no longer a tactic among many, and is instead pushed as a philosophical, moral, or religious principle, it gains a nasty, authoritarian edge. As Lance Hill writes: "By giving the luster of religious precept to a pragmatic stratagem to attract white liberals—while accommodating liberal fears of black violence—the national civil rights leadership took the high moral ground and made their critics look like nihilistic advocates of violence."[9] This moral division adds a new layer of shame and rejection onto those who take not-nonviolent action to free themselves, which, as we've seen, actually included most of the Southern movement.

The strategic maintenance of the image of nonviolence, pushed by the heads of organizations, the media, liberal politicians, and well-meaning but naive middle-class white allies alike, forced many activists into silence, keeping them from telling the truth of their experience, namely, that guns were keeping them safe, that self-defense worked. As the movement moved forward, and urban riots and rebellions spread, liberals, who had only a few years previously believed any civil disobedience was too militant and that Black folks were moving too fast, used the principle of nonviolence they now embraced to dismiss and attack the uprisings.

Police have learned this technique particularly well. Nonviolence is the essential tool in the protest policing technique of "controlled management" and the tactic of divide and conquer, as they try to "coordinate" protest marches with organization officials and protest marshals and accuse outside agitators, antifa, "white anarchists," or any other preferred boogeyman for the militancy that emerges organically from struggles for freedom. The police are helped by people theoretically on our side, who are happy to accuse anyone who acts not-nonviolently of being an *agent provocateur* and who will even turn people in for not-nonviolent acts, damning them to the terrible violence of the police and prison system in the name of pacifism.

But what is nonviolent resistance? It seems obvious, but, in fact, nonviolent resistance is an incredibly nebulous and murky concept. In practice, it can mean almost anything: Birmingham is claimed as a nonviolent success—the rioting is unmentioned or written off as unimportant or as things "getting out of hand"—whereas breaking a window on a march today, although no one is hurt, is almost always called violence.

The 2011 revolution in Egypt is still sometimes described as a nonviolent victory, despite the vast arson of police and government buildings; massive rioting in Suez, Alexandria, and Cairo; widespread looting; and the killing of over a dozen police officers. Meanwhile, the Movement for Black Lives, which, despite including looting and arson, has killed no one, is roundly condemned as too violent. Nonviolent ideologues tend to claim militant movements as evidence of their philosophy's power if the movements happen far away—geographically or historically—but they attack any and all militancy that occurs closer to home.

This open-ended definition provides for much of nonviolence's authoritarian character. Gandhi, the racist, misogynist founder of modern nonviolent philosophy, firmly kept for himself the power to determine what was violent in the Indian independence movement. On two occasions he called off strikes by his followers by calling them "violent"—forcing the movement into months of introspection, self-critique, and reorganization—because friends of his owned the factories being struck against. His anti-Blackness is now widely known: as an advocate for Indians in South Africa, he continually expressed his hatred and disdain for Black Africans, worrying that European colonizers were degrading Indians to "their level." He also believed menstruation was a sign of corruption, campaigned against contraception, believed fathers were right to honor-kill assaulted daughters, and made young female followers sleep naked in bed with him to prove his purity. All of these positions are apparently in accord with nonviolence.

In the United States in the sixties, nonviolence was equally used as a tool to bludgeon movements the powerful didn't like. Liberals used nonviolence to rail against the 1964 "stall-in" organized by Brooklyn's CORE, which would have congested traffic to the World's Fair by stalling out cars on the highway. The action was meant to focus the eyes of the city and the world on Black poverty, partially achieved by the fact that impoverished neighborhoods would be directly visible to World Fair visitors stuck on the Brooklyn-Queens Expressway. Opponents screamed that CORE had abandoned nonviolence. If causing a traffic jam is morally reprehensible violence, then nonviolence truly leaves us with almost no tools to fight oppression.

Nonviolence in the civil rights movement was mostly pointed toward gaining liberal support, instigating federal intervention in the South, and forcing the creation of new laws. But new laws are enforced by the police, and federal intervention often entails sending in the National Guard. Why does sending the National Guard to defend a march at gunpoint constitute nonviolence? Nonviolent practitioners today are happy to organize their marches in collaboration with the police, who are the main purveyors of white supremacist violence in our cities. Why is armed police protection nonviolent?

Nonviolence as a philosophy is ultimately not about reducing violence or increasing peace; it is about purifying the activist, about cleaning their hands. Nonviolence means outsourcing the power you need to meet your objectives to the police or to federal marshals—in other words, to the state. It means disavowing that power, not actually destroying it. Nonviolence is a tactic based in keeping current distributions of power in place.

As a result, in the last analysis, nonviolence is structured around victim blaming and anti-Blackness. As Robert F. Williams wrote, "Why do the white liberals ask us to be non-violent? We are not the aggressors; we have been victimized for over 300 years! Yet nobody spends money to go into the South and ask the racists to be martyrs or pacifists. But they always come to the downtrodden Negroes, who are already oppressed and too submissive as a group, and ask them not to fight back."[10]

Nonviolence puts the entire moral weight of politics onto the backs of the oppressed. It takes the history of white supremacy and settler colonialism for granted and says that the responsibility for changing the violent nature of that history lies entirely with the people who are currently crushed under that violence. But any serious engagement with history should lead us to see the wisdom in the claim made by Stokely Carmichael (later Kwame Ture) that "responsibility for the use of violence by black men, whether in self-defense or initiated by them, lies with the white community." Black people wouldn't even be in the United States, nor, indeed, would there be any United States, were it not for chattel slavery, white supremacy, and settler colonialism.

Nonviolence turns this historical accounting upside down. As anarchist theorist Peter Gelderloos writes, nonviolence advocates often argue that the state will use militant struggle or armed resistance to "'justify' violent repression. Well, to whom is this violent repression justified, and why aren't those who claim to be against violence trying to unjustify it?"[11] The nonviolent worldview, focusing entirely on protesters and not on police, ultimately obscures the responsibilities of the state, racists, and fascists, because it frames their much more extreme repressive violence as "natural" and normal. Nonviolence lets the police, and the systems that they defend, off the hook.

I want to make clear that this discussion is not meant to denigrate anyone who uses nonviolent tactics in their struggles. Most of the tactics available and desirable to us fall within the parameters of "nonviolence": discussion, education, study, community organizing, mutual aid, protest. Indeed, it is recognizing the extent of the horrible violence of the state, capitalism, white supremacy, imperialism, cisheteropatriarchy, and settler colonialism that makes me believe revolution is the only way forward.

But I do not believe that my refusal to attack property, fight physically, or make a ruckus helps us toward radical change: that refusal does not lessen the degree to which I benefit from systems of domination. It may assuage my personal aversion to violence, but history shows that it ultimately limits my ability to get free. By not lighting fires at a protest, by not defending myself from police attack, I am not successfully avoiding

violence. I believe it demonstrates a much deeper complicity with violence, for example, to let someone be arrested and taken into the carceral
system when I could prevent it, than it is to shove a cop in order to let that
person get away.

And though I don't believe that we can cleanly separate means from
ends, I also think violence is much too broad and imprecise an idea to
be a metric of tactics in and of itself. There is, in my opinion, no legitimate moral, ethical, or political equivalence that can be made between
the police murdering Freddie Gray and protesters breaking a cop car's
windows in response, and yet both can be called "violence." Similarly,
I believe that "nonviolence" has become a bankrupt concept freighted
with moral righteousness but lacking actual content. And without the political context of the sixties—in particular, the moral imperative created
by victorious anticolonial struggle in Africa and Asia—it is strategically
and tactically bankrupt, too.

The nonviolent activists of the sixties were impossibly brave, acting
with incredible discipline and restraint in the face of massive historical
and physical violence. They did so out of a commitment to freedom and
justice, and we owe them the utmost respect and honor. But most activists in the sixties also practiced or benefited from armed self-defense, and
many eventually left nonviolence behind. A vast number of participants
in the movement were involved in decidedly not-nonviolent riots and
uprisings.

This more complicated and fluid relationship to the idea of nonviolence has been lost in the intervening years. When we remove the rioters
and rebels from our image of the movement, we fundamentally misunderstand the nature of the struggle and ignore the open-minded perspectives and diverse tactics of its activists, who wanted, above all, to get free.

A TRUE LIBERATORY POLITICS IS ALSO ANTIPATRIARCHAL, AND NON-
violence advocates often claim this (indisputable) point is in their favor, arguing the existence of an inherent link between militant tactics,
machismo, and misogyny. But between the Birmingham riots and the

lead-up to the March on Washington, during the very height of nonviolent organizing, a number of Black women in the movement, many of whom had been at the forefront of militant, radical efforts, found themselves silenced.

The 1963 March on Washington, *the* great event in the history of nonviolence, and perhaps the most iconic moment of the entire struggle, shows how often *nonviolence* is actually a collaborationist and misogynist affair. Malcolm X traced the history of the march in his "Message to the Grassroots" and, later, in his autobiography. As he records it, the idea of a March on Washington, which had been present in the movement since A. Phillip Randolph's 1941 MOWM, began to percolate again among the grass roots in the North in 1962.

The march, given shape by Black labor radicals that included Randolph, was originally planned by people predominantly in the North, who focused on the intersection of racial and class exploitation. Its original goal was to fight against the "economic subordination" of Black people. March organizers began working with the heads of other movement organizations, however, and expanded the definition of the march to include civil rights struggle: it would become a "March for Jobs and Freedom." At first this only expanded its scope. The march had the support of the grass roots, and a militant plan emerged. Poor Black people were going to go down to DC however they could for two days, march on the Congress and the White House in a series of dispersed direct actions, and shut down the government.

President John F. Kennedy, just as FDR had twenty years before him, panicked in the face of the planned attack on the capital, and called a meeting with the moderate leaders of the civil rights movement, begging them to stop the march in exchange for concessions. When they told him that energy for the march was flowing from the bottom up and they couldn't stop the event, JFK graciously "authorized" an official march, which would be headed up, funded, and organized by the fine, middle-class gentlemen of the leadership and which would end with an official delegation meeting with the president. In return, the movement's leadership assured the president that the march, rather than a riotous mob of the poor descending on the seat of government, would see a polite crowd stay on the Mall for only a day—they all left that same evening!—to be shipped out without doing any damage. It would be nonviolent, racially mixed, and even the signs and chants would be controlled. Malcolm called it the "farce on Washington."[12]

This co-optation was intensified by the internal misogyny of the civil rights organizations. Dorothy I. Height, Pauli Murray, and Ella Baker record, from their positions within the leadership's inner sanctum, how the mainstream leaders were evasive and dismissive when it came to questions of gender and representation. As the major organizations came together to plan the big day, women advocated for their place at the podium. Height describes the situation:

> We women were expected to put all our energies into it. Clearly, there was a low tolerance level for anyone raising the questions about the women's participation, per se.
>
> The men seemed to feel that women were digressing and pulling the discussion off the main track. . . . It was thought that we were making a lot of fuss about an insignificant issue, that we did not recognize that the March was about racism, not sexism.[13]

Women were the core organizers of the civil rights movement. National organizers like Baker, Parks, Murray, Height, and Septima Clark did constant, thankless work building organizational infrastructure, discovering grassroots leaders, and building voting drives and freedom schools (which taught reading and basic political literacy) in towns all over the South. Meanwhile, organizers like Gloria Richardson, Daisy Bates, Fannie Lou Hamer, Ruth Batson, and Amelia Platts Boynton emerged from their communities to lead the most exciting and militant local struggles in the country.

But as planning for the March on Washington was coming together, despite the fact that much of the work for the march itself was being carried out by women, it was made clear that no women were going to be allowed to speak at the dais. Despite the angry protests of many women leaders, "the organizers gave a number of us prominent seats on the platform. We were seated. In all the March on Washington pictures, we're right there on the platform. There were several women who just refused to do anything. Some were so angry that they didn't really want to take part."[14]

Pauli Murray sums up this anger well: "It was bitterly humiliating for Negro Women on August 28, to see themselves accorded little more than token recognition in the historic March on Washington. Not a single woman was invited to make one of the major speeches or to be part of the delegation of leaders who went to the White House. The omission was deliberate."[15]

The patriarchal erasure of these women from the struggle's most historic moment is of a piece with the anti-militancy of the affair, which at the last minute refused SNCC's John Lewis his speaking role until he removed language promising revolution and criticizing JFK's civil rights bill. Patriarchy and *anti*-militancy are part of the same political program.

These days, however, those who violate absolute nonviolence and act militantly are often accused of being macho, immature, middle class, and in league with the police. The fact is, the nonviolent wing of the movement was most pronounced in its misogyny, most middle class in its leadership, and most complicit with the state. Whereas the overwhelming majority of famous figures in the pantheon of the Black Freedom movement are men, it is Black Power, and in particular the Black Panther Party (BPP), that is singled out for accusations of misogyny and machismo.

But the idea that the BPP was *particularly* misogynistic is simply not true. At its height, two-thirds of the BPP membership were women. The vast majority of BPP activities, a wide range of "medical, housing, clothing, free breakfast and education programs," were run and organized by women.[16] It was this work, in support of the armed self-defense, that J. Edgar Hoover thought made the BPP particularly dangerous, because with these programs the Panthers could win mass appeal and receive support from many sectors of society. As Panther Frankye Malika Adams said, "Women ran the BPP pretty much. I don't know how it got to be a male's party or thought of as being a male's party." BPP rallies featured women standing shoulder to shoulder with men wearing the same uniforms. It was, furthermore, the only major organization of the period to be publicly led by a woman: Elaine Brown chaired the BPP from 1974 to 1977, and it was one of the only organizations to officially take a position on women's liberation.[17]*

This is not to deny or excuse the fact that the BPP was afflicted with patriarchal and misogynist views and practices we would find objectionable today (nor to say that there aren't many of the same problems in our movements now; they're just not as explicitly expressed). Women still did the vast majority of the caring, cooking, and cleaning and were expected to raise children and do the social services and administrative work while men were chosen for media appearances and glamorous direct actions. The BPP traded in macho rhetoric, and Eldridge Cleaver's best-selling *Soul on Ice*, written in 1965 before he was a party member but published in 1968 and associated widely with the Panthers, has a horrific passage of rape apology and misogynoir in its opening pages.

But even though these facts are relatively common knowledge about the Panthers, we rarely, if ever, hear about the rampant misogyny of the white middle-class peace movement, hippie culture, or the civil rights mainstream. It is not to deny the misogyny of the party to ask: Why is the BPP so often singled out for its machismo? I believe that it is partially because of its mass lower-class character.[†] But it is also the result of a

---

*SNCC, the most militant of the civil rights groups and the organization that first declared and popularized Black Power, was founded and coordinated behind the scenes by Ella Baker, cultivated women leaders like Fannie Lou Hamer, and had women in all ranks of its leadership. On the other hand, the "cultural nationalist" organizations within the Black Power tendency, such as Ron Karenga's US (United Slaves) and the Nation of Islam, had strongly proscribed positions for women built into an explicitly chauvinistic ideology of "natural" gender roles. But these organizations were opposed to political struggle, let alone revolutionary politics, believing instead in individual uplift, Black capitalism, and cultural cohesion as the goal. Historically, the *less* militant or revolutionary the organization, the less liberatory its gender politics tended to be. This is not without exceptions and is *definitely* not an excuse for male revolutionaries to rest on their laurels and not explicitly struggle against patriarchy within themselves, their communities, and other organizations. It is, however, reason to question received narratives around militancy and machismo.

†The poor, less sophisticated at hiding their patriarchal opinions and more frequently punished for their violence, are always accused of greater misogyny than the rich and middle classes, who can more easily keep their violence behind closed doors and who organize and systematize their patriarchy through fraternities, business clubs, family life, sexual control of employees and staff, and other such strategies.

general attempt to connect militancy to masculine posturing—a percep-tion not always discouraged by male activists—in order to discredit not-nonviolent tactics.

Not-nonviolent tactics are not just decried as macho, however; they are often treated as evidence of "provocateurs." The supposed moral su-periority of nonviolence, and the connected belief that "violence" is what the state wants us to do, often sees liberals and well-meaning activists accuse anyone who escalates conflict of being a government agent at-tempting to discredit the movement. This acts as a direct brake on street action and serves to unnecessarily divide us in the streets.

Is it any surprise, then, that in many public schools and public ac-counts, the Black Power movement, if taught at all, is viewed as a mili-tant error, an excessive overreaction, while the civil rights movement is reduced to King's "I Have a Dream" speech given at the march? That march was the product of a series of sellouts and silencings, of nonviolent leaders dampening the militancy of the grass roots, of middle-class leaders taking control of a working-class movement, of government-sanctioned protest replacing mass insurgency, of men taking credit for the work of women. That the march was an inspiring and historic moment cannot be denied—but it was also mostly a symbolic one, one that sapped move-ment energy and focused it into a daylong rally. It is not militancy but nonviolence that truly helps the state.

chapter eight | # CIVIL RIOTS

T HOUGH INCREDIBLY IMPORTANT, THE WINNING OF NATIONAL CIVIL rights legislation and legal desegregation through these most visible campaigns in the South was not the apex of the movement's power or achievements. The fall of Jim Crow prepared the terrain for a more radical restructuring of American society—it was, in many ways, only the opening part of the struggle. However, history does not unfold like a book, and we must also push against the idea that the movement simply grew progressively stronger and more radical until it climaxed in the Black Panther Party and various revolutionary tendencies of the late sixties and early seventies. Following the premise that looting represents an incredibly powerful tactic in the revolutionary strike against white supremacy allows us to focus on the string of hundreds of urban riots from 1964 to 1968 as an escalation of the movements already in progress, an escalation that most acutely demonstrated the extent and breadth of white supremacy and offered the most prolonged and successful attack upon it.

Otherwise, the riots and uprisings that explode onto the scene in the Northeast in 1964 seem inexplicable or somehow related only negatively to the Southern movement: If the country was really experiencing a transformation of race relations, why were things still so bad in the North?

Whereas de jure segregation may have been a Southern thing, de facto segregation through redlining, public schools, and racist unions and hiring practices was no less prevalent in the North. Protests for housing, employment, and educational justice were widespread in this period; for example, in the years preceding the Watts rebellion, 250 civil rights protests took place in LA.

And it wasn't just legislative victories these protests achieved: rioting won huge concessions in the form of cash and programs, federal funding that flowed into cities and ghettos through the seventies. This cash neither solved the problems the riots fought against nor survived the rightward swing, neoliberal cuts, and restructuring that started in the eighties. But it is still a significant historical fact of the period, and one that is often disconnected from the "movement" proper.

What else shifts in the narrative of the Black Freedom movement if you focus on the urban riots rather than the more formal movements surrounding them? I do this not because I believe that the major riots of the 1960s are the only or even the most important component of the movement. But in most histories the riots themselves, which make up a huge and crucial part of the experience of the people who fought for their freedom, tend to be narrative blank spaces.

Carefully investigated contemporaneous sociological studies and government reports, such as the McCone and Kerner Commissions reports, tended to treat riots primarily as "outbursts," reflex actions responding mechanically to the tragic conditions of the ghetto. Focused on discovering riots' causes in order to prevent future occurrences through federal government action, these studies decontextualize the riots from the broader movement. They instead portray riots as resulting from the existence of pathological communities and criminal depravity and defined by poverty, broken families, and general social collapse. Riots were seen as criminal, and the explosion of riots all over the country was explained as a kind of "infection" spreading senselessly through imitation and desperation. If, following Christina Sharpe, anti-Blackness is the weather, then these riots appear as hurricanes or flash floods, a terrible fact of the climate that must be accommodated, against which infrastructure (po-

lice, prisons, insurance, national guards, curfews, deescalating "leaders")
must be built but about which nothing can be done.[1]

Even in excellent, vital histories that reject the pull of this anti-Black
narrative, riots are often treated like signposts, objective markers of racial
tensions. They are treated as a natural and naturalized fact rather than as
serious and focused bursts of grassroots movement, organization, struggle,
and rebellion. But these riots often manifested as crucial moments that
molded activists, radicalized masses, and transformed the movement's
trajectory.

DESPITE THE NATIONAL AND HISTORICAL FOCUS ON THE MARCH ON
Washington, it was the preceding struggle in Birmingham, the "duel of
rocks and fire hoses," that pointed in the major direction the movement
was headed. Through 1963 and 1964, as movements proliferated across
the South—including the incredibly important grassroots organizing of
the Mississippi Freedom movement, whose 1964 defeat at the Democratic National Convention would convince most SNCC activists that
there was no future for them in federal politics or the Democratic Party—
urban rebellions also began to pop off, including the early rebellions in
Cambridge, Maryland.[2]

I'm not surprised if you haven't heard of Gloria Richardson and the
Cambridge, Maryland, civil rights struggle she led; I hadn't until I re-
searched this book. But considering her fame during the movement, we
absolutely should have known about her. Richardson "received nearly
daily front-page coverage in local and national newspapers in 1963 and
1964." And yet, "Gloria Richardson and the Cambridge Movement were
not mentioned by the authors of the leading studies of the Civil Rights
Movement."[3]

Cambridge is a picturesque seaside town, geographically isolated
from the mainland of Maryland. In the fifties and sixties, its Black in-
habitants were desperately poor. As in so many towns across the country with large Black populations, in the wake of the 1960 student sit-in

movement—and further influenced by a Freedom Ride that came to Cambridge in 1961—civil rights organizing began to grow in Cambridge. At the age of thirty-nine, Gloria Richardson, the respectable manager of a local pharmacy, was voted leader of the Cambridge Nonviolent Action Committee (a local branch of SNCC), the organization at the center of the Cambridge movement.

The Cambridge movement started with sit-ins against business segregation, but its demands always included economic justice as well, in particular, economic justice related to poor housing and hiring opportunities. The movement was incredibly active. At its height from 1962 to 1964, Cambridge activists "regularly sat-in at movie theaters, bowling alleys, restaurants, and other public places; marched in the streets of Cambridge; picketed downtown businesses; wrote letters to newspaper editors; and occasionally responded to violent attacks with violence of their own."[4] But it was the last fact that made Richardson (and her movement) both famous and a kind of pariah.

Richardson and the Cambridge movement openly disavowed nonviolence, choosing to fight back against white racists who attacked their sit-ins, pickets, and marches. On June 12, 1963, protests turned into full-fledged rioting, with Molotov cocktails and shootouts between Black activists and white racists and police. The National Guard was sent in and would remain in Cambridge for months. Nevertheless, Richardson refused to disavow the riot or her participation in it.* Nor should she

---

*Richardson was also controversial for her anti-elections stance. In an attempt to buy off the movement, the Cambridge town government put a desegregation bill up for referendum. But Richardson "opposed this measure because she believed that equality had already been guaranteed by the U.S. Constitution." She pointed to the fact that many in her movement were Korean War vets—they had already earned the right to vote by fighting for the United States. "In addition, Richardson pointed out . . . that African Americans in Cambridge had been participating in elections for nearly one hundred years and it had not significantly changed the quality of their life." She argued this directly against the NAACP, Adam Clayton Powell, Robert Kennedy, and MLK. On her advice, the Black community boycotted the vote and refused to legitimize the local government. This move kept the movement in the streets and kept it focused on its core principles of economic justice, jobs, homes, and food for all. A year later, when the Voting Rights Act made desegregation the law of the land anyway, she was proven right not to have traded a street movement for such concessions (Jeff Kisseloff, *Generations on Fire: Voices of Protest from the 1960s, an Oral History* [Lexington: University of Kentucky Press, 2007]).

have, because their tactics worked: the Cambridge movement was wildly successful, winning desegregation of transportation, schools, the library, the hospital, and other public accommodations within a year. They demonstrated, even more clearly than Monroe, the continuities between fighting for civil rights and economic justice and between protest and violent insurrection.

Cambridge also shows that urban riots were hardly a Northern phenomenon: the first two famous ones in the movement, after all, took place in Birmingham and Cambridge. A riot had broken out a year earlier, in 1962, in Kinloch, Missouri, a small suburb of St. Louis, after police killed a Black teenager, with another in North St. Louis in June 1964. A riot in Jacksonville, Florida, in the spring of 1964 gained nationwide attention, because Black students attacked police and vigilantes with rocks. But these uprisings are not always included in histories of 1960s urban riots, which traditionally begin in the North with the famous Harlem Riot of 1964.

That riot began on July 16 after police killed a fifteen-year-old boy, James Powell, shooting him down in the streets. CORE had planned a rally in Harlem that day for three civil rights activists whose disappearance in Mississippi was provoking national outrage: James Chaney, Michael Schwerner, and Andrew Goodman.[†] At the last minute, CORE changed the subject of the rally to justice for James Powell and against police brutality. This is a crucial moment of continuity and connection. The struggle against Jim Crow and white violence, for civil rights and economic justice, in North and South directly transformed—through literally the same demonstrations, infrastructure, and organizations—into urban rebellions, rebellions that would bring the United States seemingly to the edge of revolution by 1968.

Because that day in July 1964 people didn't just want to rally. They marched and then ran through the streets, fought with police, smashed

---

[†]The three activists had gone south to participate in SNCC's Mississippi Freedom Summer, but they had been arrested by Mississippi police and then turned over to the KKK and lynched. Their disappearance was a huge news item all summer and focused the nation's eyes on Mississippi's horrific violence. Their bodies were found at the end of the summer, and only decades later would the real story of police and KKK collusion come out, though it was widely suspected at the time.

store windows, and lit fires. Rioting lasted for two nights when no charges were brought against the cop, at which point Brooklyn CORE called a rally in Bedford-Stuyvesant, a neighborhood in north Brooklyn. That rally also turned into a riot. For six nights total, fighting with police, looting, and arson spread across Harlem and Bed-Stuy.

Inspired by the events in New York and sparked by local outrages, uprisings against white supremacist police violence ran rampant across the country. First upstate to Rochester, New York, then across the Hudson to Jersey City. The next riots also took place in New Jersey, first in Paterson, then Elizabeth. A riot popped off in Dixmoor, a Chicago suburb. Next a major riot erupted in Philadelphia. All of these riots occurred within six weeks of each other, July–August 1964.

Activists and revolutionaries participated in and pushed forward these uprisings. As we've seen, CORE called the rallies that began the New York riots. Martially trained Black Muslims deployed their skills in the streets, playing a particularly important part in Rochester. Malcolm X had just split from the Nation of Islam and, rejecting its policies of separatism and political disengagement, was in the process of building an independent, revolutionary Muslim tendency: his followers were most present in the fighting. Members of the Revolutionary Action Movement—a Marxist Black nationalist revolutionary group—agitated, propagandized, and fought as well, particularly in Philadelphia, where they had a large presence as a result of organizing successfully there for two years.

Though these riots were sparked by instances of police brutality, rioting isn't simply a mechanical reaction to police violence: it's not a knee unbending beneath a doctor's hammer. If it were, riots would occur every day in every city in the United States. Riots, instead, emerge out of movement.

Sometimes they come out of that subterranean, invisible but ongoing movement for freedom, justice, and Jubilee that Karl Marx called the "historical party" that runs through the entire history of capitalism, reappearing seemingly suddenly and spontaneously (though specific histories of uprisings always tell a more complicated story of rising local tensions and grievances). But uprisings occur much more frequently when social movement is highly visible, agitating, and powerful. Riots transform the consciousness of their participants, widen the group of people taking part in political action, and usually produce a new generation of revolutionaries, opening up new directions for further action.

CHARLES FULLER, WHO WOULD EVENTUALLY GO ON TO WIN THE Pulitzer Prize for drama, was a young writer just starting his career when the Philadelphia uprising occurred. In the important Black arts newspaper *The Liberator*, he described walking through town the morning after the riot began. His essay captures beautifully the transformations of consciousness created by these uprisings. Rather than frightening him and making him feel unsafe, the riot flipped the normal racial order, and its distribution of safety and violence, on its head: "Then you slow down, and stop in front of the first store whose windows haven't been smashed, and you read the sign: 'THIS IS A BLACK WOMAN'S STORE!' and somehow you feel good. You tell yourself again, you are safe because you are black."

He experiences "an unbelievable courtesy" as he walks through the streets, a feeling of solidarity and mutual respect: "Maybe it's the tension, maybe it's the power the people feel they possess, but no black man is discourteous to another black man. Somehow, in this sea of black faces it no longer becomes necessary to fear one another." This experience of disappearing fear and rising strength and cohesion is described everywhere riots happened across the period and is described today in the wake of antipolice riots. That particular feeling takes months to fade, and most who experience it remember it their whole lives. Many become activists, revolutionaries, or otherwise socially active. Dozens of social, cultural, and political groups and groupings pop up to carry that feeling forward.

Within the atmosphere produced by riots, looting then functions to tie that sense of community to a questioning of the historical ties of white supremacy, property, and the law. "You go past a 'Fish-Fry' joint where some drunken broad in her fifties steals a white cooking apron and walks away satisfied. You ask more questions, and you tell yourself unbelievingly that she just wanted a souvenir, and you realize there is more than that going on inside her, that somehow she has lashed out at every white store owner on the Avenue, has gotten back all the hurt she suffered; you quickly dismiss this idea, and call her a thief."[5]

Reducing looting and rioting to a question of crime, calling the looter "just a thief," as Fuller ironically suggests, serves to mask the liberatory content of the action taking place.[6] In the midst of the uprising, onlookers and participants alike begin to question the ideology supporting property and commodity, order and law. As such, looting represents a fundamental threat to a society ordered by white supremacy, a threat that often goes beyond the boundaries that activists or even self-proclaimed revolutionaries feel comfortable with.

These riots all came immediately after the passage of the Civil Rights Act of 1964, which finally, legally declared the end of segregation. The Harlem Riots took place only fourteen days afterward. As liberals declared victory, and an end to racial discrimination, Black people north and south called bullshit.

But the riots did more than just express a voice. Riots are more than just the "language of the unheard," as MLK called them. Riots give birth to revolutionary transformation. The three largest riots of the period, Watts, Newark, and Detroit, created three different but powerful revolutionary movements in their wake, each indicating the degree to which riots expand and empower political consciousness and action, and the three together demonstrating how they can do so in unpredictable directions.

THE TENSION BETWEEN LIBERAL DECLARATIONS OF VICTORY OVER racism and the real lived experience of Black people in America exploded into full contradiction with the Watts Uprising in LA. The passage of the Voting Rights Act, on August 6, 1965, was widely described as a revolution in race relations, an epochal victory of the civil rights movement. Five days later, on August 11, something that looked like an altogether different kind of revolution broke out.

That afternoon, twenty-one-year-old Marquette Frye was pulled over by a California Highway Patrol officer not far from his house in South LA. In the passenger seat was his younger brother Ronald, just home from the Air Force. As Marquette was interrogated outside the car, a crowd gathered, mostly watching and cracking jokes. Ronald ran home to get their mom, Rena, who arrived and began berating Marquette for drunk driving. A second cop car arrived. Those officers began to harass and yell at the Fryes. One officer bashed Marquette on the head with a baton. Rena jumped forward at him, and an officer slapped her, twisted her arm behind her back, and handcuffed her. Another beat Marquette and arrested him. The crowd jeered as all three were beaten, stuffed in the back of cop cars, and driven away. As news and rumors of the beatings spread, people poured into the streets in protest.

What followed was six days of "insurrection against all authority," as the local CBS radio station reported it. "If it had gone much further," the news report said, "it would have become civil war."[7] More than 950 buildings were damaged, and 260 were totally destroyed. Looting and property destruction amounted to over $40 million in damages—nearly $330 million today adjusted for inflation.

But the destruction was hardly wanton or senseless. Almost no homes, schools, libraries, churches, or public buildings were even partially damaged. The use of arson was strategic and controlled. The majority of Black-owned businesses were not looted, nor were those businesses that were seen as dealing fairly with the community. Signs went up saying "Black-owned" or "soul brother" and the like, which would (usually) protect a shop from rioters. On the other hand, businesses that had traditionally exploited people, in particular pawnshops, check-cashing stores, and department stores that operated aggressively on credit, went up in flames. Credit records were usually destroyed before anything else took place. Brave rioters even made attacks on police stations; one was set alight.

The tactics were simple but effective, as Gerald Horne records in his important history of the Watts Uprising, *Fire This Time*. One common tactic saw a group of rioters, usually young men, drive up to a business, hop out, break out the windows, then drive away. Then cars of looters, a much more mixed group, split between men and women, young and old, would arrive and work to empty the store. The store would only be set alight once credit records had been destroyed and goods had been fully looted. Rioters usually remained nearby to make sure the building burned, attacking firemen with bricks and bottles if they tried to put out the flames before the fire had fully consumed the hated business.[8]

Tactics reflected effective communication and mobility among the rebels. Rioters transmitted information over the radio waves, used payphones to spread intel, and listened in to police broadcasts to see where cops would be deployed. False reports were called in to send police scrambling, at which point areas they'd just "pacified" could be retaken. In areas they didn't entirely control, rioters focused on hit-and-run strikes, then dispersing quickly to reappear elsewhere. All of these tactics would be adopted and practiced, with local modifications, in other riots throughout the period.

The media described these as guerilla tactics, and police and reactionaries compared the situation in Watts to fighting the Viet Cong or the Mau Mau of Kenya. Rioters often appreciated the comparison: many, encouraged by the thought of Malcolm X, Revolutionary Action Movement (RAM), Robert F. Williams, and local militants, understood their actions as guerilla warfare, too. Other rioters tied their actions to anticolonial struggle via resistance to imperialist war. Many men of draft age interviewed afterward said something very similar to what one rioter told SNCC newspaper *The Movement*: "I'd rather die here than in Vietnam."[9]

The predominantly white, middle-class, university-based antiwar movement failed, however, to see the crucial anti-Vietnam dimension of the riots, and therefore failed to form unity with rioters, which it might have done by creating defense committees or solidarity demonstrations. The Vietnam War and the movement against it were ramping up across the years of the urban rebellions, and this connection might have helped transform the antiwar movement in a truly revolutionary direction. Rather than listen to or organize with rioters, all but the most radical tended to see Watts only as a "race thing," failing to understand the links among revolution, antiracism, and anti-imperialism—links that had been at the forefront of Black radical theorizing for decades and that were increasingly spreading through the Black Freedom movement at large.

Only too late, once the riots had mostly subsided after 1968, did large sections of the antiwar movement recognize these connections. This same fatal reactionary error is being made today by members of the social-democratic Left who say focusing on race (or "identity politics") is wrong, that we should focus instead on class. They fail to recognize the degree to which Black Freedom struggles are already about class and race, something they would realize if they simply listened to the people taking part in those struggles.

As in Philadelphia, the action in Watts greatly increased feelings of strength and unity. As Jimmy Garrett recorded in *The Movement*: "The unity came out in the words 'Burn baby burn.' It expressed itself Friday night on 42nd street and Avalon boulevard when a young Negro stood in front of a Negro business shouting 'Don't bother this one, He's a brother. He's a brother.' It showed when another young Negro politely asked a woman her size, then stepped through a broken window of a dress shop to pick out ten or twelve dresses. It was seeing people with their heads up and smiles on their faces."[10]

Not some dour, grim thing, Watts, like most major riots, took on a carnivalesque, celebratory atmosphere. Participation was widespread. Gerald Horne quotes one report that said one in seven residents of the affected area took part. The Kerner Commission, formed to study the riots of 1967, indicates that 18 percent, or nearly one in five residents, participated in those urban uprisings. Not some tiny cabal of troublemakers, rioters *were* the community: those numbers mean nearly everyone had an active participant in either their family or among their friends.

The cops, for their part, practiced vicious collective punishment on Black people. The first thing the police did when looting broke out was deploy to protect the banks, which they prioritized over pawnshops full of guns and even their own precinct houses. After the second day, the governor declared a curfew, enabling police to carry out mass arrests of anyone on the streets. On top of police, fourteen thousand national guardsmen were sent into the curfew zone. Two days after rioting ended, on August 18, LAPD attacked the Nation of Islam mosque in Watts—the most visible symbol of Black organization in the ghetto—firing hundreds of rounds into the mosque, absolutely riddling it with bullets. It was a miracle they killed no one, although they injured a number of nation members, mostly with flying glass shards.

Over the course of the riots, 3,438 people were arrested, the vast majority of them with no criminal record. Over 1,000 people were injured, mostly civilians beaten or shot by police forces. And 34 people died, all but 3 of them civilians killed by LAPD or National Guard, while the remaining three included a firefighter killed by a falling wall and two police officers killed by friendly fire.

Most of those killed were shot for looting. But all the police and National Guard murders were ruled justifiable homicides. As Horne writes, reviewers "were not concerned about the propriety—legal and otherwise—of a shoot-to-kill procedure directed at unarmed suspects in the midst of committing what were arguably misdemeanors."[11] Property is always valued over life, particularly Black life, in this society. But in the liberated, carnival atmosphere of the riot, the enjoyment of everything by everyone—looting—overturns this logic. The celebration of freedom and life overcomes all notions of law, property, and commodity. Police make looting a capital offense in a riot precisely to reassert their system of values. The media, police chain of command, judiciary, and local and federal governments all support them: this is the essence of their job. Killing for property is restoring order, because worship of property at the expense of Black death is what American order is.

The LAPD had already earned its reputation as one of the most violent, racist, and out-of-control police forces in the world before the riots. In the wake of the Watts Uprising, rather than trying to improve their relations with the community—police brutality started the riot and was one of the main issues cited by rioters, after all—the LAPD increased its military capacity and developed more explicitly counterinsurgent forces. All police "innovations" come in response to struggles and uprisings by the people, because it is these uprisings that police exist to destroy. The LAPD instituted constant helicopter flyovers, "eye-in-the-sky" policing, which persists today, and introduced a comprehensive computerized control center for tactical domination of all of LA.

The most famous result of this is the SWAT—special weapons and tactics—team. These famous paramilitary police squads developed in LA in response to the riots. But they were introduced on the national stage when they first went into action in a 1969 standoff and raid of the offices of another major organizational legacy of the riots, the Black Panther Party.

The Watts rebellion helped launch Black nationalism and more militant revolutionary Black politics into the mainstream. Polls showed that after Watts, "civil rights" replaced Vietnam as the number one political concern of Americans.

In LA, the riots led to creation of the Black Congress, an umbrella organization brought together from a series of Black nationalist and revolutionary organizations. These groups, most of them formed and all growing exponentially in the wake of the riots, included Ron Karenga's United Slaves (US Organization); the Community Alert Patrol, which developed armed patrolling of the police, which would become the founding principle and practice of the Black Panther Party; the Black Student Alliance, a variety of civil rights and antiwar groups; and a Revolutionary Action Movement–led Black Panther Party chapter.*

Most of the revolutionary organizations and activists in LA in the following years passed through the Black Congress. A yearly Black nationalist arts festival was organized to keep the spirit of Watts alive, and the street gangs that took part in the riots declared a truce, many of them reorganizing as the radical Sons of Watts, most of whom would later become Black Panther Party cadre. Two months after the uprising, rioters and activists turned an abandoned furniture store into the Watts Happening Coffee

---

*This party was not originally connected to the Black Panther Party for self-defense that emerged in Oakland, California. Both groups independently took their name from the Mississippi Black Panther Party, led by Stokely Carmichael, which emerged in 1966. The LA group was largely led by RAM militants, but it would eventually be subsumed by the Oakland BPP, a final moment in the collapse of RAM power and influence; the group was largely defunct by 1967.

House, a gallery and performance space that became a major center of both artistic and revolutionary practice in LA. The LAPD, of course, did everything it could to arrest, harass, infiltrate, and destroy this flourishing movement of working-class culture and democracy.

But Watts was incredibly important state- and nationwide, and its most famous child is probably the Black Panther Party. BPP members took their uniform—black pants, leather jackets, and dark turtlenecks—from Watts rioters. But the connection went much deeper. In *Revolutionary Suicide*, BPP founder Huey Newton begins a chapter on the formation of the party with an analysis of Watts. As he wrote, he and cofounder Bobby Seale "had seen Watts rise up the previous year. We had seen how the police attacked the Watts community after causing the trouble in the first place. We had seen Martin Luther King come to Watts in an effort to calm the people, and we had seen his philosophy of nonviolence reject-ed."[12] It was this, combined with the increasing violence of the Oakland PD, that led them to conceive of and create the party in 1966.

And Watts remained a touchstone of BPP analysis. As Newton said in a speech called "The Correct Handling of a Revolution," rioting like Watts was politically powerful because it could not be reinterpreted nor easily recuperated by the press. In Watts, "the economy and property of the oppressor was destroyed to such an extent that no matter how the oppressor tried in his press to whitewash the activities of the Black broth-ers, the real nature and cause of the activity was communicated to every Black community."[13] The Panthers aimed to produce similarly unambig-uous actions through both their armed actions and their powerful com-munity programs.*

But the uprisings also gave the BPP its potential base and its sense of purpose. As Elaine Brown, chairman of the BPP for three years, ex-

*The range of programs was immense. They "eventually included the Free Breakfast for Children Program, liberation schools, free health clinics, the Free Food Distribu-tion Program, the Free Clothing Program, child development centers, the Free Shoe Program, the Free Busing to Prison Program, the Sickle Cell Anemia Research Founda-tion, free housing cooperatives, the Free Pest Control Program, the Free Plumbing and Maintenance Program, renter's assistance, legal aid, the Seniors Escorts Program, and the Free Ambulance Program" (Joshua Bloom and Waldo Martin, *Black Against Empire* [Berkeley: University of California Press, 2013]).

plained the party's purpose, "those rebellions, from Harlem to Watts, had been endorsed by the entire black underclass, shouting 'Hallelujah.' The party intended to educate and politicize that mass of energy, creating vanguard soldiers from the hard core and a mass of black people ready for revolution."[14]

The Watts (and other) riots demonstrated to the BPP that the time was right for a revolutionary party, an organization with an explicitly not-nonviolent philosophy and one aimed toward total social transformation.

The Panthers' strategy was based on directly organizing the poor, the unemployed, the socially marginalized, and the criminal gangs of the ghetto into a revolutionary party. This may seem to make their politics a "natural" fit with riots, which we are taught to incorrectly presume are carried out by the most isolated, alienated, and criminalized in society. But it was hardly the only form of organization born in the flames of looted department stores. In Newark, a movement focused on gaining local political power and pushing cultural and social transformation through control of existing city structures—a favorite dream of reformers and those revolutionaries who disdain insurrection—rose out of a massive riot's ashes. A few weeks later, insurrection in Detroit gave birth to a radical labor movement, precisely the kind of movement that many "socialists" who condemn rioters claim they would support.

BY THE TIME NEWARK WENT UP IN FLAMES, ON JULY 12, 1967, RIOTS had seemingly become a fact of American life. "In 1964, 15 urban rebellions shook the country; in 1965 there were 9; in 1966: 38; in 1967, 128."[15] People talked about the "long, hot summers" of riots; they were the new normal. The political temperature in America was rising.

Civil rights struggles continued to move in the streets, including fights for welfare, tenants' rights, school busing, sanitation, electoral representation, and many other issues, large and small. But despite the passage of civil and voting rights acts, conditions on the ground were changing only slowly in the South. SNCC organizing grew increasingly militant, and nonviolent marchers in Mississippi and Louisiana were now protected by an openly armed movement bodyguard, the Deacons for Defense. During one march in 1966, Stokely Carmichael and marchers proclaimed their goal was "Black Power!" The motto spread like wildfire across the country, giving a name to the growing militancy and terrifying white liberals, most of whom were showing their true colors and turning away from the movement.

While SNCC deepened the struggle in the South, Martin Luther King's SCLC moved north. There they found that although economic and housing discrimination created much the same conditions as in the South, nonviolent marches were much less effective. When MLK marched in Chicago, unlike in small Southern towns, thousands of white supremacists could come out to a counterprotest, an incredibly threatening and disempowering experience. Mayor Richard Daley also demonstrated the anti-movement efficacy of Northern Democratic politicians, as he appeared publicly to negotiate and accept movement demands while actually stonewalling on all but the most minor concessions.

As a result of these experiences, MLK grew increasingly radical and pessimistic about reform. He began believing that Black people were "integrating into a burning house" and that a more fundamental, socialist transformation of society was required. By 1967, he was arguing for radical, fundamental change, because "only by structural change can current evils be eliminated, because the roots are in the system rather than in man or faulty operations." As he would put it in a speech in 1967: "It didn't cost a penny to deal with lunch counters and integrate lunch counters. It didn't cost the nation one penny to guarantee the right to vote. . . . It is much easier to integrate a lunch counter than it is to eradicate slums."[16] The country wasn't willing to do the latter, and, as more and more activists recognized the fact, they started proclaiming their allegiance to revolution.

Those in power were forced into giving concessions, and they did so with money: federal funding to cities, towns, and social initiatives increased dramatically. Liberals hoped to mitigate the effects of rioters' victory by buying off the rioters' allegiance, producing government programs that would co-opt and contain activist energy, bringing their grassroots organizing effort into working for government programs, as their predecessors had done with the New Deal. This had partially worked in 1963 and 1964, when CORE and SNCC activists in the South focused their efforts on voter registration despite the fact that locals consistently wanted them to tackle economic issues; they were receiving much of their funding from Democratic Party organs anxious to keep their hold on the South, and so kept the focus on elections.

President Lyndon Baines Johnson's attempts to tackle the racial and economic crises of the period, his War on Poverty and Great Society programs, were despised by white reactionaries, while in radicalized poor and Black communities they were recognized as insufficient and ineffective Band-Aids. In most cities, War on Poverty programs just increased funding to existing infrastructure, thus doubling down on education, youth, and job training programs that were already failing Black ghetto residents. Mired in bureaucratic problems, based in an analysis that saw both unrest and racial discrimination as crime—which is to say, as problems caused by individuals—Johnson's programs couldn't offer the fundamental transformation and empowerment the movement pointed toward. And anyway, the cost of the War on Poverty paled in comparison to the cost of the war on the impoverished people of Vietnam; as many activists pointed out at the time, imperialist war in Vietnam kept the ghetto poor.

The lead-up to the Newark uprising was marked by conflict around all these problems. Increasing grassroots activity and increasing awareness of the limits of political participation marked the years before the riots in Newark. From 1965, Black women, as they always do, had taken the lead in organizing, pushing for maximum benefit from the new War on Poverty programs. They tried to take control of the local Area Boards that distributed funds, they educated their neighbors and communities on how to apply for grants and foundations, and they built programs for housing stock improvement, social centers, and other such projects. But all of this required constant, exhausting struggle with the government bureaucracy, struggle that often failed to achieve activists' goals.

There was also an ongoing, powerful antipolice movement in Newark, which had organized massive rallies and memorials for Black residents murdered by police. Only a few weeks before the uprisings, police on the East Orange–Newark border had raided, fought with, and arrested Nation of Islam militants, increasing tensions. And Amiri Baraka and his Spirit House group were transforming and politicizing the culture of Newark with Black nationalist poetry readings and street theater, performances that not only featured political themes but also became, themselves, rallies and protests.*

It is in this context that Newark police ruthlessly beat and arrested cab driver John Smith on the night of July 12, 1967, setting off six days of massive rioting. The police and National Guard killed 24 people. "More than 1,100 sustained injuries; approximately 1,400 were arrested; some 350 arsons damaged private and public buildings; millions of dollars of merchandise was destroyed or stolen; and law enforcement expended 13,326 rounds of ammunition."[17] As in Watts, the people held the initiative on the first few days, after which point massive violence, collective punishment, and repression on the part of police and the National Guard began to win the struggle.

Looting was massive and organized. The rioters used Molotov cocktails in attacks on police and property. A few months before the riots, an anonymous pamphlet had circulated with instructions on how to make them. Despite this militancy, though, the rioting in Newark was experienced as a massive party. Indeed, "on a profound level, the gleeful spirits of the riot crowds disturbed public officials as much as the prospect of violence. When Newark's police director Dominick Spina toured the riot scene with Mayor Addonizio and Governor Hughes . . . Hughes was said to have been particularly 'appalled at the holiday air he felt in the ghetto.'"[18] The experience of pleasure, joy, and freedom in the midst of a riot, an experience we almost never have in these city streets where we are exploited, controlled, and dominated, is a force that transforms rioters, sometimes forever: the experience of such freedom can be unforgettable.

And it was movement people fighting in the streets. The riots kicked off after demonstrations were organized and CORE activist Robert

---

*This tradition has been powerfully continued in the current movement by political prisoner Ceebo Tha Rapper, an LA artist who, after the August 2011 murder of his cousin Ezell Ford, spearheaded the movement for Ford, writing songs and shooting music videos about the movement that were themselves staged as protests.

Curvin appealed to crowds outside the precinct house where Smith was being held. In one of the most infamous moments of the riot, Amiri Baraka was pulled from a car by police and beaten within an inch of his life. The people fighting in the streets in Newark were not sudden opportunists; they had been educated and politicized by years of steady movement and struggle.

As in Watts and other cities, signs in windows protected Black-owned businesses from attack, although in Newark this had a sinister twist: in the final days of rioting, police and National Guard drove through town shooting out the windows and shooting up the businesses that rioters had carefully protected. Police again killed on sight for looting, for example, shooting Billy Furr, twenty-four, in the back, murdering him directly in front of a reporter and photographer for *Life* magazine. Furr had been looting a six-pack of beer; the photos of his murder were seen by millions.

But many were also killed as police, "fighting against snipers," fired indiscriminately into apartment buildings and homes. Though some people in Newark fired guns at the police, these shots were much less widespread than reported. Where shooting did occur, it tended to be warning or pot shots, fired to keep police and firemen away from areas of looting and arson.

Still, media, police, and national guardsmen hysterically circulated the idea of sniping to justify collective punishment. Across the riots of the period, dozens of people were murdered in their homes by police and guardsmen firing into apartment buildings "in fear of snipers." The chain of command told guardsmen that they were heading into an area of massive sniping to terrify them and authorize them to murder Black civilians. The media, embedded as it was in police stations and guard posts, reported on this "widespread" sniping, thus deepening repressive forces' fear on the ground while explaining the repression to the rest of the country. White supremacist forces always play the victim to justify their ongoing anti-Black oppression.

But despite the repression, the uprising marked an important turn for the Newark movement. Its many trends—Black nationalism, Black arts, antipolice activism, welfare activism, and Black community control—consolidated and grew into a unified movement for Black Power after the riots. The movement's center formed around the Community for Unified Newark (CFUN), an umbrella organization that had begun life as the United Brothers. The United Brothers literally formed as concerned activists gathered at Amiri Baraka's bedside while he recovered from the police beating he endured in the riots. As Komozi Woodard writes, "The Black Power movement rose like Phoenix out of the ashes of the Newark Rebellion. CFUN came to symbolize the politics born of the urban uprisings."[19]

Rather than forming a national, militant revolutionary party like the Panthers, CFUN took a different approach to addressing the political and economic crises of the ghetto. As Woodard records, CFUN

> ran candidates for public office, fashioned public policies, advocated reforms, mobilized huge demonstrations to resist President Richard Nixon's political reaction, and, above all, established an elaborate network of institutions, programs, and business . . . the Spirit House Movers and Players, for drama and poetry; the African Free School, for early childhood education; the *Black NewArk* newspaper, for local communication; the *Unity & Struggle* newspaper, for national politics; Events, Inc., for public relations; Proposals, for development grants; and Kawaida Towers and the NJR-32 Project Area Committee, for urban planning and community development.[20]

The full story of CFUN, and the inspiring struggle for political transformation in Newark, is beyond the remit of this book. But the movement in Newark points to the fact that hardly an instigator of only openly insurrectionary politics, riots, and uprisings can inspire and expand movements that are based around predominantly nonviolent community campaigns for political, cultural, and social power. There is nothing "riot-like" about the activities or tactics of CFUN; nevertheless, it was born as Newark burned. And insurrection in Detroit would move out of the streets and into the factories, giving birth to one of the last major, radical US labor movements of the twentieth century.

LATE IN THE NIGHT OF JULY 23, 1967, SIX DAYS AFTER THE SMOKE HAD cleared over the Newark skyline, Detroit police raided an unlicensed after-hours drinking club (a "blind pig"). Rather than a few drunks, police were surprised to find more than eighty partiers, celebrating two veterans' safe return from Vietnam. Rather than disperse the crowd, police decided to arrest and brutalize them all.

Five days later, 43 people were dead, 1,189 were injured, and 7,200 were in jail; 1,300 buildings were utterly destroyed, and 2,700 businesses had been looted. Other than the Los Angeles riots of 1992 and the New York City Draft Riots of 1863, this was the largest riot in American history.

The American auto industry, centered in Detroit, was the engine and center of American capitalism for the first half of the twentieth century, and, as is inevitable in major centers of capitalist dynamism and power, Detroit featured some of the most dramatic social conflict in the country. The Detroit strike of 1933 and the Flint sit-down strikes in 1936–1937 against General Motors were among the hardest fought in the Great Depression. The Detroit race riots of 1943 had been the largest and most violent of the twentieth century.

But white flight, automation, and deindustrialization meant Detroit was in trouble by 1967. Detroit and the car industry were no longer the driving economic power in American society, although it was hard to recognize this from the inside at first. The full fallout and effects of these trends would only be recognized in the decades following the riots. (As a result, white folks have often blamed Detroit's decline on the riots, despite the simultaneous industrial decline of the entire Midwest.)

It's not surprising the riots traumatized and terrified the white powers of Detroit. Unlike in Newark and Watts, where fear of snipers was mostly unjustified, Detroit saw some actual sniping. The first night they were deployed, the National Guard indiscriminately fired machine guns from the street into apartment buildings, claiming they were fighting snipers, killing nine—none of whom were proven to have weapons. Looters were shot on sight—a direct order from the National Guard command hierarchy—and police and guardsmen were caught moving and rearranging bodies to indicate the people they killed had been looting. In the face of this violence, snipers started shooting back. Things got so serious in

Detroit that LBJ sent in the 82nd and 101st Airborne divisions of the US Army, which had seen combat in Vietnam. Rolling through Detroit in tanks and armored personnel carriers, soldiers came straight from murdering Vietnamese people to attack and murder Black Americans.

Many radicals fetishize military-style conflict as the sign of true revolutionary potential. This was especially true of the movements of the late sixties and early seventies, that all proclaimed armed struggle and saw the "guerilla" as something of a revolutionary saint. But the revolutionary content of the riots does not lie mainly in these military aspects. The shooting is a small piece, not the main component of the attack on white supremacy, the state, property, and the commodity. Whereas armed self-defense will always be an important part of struggles for liberation, the arms themselves have no magical property to make our movements more serious, more revolutionary, more powerful. The power of the attack on white settler society is seen instead in the broad lawlessness, property destruction, looting, and cop-free zones produced by the riot and is reflected in the attendant sense of freedom, unity, and radical safety felt by the rioters.*

Detroit was in full-blown insurrection. Arsonists in Detroit controlled their fires much less effectively than rebels had in Newark and Watts, as a strong wind was blowing off Lake Erie throughout the days of the riot. As a result, fires spread much farther in Detroit, destroying many homes, not just businesses. But despite this, participation in rioting was truly

---

*The shooting of a few cops and soldiers may well be necessary in the course of a revolutionary struggle, but the emphasis on snipers by the police and media isn't merely a repressive justification strategy; it is also a kind of strategic optimism: the state wants to face its enemies in a military conflict, not a social one; the state wants to fight an army, not a mob. Armies, even (perhaps especially) guerilla ones, are shaped around technical expertise and organization, supply lines/chains and logistics, hierarchy, the harshest discipline, right to punishment up to and including death, laws of conduct, and an overarching force of social unification. These are all core factors of a state: any army must become a functional state in miniature. Thus, even if the revolutionaries win the war, the state will persevere, merely transferred to more progressive bureaucrats. Real revolution will have been prevented in the militarization of the conflict, which really means the bureaucratization of the revolutionaries. This, no doubt, must be one of the basic lessons of the twentieth-century revolutions and anticolonial victories that in many places dramatically improved daily life but everywhere failed to revolutionize it.

widespread. In Detroit, as Malcolm McLaughlin records, "the Kerner Commission's researchers were surprised that half of the seven thousand people arrested had never been in trouble with the law before. It seemed that 'people who weren't involved in things' before were 'getting involved in this.' Even 'people who are living relatively stable lives' had become 'involved in some connection with the disturbances.'"[21]

Widespread popular participation by previously uninvolved or un-radicalized people in mass illegal activity points to the desire for and possibilities of a more total social transformation that rests within every-one, not just the already activated, and is one of the vital facts marked by urban uprisings.

Community leaders and nonviolence advocates appeared on the scene to try to calm the situation and were rebuffed. US representative John Conyers was shouted down when he tried to address a crowd, while MLK, who had been heckled in Watts, was laughed at in Detroit. Non-violence was utterly rejected by a crowd made up of perhaps 20 percent of the population: nonviolence as a philosophy had been fully defeated in the streets. Echoes of this rejection of elite leaders reverberated during the Ferguson uprising of 2014, when professional de-escalators Al Sharp-ton and Jesse Jackson, sent in to discipline and shut down the crowds, were instead booed off stage and out of town.

As in most of these riots, the community was instead led by a core group of rioters, mostly but not exclusively young men. That "leader-ship," however, meant inspiration through direct action rather than a more traditional sense of the word. Lead rioters would break windows, knock down doors, throw the first rock, light the first Molotov, or commit an initial act of looting to "create permission" for the crowd to act sim-ilarly. Action inspires action, and though those lead rioters were often organized among themselves, communicating with radios and phones, heading out to vulnerable spots, and fighting or avoiding police in a sys-tematic fashion, they did not lead in the sense of giving orders, building hierarchies, or drawing boundaries.

Detroit was home to one of the foremost theorists of this kind of in-surrection. Reverend Albert Cleage, who ran the Black nationalist Shrine of the Black Madonna, had organized and led what had been to that point the biggest civil rights march in history. In the spring of 1963, he and Dr. King marched at the head of 200,000 people through downtown Detroit—a crowd only surpassed by that of the March on Washington. But after the March on Washington, and in particular the violence of Birmingham, Cleage's thinking took a dramatic, militant turn, and he began arguing for a "strategy of chaos"—rejecting nonviolence, his strategy called for using retaliatory violence and escalation, increasing the intensity and spread of riots until demands were met. "We'll get what we're after or we'll tear it up!" was the strategy's summation. In the years leading up to the riots, he was increasingly involved in organizing with the workers in Detroit factories.

So when the army finally succeeded in putting down the uprising, political organizers, including Cleage, got to work. As activist-historians Dan Georgakas and Marvin Surkin write in their seminal *Detroit, I Do Mind Dying*:

> An attempt to organize the power of the Great Rebellion into a political force capable of restructuring American society began as soon as minimal order had been restored by the National Guard and police. Black-owned newspapers and organizations of black industrial workers began to present a series of programs and revolutionary visions in sharp contrast to the ideas put forward by the [government and labor bureaucracy response to the riots, the] New Detroit Committee.[22]

That organizing first manifested in the collective Inner City Voice, which published a newspaper of the same name and which "was to be a positive response to the Great Rebellion, elaborating, clarifying, and articulating what was already in the streets."[23] *Inner City Voice* pushed forward the cause of the Great Rebellion and its "shopping for free," referring to the rebellion as "the general strike of '67."

The Voice eventually became DRUM, the Dodge Revolutionary Union Movement, a Black workers' organization instigating revolutionary unionism within the auto industry. Within months of becoming DRUM, members had instigated a wildcat strike at Dodge's biggest plant, Dodge Main, involving four thousand workers. DRUM (and other revolutionary movements in the auto industry) came together to form the League of Revolutionary Black Workers, which struggled against the bosses and the United Auto Workers (UAW) alike. The UAW was, like most in the United States, a racist union—Black workers were completely underrepresented in union positions and many unionized shops within the plants were still entirely white—and the top of the UAW bureaucracy were as rich as many in the higher ranks of the auto industry and a key part of the Detroit power structure. The league created a militant labor power to counter the UAW and fight for real worker control of the factories and the community.

The League of Revolutionary Black Workers balanced on the cutting edge of a massive wave of radical labor action: the period of 1967–1974 saw the most yearly strikes and days lost to strike action in the United States since 1946. For years league members broke down racial barriers in the auto industry, organized massive strikes, and created a militant labor culture unseen since the forties, one that merged with the Black radical tradition and antiracist struggles of the sixties to form a revolutionary Black labor movement. This movement, too, was born of riots.

LESS THAN NINE MONTHS AFTER THE DETROIT RIOTS, MARTIN LUther King was assassinated, shot down on a motel balcony in Memphis, Tennessee, on April 4, 1968. Memphis rose up in rebellion. Within a week, riots had spread to 125 cities, where massive rioting was met with equally massive deployments of the US Army and the National Guard. The insurrection in DC got within two blocks of the White House, "and machine guns were mounted on the Capitol balcony and the White House lawn. Forty-six people were killed across the country, 2500 were injured, and it took 70,000 federal troops to restore order."[24]

The April uprisings in 1968, taking place during Holy Week leading up to Easter, created the largest disorder in America since the Civil War,

yet remain wildly understudied, theorized, or historicized. This silence
on the part of historians, scholars, and activists has been deafening.* The
shock and trauma of King's murder overshadowed the rebellion that it
caused, and the massive, furious, unorganized, and spontaneous nationwide uprising fits neatly into few theories of protest or revolution. Unlike
other riots, perhaps, the fact that it was an act of pure mourning, grief,
and rage made it hard even for its participants to summarize afterward.
Or maybe the riots felt so natural, so immediate, so *appropriate*, even
those who would normally marvel at their scale fell quiet. Or maybe the
state's massive project, begun immediately upon his death, of recuperat-
ing the image and meaning of King played an active part in enforcing this
silence, this forgetting, and so the riots are seen more as a simple funerary
reaction than an uprising so fierce the government feared the Capitol
would fall. It is, no doubt, some combination of all of these factors. In any
case, the Holy Week uprisings seemed at the time to be a turning point
in American disorder, and even after the fires had smoldered, revolution
seemed just one more "long, hot summer" away.

King had been in Memphis that spring to assist in radical Black labor organizing there. He had spoken to a crowd of fifteen thousand on
March 18, calling for a general strike. The march he led from that speech
resulted in rioting and looting—even his physical presence no longer
guaranteed nonviolence. But in those last years he had begun to speak
about a socialist transformation of America, and though he wasn't calling for violent revolution, neither was he chastising or rejecting rioters
anymore.

Unlike the uprisings of the previous summers, the Holy Week riots had
no local instigating incidents of police brutality. Instead, the importance
of Martin Luther King and the decade and a half of Black liberation struggle had pushed the Black community to the point of proto-revolutionary
agitation and organization. People poured out of their houses wherever

---

*As recently as 2018, in a book on the riots of the 1960s, historian Peter Levy could write
that, beside a single volume written in the immediate aftermath of the riots, these uprisings "have received remarkably little attention . . . scholars have virtually ignored them"
(Peter Levy, *The Great Uprising* [Chelsea, MI: Sheridan Books, 2018], 154).

they were and tore shit up, trying to dismantle the system that murdered King—the very face of the respectable, peaceful movement the white power structure claimed it wanted to do business with.

With Dr. King's death, as Stokely Carmichael put it, "Nonviolence was dead." At that point, organizing for the revolution seemed to be the most realistic way forward. This sense was not purely an American one, though: the feeling was global. The Cultural Revolution in China was at its height, and around the world radicals were taking inspiration from the apparent deepening of the Chinese revolution. Although Che Guevara had been killed the previous summer in a disastrous guerilla campaign in Bolivia, where he and his comrades were executed by CIA-backed forces, he had become a global martyr and symbol of the era. The Cuban Revolution he helped win was going strong, forming a new pole of radical leadership distinct from China and the USSR, the latter of which most revolutionaries in the sixties recognized as a reactionary, capitalist state.

And while many of the revolutionary pan-African and socialist movements were on the back foot in Africa—particularly devastating was the ousting of Ghanaian president Kwame Nkrumah in 1966 and the collapse of the revolution in the Congo—others, such as the struggle of the PAIGC and Amilcar Cabral in Guinea-Bissau, the increasingly successful war for independence in Angola, and the ongoing socialist collectivization of "Ujamaa" practiced by Tanzanian president Julius Nyerere, seemed to point to an African continent in the midst of revolution. The riots of April 1968 in the United States were followed closely in May by massive riots and a general strike in Paris that almost toppled the government. Salvador Allende would be elected in Chile in 1970 on a wave of socialist agitation already making itself felt. Meanwhile, the Tet Offensive, launched in January 1968, saw the peasants of North Vietnam winning a war against the world's great imperial power.

And so in the wake of the April uprisings, and in light of all these facts, explicitly revolutionary movements across the country exploded onto the scene. Following the Black "screaming queens" of the Compton's Cafeteria rebellion in 1966, Black trans women again pushed forward the revolution, leading the Stonewall uprising in New York City in 1969 that gave birth to the queer movement. Within a few years, hundreds of queer advocacy organizations had sprung up across the country. The American Indian Movement, formed in the summer of 1968, occupied Alcatraz Island in San Francisco in November 1969, centering national attention on their militant demands and the continued colonial genocide of Indigenous people. The Alcatraz occupation would only be forcibly evicted by federal troops nineteen months later, and the movement built strength and power, climaxing in the occupation of Wounded Knee in 1973. The Black Panther Party achieved its meteoric moment of national prominence from 1968 to 1971. As the state increasingly turned to repression to tackle these growing movements, the prisons, too, exploded into organization and action, most famously with the riotous takeover (and police massacre) at Attica in 1971. That was only one of dozens of prison uprisings in the period.

The antiwar movement also radicalized. Students, sometimes armed, occupied and took over university campuses across the country—this reached its apotheosis with the National Guard massacre of four protesting students at Kent State on May 4, 1970. The Chicanx wing of the antiwar movement organized a march under the banner of the Chicano Moratorium and rioted in East LA in August; police killed four of their number. Although popular histories sometimes point to the Weathermen—a group of white antiwar radicals who favored pursuing riots, bombings, and guerilla attacks on the state—they were more exemplary of a trend than the crazy radicals at the fringes they are usually described as. It is little remembered now, but the period was one of massive left-wing terrorism: between January 1969 and the spring of 1970 there were 4,330 bombings in the United States.

Massive movements emerged from within Chicanx, Asian American, and Puerto Rican communities—most famous among them the Young Lords, Asian Americans for Action, and the Brown Berets. Workers organized an awesome wildcat strike wave from 1967 to 1974, feminism was transforming awareness across the country as consciousness-raising groups, books, and demonstrations proliferated, people with disabilities were organizing and fighting for accessibility and freedom, and a mil-

itant movement of poor mothers was fighting a winning fight for welfare. American soldiers in Vietnam were refusing their orders and killing
their officers at record rates; "fragging" was such a problem that the army
seemed on the verge of total collapse. Everywhere you looked America
seemed ready to explode.

A wide range of movements were thus radicalized and activated by
national Black insurrection and international Third World revolution.
As Keeanga-Yamahtta Taylor writes, "When the Black movement goes
into motion, it destabilizes all political life in the United States."[25] Black
struggle had opened the door for revolutionary movements to blossom
across the country, and it was the riots of 1964–1968 that seemed to indicate that the end of American empire was imminent and that the revolution only needed to be organized.

But the riots didn't come back: there were no more long, hot summers.
Without the mass energy and intense threat to the state the riots posed,
white retrenchment and reaction slowly retook control. The COINTEL-
PRO program, run by the FBI and police across the country, would kill
more than twenty Black Panthers and imprison more than a thousand,
would murder dozens of American Indian Movement militants, would
attack, disrupt, and infiltrate the Puerto Rican independence movement
and the radical antiwar groups. Rather than social reform, the United
States built its massive prison system, which grew partially as a way of
guaranteeing the revolutionary movements of the 1960s and 1970s would
not be repeated. Though America lost the Vietnam War, the main lesson
the military learned was that a mass, drafted army in a long, drawn-out
war was too dangerous for morale. So the United States abolished the
draft and developed a volunteer army made up of only the poor and the
patriotic, and it increasingly privatized its military, pointing future US
strategy toward global police action, assassination, and special forces intervention rather than massive ground war.

Without increasing street action, the movements of the late sixties
and seventies fell to repression, fizzled out, or devoured themselves
through splits and infighting. Most of the political gains of the sixties have
since been taken away by generations of "tough on crime" politicians,

Republican and Democrat alike, and the successive crises of the global capitalist economy, expressing themselves in more and more dramatic debt bubbles since 1973, have wiped out much of the social progress.

Another revolutionary period ended in defeat. Although many of the victories have been wiped away, we can resist the suppression and deformation of its history. The centrality of rioting and looting to the period was intimately understood by its activists, rebels, and revolutionaries. But their voices have all too often been silenced or co-opted by liberal historians and conservative politicians.

The question of nonviolence and the efficacy of rioting has once again been put on the table in Ferguson, Baltimore, Milwaukee, and Baton Rouge, in Charlotte, Chicago, Oakland, and Minneapolis, in Charlottesville, Berkeley, Hawaii, and Puerto Rico. We can no longer afford to misunderstand the sixties, to excise the riots and refuse to recognize the vital role they played in the upheavals that shook America to its core. We must do away once and for all with the myth of nonviolence and with the false moral divisions between uprising and social transformation, between insurrection and movement, between looting and boycotting, between rioting and community organization. As Shakur Assata reminds us, it is our duty to win.

chapter nine | **THE INHUMANITY OF LOOTERS**

THE REVOLUTION PROMISED IN THE FIRES OF THE LONG SIXTIES failed to materialize, and the victories and reforms won proved vulnerable to counterattack by state and capitalist alike. The decline of mass movements was met with a similar decline in the living and working conditions of the masses. However, the movements had broken many of capitalism's favored methods of control at the same moment that capitalism was running up against important internal limits. So capital, responding to its own internal crises and the crises caused by decades of upheaval, changed tack while doing everything it could to co-opt, defang, slander, and bury once and for all the protagonists of that upheaval. This new strategic program has often been referred to as "neoliberalism," and neoliberals would begin their five decades of capitalist restructuring while the embers of the failed revolutionary movement burned out. One of the tactics in this repressive struggle was the total vilification of the rioter and the looter.

Capitalism has been in continuous slow-moving crisis since 1973. In the immediate postwar period, profits and wages in America and in Europe rose in tandem, as domestic consumerism led to production of more consumer goods, which led again to more consumption in a virtuous cycle. All of this was made possible only by the neocolonial extraction of raw materials from the Global South. But even with continued imperial domination, American and European consumerism hit serious limits. At some point near the end of the "golden years" in the sixties, workers started saving and investing their money rather than spending it on ever more elaborate and senseless consumer goods. Meanwhile, the manufacturing economies in Japan and Germany had recovered from the rubble of World War II, providing serious competition for US corporations. Just as importantly, class struggle was winning victories for workers, forcing increasingly expensive concessions from both state and capital.

As rioters, protesters, and strikers continued to force wages higher and increase state programs, and as automation increased global productivity to be faster than consumption could absorb, corporations suddenly couldn't sell enough of their products and profits began to stall out. This crisis came to a head in the crash and recession of the early 1970s—most of that decade saw severe economic retrenchment, stagnation, and collapse, as municipal and state governments went broke and jobs disappeared. But a total reckoning was staved off by the ending of the Bretton Woods agreement and the "floating of the dollar," which decoupled the value of the dollar from real value in gold, fully transforming the US state and the Federal Reserve into the backbone of global capital.

The crisis of profitability has never been resolved, but floating the dollar gave space for a number of strategies to manage it. The violent impact of the earliest of those strategies—globalization, consumer debt, service economy development, financialization—was at first lessened by domestic concessions won by the uprisings of the sixties and seventies and papered over by consumer debt. But in the late seventies and through the eighties, as working-class power faded, capital took the offensive—most infamously in the administrations of Ronald Reagan and Margaret Thatcher—and pushed forward strategies of austerity, union destruction, repression, and privatization. These strategies all combined to more or less guarantee profit and GDP growth in the medium term at the expense of long-term social stability.

The inability of the government and the market to truly provide a response to this crisis became obvious in the widespread destruction and

slow recovery initiated by the 2008 financial collapse. Finessing the unemployment numbers has become the only jobs program the government takes seriously, as stable, long-term jobs are replaced with low- and
minimum-wage, part-time, precarious, and seasonal work. People who
work three jobs but can barely pay the rent or who only get fifteen hours
a week at Target and live one illness away from total penury are gleefully
declared "employed!" by liberal metrics of economic health. The disabled, imprisoned, undocumented, long-term unemployed, and otherwise marginalized people are permanently cut out of the "official" labor
force statistics, further reducing unemployment numbers without changing material conditions.

The official poverty threshold is similarly kept absurdly low, not track-
ing changes in costs of education, health care, rent, or debt levels to hide
the fact that some 30 percent of Americans live in poverty while another
20 percent have a higher income but are only three months of unemployment away from total poverty. Misery spreads everywhere while politicians, economists, and the media gaslight the population with reports of
recovery and economic strength. Wealth concentrates in an increasingly
small and increasingly rich capitalist class. At the time of this writing,
it seems the dam has finally broken on this strategy, as the shock of the
coronavirus shutdown has popped the fragile bubbles resting atop five
decades of debt and logistic schemes and created unimaginable unemployment alongside mass death.

American triumphalism over the fall of the USSR, the victory of
global capitalism, and the "end of history"—the idea that political transformation is over and that instead we will merely witness the global spread
and increase of liberal democracy and wealth—has been revealed for the
farce it always was. In truth, capitalism is gorging itself on the planet, destroying the earth in a horrific ecological crisis that, rather than attempt
to solve, it merely schemes to profit off of even further. It is also killing
off the nation-state, the main form of political power it has relied on over
the last century and a half; governmental bodies such as the EU and
concepts such as "global cities" are testament to the fact that capitalism
requires openness to a total system of global flows more than it does the
development of profits through social spending and trade imbalances.

Rather than a world of harmonious liberal democratic nations, capitalism instead seems to be headed for a proliferation of high-tech, authoritarian city-states that compete for resources against the backdrop of migration, employment, pandemic, and starvation crises in widespread hinterlands full of populations made surplus by automation and ecological collapse.[1]

But this era of general crisis that began in the seventies did not see a proliferation of mass movements in the United States. Instead, a wave of revolutionary fervor faded and fell to repression. Although social movements existed in the period—in particular, the gay-led AIDS movement, the antinuclear movement, Jesse Jackson's Rainbow Coalition, animal rights, and alter-globalization—they often got bogged down in electoral or nonprofit "single-issue"-style campaigns. And though instances of anti-white-supremacist rioting and looting took place—most significantly in LA in 1992, but antipolice riots popped up every few years throughout the period—they mostly failed to initiate a cycle of social transformation.

Without a broader movement context, rioters increasingly appeared as simple pariahs. Looting became the prototypical evidence of Black pathology and crime. As the political center of gravity in America definitively shifted to the white suburbs, even liberal explanations of rioting and looting, such as those put forward by LBJ's Kerner and Governor Brown's McCone Commissions, were rejected. Sociology was dismissed for psychology, and narratives about looting and rioting were explained as a question of culture, crime, and family. This newly re-racialized definition of looting would reach its horrific apotheosis in New Orleans in 2005, when police and white vigilantes murdered Hurricane Katrina refugees with impunity under the aegis of "stopping looting."

DEPENDING ON WHERE YOU LOOK IN THE WORLD, YOU WILL GET A different historical moment to date the end of the revolutionary wave of the sixties: the police standoff with United Red Army militants in the Asama-Sansō incident in Japan in 1972, the coup unseating and killing Chilean Marxist Salvador Allende in 1973, the end of the Cultural Revolution and China siding with right-wing rebels in Angola in 1975–1976, the murder of Red Army Faction (RAF) revolutionaries at the end of the German Autumn of 1977, the precipitous decline of the autonomous movement after Aldo Moro's kidnapping in Italy in 1978, and so forth.

For the US movement, historical accounts converge consistently around the end of the Vietnam War in 1975, as the antiwar movement provided the most consistent activist base for mass action across the United States, particularly after the split and collapse of the Black Panther Party's national membership in 1970–1971. But perhaps the one moment that most solidified the turn in national politics away from upheaval, social justice, and equality and toward that reactionary suburban politics of white grievance and white vengeance known as "color-blindness" and "law and order" was the blackout looting in New York City in the summer of 1977.

A massive power failure on the brutally hot night of July 13, 1977, instigated by lightning striking electric lines north of the city, plunged New York City into darkness. People spilled out into the streets to help one another, to party, and to loot, burn, and fight with police. Over sixteen hundred businesses were looted in the twenty-five hours of blackout, and forty-five hundred people were arrested—the largest mass arrest in New York City history.

Looting mostly took place in poor Black and Latinx neighborhoods. Arson and looting were so dire in Bushwick that business owners refused to move back into the neighborhood for a decade after the blackout, but more than thirty neighborhoods in the city were affected. The most brazen acts of looting included teens driving fifty Pontiacs directly out of a showroom in the Bronx. The widespread looting of otherwise unaffordable turntables and mixing equipment is often cited as a crucial moment in the birth and growth of hip-hop and DJ culture.

During the looting, Black businesses were targeted just the same as white ones. Without the clear racial demarcation between businesses that many pointed to in the sixties as evidence of looting's "political" nature, and without an initiating event of police brutality, defense of the looting required directly challenging class society, not just racism. It required directly aligning with the "antisocial" actions of the proletariat in making their own lives better at the expense of law and order. You'd have to stand with them as they acted outside and against white supremacist commodity society, even when they were not legibly "protesting" it.

But the riots not only lacked an obvious political content, they also lacked a movement. The rise of the Black middle classes after civil rights victories had, by 1977, reinforced and widened a significant class line within Black communities. Income, wealth, and unemployment rates of poor folks in the late seventies were often worse than they had been in the sixties, but a small class had benefited. Black middle-class business owners and politicians, who had replaced movement leaders as "representative voices," disavowed the looting: after all, it attacked their interests. The editorial board of Harlem's *Amsterdam News* led the charge for the Black middle class, writing an excoriating denunciation of the looting that was reprinted in papers throughout the country to provide cover for more openly racist antilooting positions.

Arrested looters, meanwhile, were processed with a deliberate slowness that left thousands in horribly overcrowded cells for five or six days in the middle of a record heat wave. Given rotten food and insufficient water, they languished in collective punishment. "We slept on the floor with our hands next to our body like the slaves brought over from Africa," one arrestee testified. It was a rather direct example of what Christina Sharpe calls Black life "in the Hold." As a way of reasserting property relations after an act of looting, the state turns to its foundational strategies and reintroduces the logistical techniques of the slave ship. Looters are punished for their act by the traumatic (re)experiencing of the conditions of the slave ship, an experience that shadows all racialization and all property relations in America.[2]

But police, judges, and the mayor played down this horrific violence, instead participating in a broad dehumanization of the looters. They used the fact that the municipal government of New York City was in dire financial straits—nearly bankrupt, it had been devastated by white flight and by the general economic downturn of the seventies—to falsely claim they couldn't afford to process looters in a timely fashion.

The poverty in the city *was* immense. Liberal economic and social welfare policies had utterly failed to rectify the situation, as Great Society programs, already too small to combat the problems of the late 1960s, were completely insufficient in the face of the collapse and stagnation started in 1973. White flight into the suburbs decimated the city's tax base at the same moment that the economy went into crisis. What the programs had done, however, was give white people an excuse to blame the Black and Latinx poor for their own condition. After all, hadn't they been receiving welfare, War on Poverty programs, affirmative action, and all sorts of other special treatment from the government?

In his history *Blackout*, James Goodman traces how this shift was made visible through the *New York Times* coverage of the blackout. The editorial board at first attempted to explain and understand the looting through the familiar liberal sociological lens of poverty, unemployment—which was at Great Depression levels in Black and Latinx communities—and lack of services. But white subscribers, many of them now living far outside the city, wrote in by the thousands, objecting, calling the looters "animals" and "parasites." Such "debates" happened in media across the country, and it was the white suburban voice—which included not only the newspapers' and TV stations' owners and editorial boards but also the majority of paying customers—that won out. The looting, white people insisted, was not about poverty—after all, weren't they living high on their welfare checks?—but about the degradation of morals and a culture of lawlessness, laziness, and entitlement.

There would be no government inquiry, no sociological study: the looters would not be asked why they had done it. The mayor, Democrat Abraham Beame, lost the mayoral primaries that fall to conservative Ed Koch in large part as a result of the blackout rioting. Koch fomented outrage and blew dog whistles, criticizing Beame for not bringing in the National Guard and not letting police attack looters more violently, riding "law and order" racism straight into Gracie Mansion.

The widespread dehumanization of looters and arsonists, of *criminals*, in the aftermath of the blackout helped consolidate the new white supremacist politics of "color-blind" mass incarceration, precarity, poverty, and police murder. Looting became an excellent symbol for this new form of the old racial politics: it can be easily pointed to as a form of the "shamelessness" of criminals. Taking place during mass unrest, it can be treated as representative or reflective of a (Black) cultural or social attitude as well as a general societal breakdown of law and order that requires more authoritarian politics to "renew" the country. Meanwhile, looting's submerged history as a racialized relationship to property is safely evoked without directly using "racist" language. "Looter" becomes a perfect color-blind dog whistle.

This is why, on whitehouse.gov, Donald Trump's administration could write, on their special "Standing Up for Our Law Enforcement Community" page: "Our job is not to make life more comfortable for the rioter, the looter, or the violent disrupter. Our job is to make life more comfortable for parents who want their kids to be able to walk the streets safely. Or the senior citizen waiting for a bus."[3] The "rioter" and "looter" is summoned as an innate enemy of the government and of the people, of "us." What about the Black parents who just wanted their kids, like Michael Brown, "to be able to walk the streets safely"? Black mothers and fathers are here purposely excluded from the body politic, and yet the government hasn't directly used any racialized language. Anti-rioting is one of the major ways ethnonationalist power talks about its work of racist oppression.

By the time a massive uprising broke out in Miami in May 1980, in response to the acquittal of four police officers who had murdered Arthur McDuffie after he ran a red light, these notions were firmly in place. The uprising is little remembered now outside of Miami, but it was larger by many metrics than Watts. More than four thousand police and National Guard were deployed, and they were joined by white vigilantes. Together they killed fourteen people, while four people were killed by rioters. A hundred million dollars in property was looted and destroyed.

But the Miami uprising was not analyzed or discussed as the riots of the sixties were in terms of inequality and racism. Instead, the Miami uprising was understood and analyzed through the subtly different "color-blind" lens of "racial tensions," which implies that white people having racist feelings and Black people experiencing the effects of racism are equivalent. Liberal commentators' lines shifted, replacing unemployment and poverty with concepts like "hopelessness" and "despair."

It's not that affect and emotion are politically unimportant—quite the opposite: anger, rage, and mourning are all crucial motivations of people rising up. Rather, liberal explanations of riots as caused by "poverty" are just as lacking and ahistorical as neoliberal evocations of "despair." But the turn to moral and psychological explanations for unrest marks a transition to a frame that deemphasizes systems and structures in favor of individual responsibility, family values, and "culture."

The Miami uprising barely made the national news, and it was quickly erased from the historical memory of the era. President Jimmy Carter, facing a primary challenge from Ted Kennedy, was campaigning on a promise of stability and competence. He ignored the Miami riots; his administration hardly mentioned them. As historian Manning Marable records: "The Miami rebellion was the first major racial uprising in twelve years—yet it failed to make the front pages of white America's two prestige news weeklies, *Time* and *Newsweek*."[4] The white people of the country didn't want to talk about Miami, and the memory of the massive revolt was quickly buried under the rising tide of suburban conservatism that would bring Ronald Reagan to office in a landslide election five months later.

THE LARGEST US UPRISING IN THE TWENTIETH CENTURY WOULD NOT be so easily ignored. Broadcast live on TV, while newscasters mouthed platitudes and expressed shock and outrage over news helicopter–captured images of crowds moving through South Central LA's sprawling freeways and parking lots, the 120 hours of rioting and looting that shook Los Angeles in 1992 seemed to inaugurate a new era of resistance. Whereas Miami had largely been fought along Black versus white racial lines, the LA riots quickly became ethnically diverse: "Of the first 5,000 arrests 52 per cent were poor Latinos, 10 per cent whites and only 38 per cent blacks."[5] The riots were an uprising of working-class Angelenos that were initiated by a clear instance of anti-Black oppression and violence. Resistance emerged along lines of a class solidarity with Black Angelenos against the police, white supremacy, and capitalist domination.

Rioting was sparked when four police officers, whose beating nearly to death of motorist Rodney King for speeding was captured on camera and aired widely, were acquitted on April 29, 1992, at a trial moved from LA to lily-white, hyper-conservative Simi Valley.[6] As that famous chant that spread nationally from the LA uprising goes: "No Justice, No Peace!" But the acquittal was only one instigating incident. The LAPD is consistently rated as one of the most violent, racist, and fascistic police forces in America, and police abuse, racism, and murder had escalated in the years leading up to the riot. Another important incident had occurred six months earlier, when a Korean store owner, who had murdered fifteen-year-old Latasha Harlins for supposedly stealing a bottle of orange juice, was convicted of manslaughter but received only a $500 fine and community service. The murder was caught on camera, and the $1.79 to pay for the juice was found in Latasha's hand.

These meant one angle of the riots was a racial battle between Black people and the Korean immigrants who had come to own and manage most of the businesses in South Central. Rioters systematically attacked Korean businesses, and a television crew happened to be present for a gunfight between Korean store owners and Black rioters. But much as Watts was sometimes described as an anti-Semitic uprising, because Jewish businesses were frequently targeted for destruction, actual "anti-Korean" sentiment was contingent and largely beside the point. Instead, just as Jews were in 1965, Koreans in 1992 were "on the front-line of the confrontation between capital and the residents of central LA—they are the face of capital for these communities."[7]

This racial pattern is a common strategy settler-colonial society uses to deflect and misdirect tensions in the urban environment. Forming a "buffer class" of ethnic entrepreneurs with easy access to small business loans and support, these small shop owners perform the daily exploitation of capital and as such perpetuate and absorb much of the violence of the system in exchange for generational entry into the middle class and whiteness. Black people are thus constantly kept at the bottom of the racial hierarchy, while immigrant participation in American citizenship is predicated on the expropriation of Black communities and the reproduction of anti-Blackness.

The media further attempted to frame the riots as race riots by focusing on the beating of Reginald Denny. Denny, a white truck driver, had the misfortune of driving through an intersection where the police and National Guard had just been violently battling a group of Black teenage boys. Rioters pulled Denny from his truck and brutally assaulted and robbed him. Footage of the beating was caught by a news helicopter—and newscasters conveniently ignored the police violence preceding his attack and almost never showed the subsequent rescue of and care for Denny by other Black rioters, who quickly took him to a hospital, saving his life.

But while these media narratives failed to contain the anger of rioters, neither do they sufficiently explain it. At the time the nature of the uprising was such that even *Newsweek* reported that "what happened was not a 'race riot' but a 'class riot.'"* Black people were not the only ones rioting. One of the most revolutionary aspects of the LA rebellion was that the pattern that took a decade to unfold in the civil rights era—Black people rising up and in turn encouraging the rest of the working class to insurrection—happened instantaneously. "The rebellion started among black people, spread immediately to involve Latinos in South Central (which is about 42 percent Latino) and Pico Union, and then brought in unemployed white workers from Hollywood in the north to Long Beach in the south and Venice in the west."[8] And the rebellion spread quickly to other cities. Looting, rioting, fighting with the police, arson, and massive infrastructural shutdowns popped off in San Francisco, the East Bay, San Diego, San Jose, Tampa Bay, Las Vegas, Seattle, Rochester, and Atlanta, and "there were smaller riots in Riverside, California, Denver, Miami, and Peoria and Springfield, Illinois. Riots broke out in various locations in Maryland, New York, Ohio, Tennessee, Texas and Alabama."[9]

Over a billion dollars in damages was done, and sixty-three people died, the vast majority of whom perished at the hands of the fourteen thousand police, FBI, Drug Enforcement Administration, National Guard, federal marshals, border patrol agents, Army service members, and Marines deployed on May 2 to put down the riots. More than eleven thousand arrests were made, and a conservative estimate has 150,000 people participating in the uprising.

---

*As is one of the core arguments of this book, such a clean distinction between class and race is untenably problematic. But this does show that the strategy of explaining everything solely through a nonclass, nonintersectional white–Black racial lens had failed.

The main aspect the rioting took was looting and arson: direct expropriation of wealth and attacks on property. Unlike in Detroit in 1968, there was little sniping at police (though rioters were definitely armed). As journalist Mike Davis recorded at the time, "The gangs have refrained from the deadly guerrilla warfare that they are so formidably equipped to conduct." As with every uprising, while (often gang-affiliated) youth performed most of the combat, the looting crowd was diverse. "Men and women, Black and white, young and old. People have brought their children out here!" one gobsmacked TV journalist reported. A rioter interviewed on live TV said, "Look around you! These people are not thugs and gang members, these are women, children, babies, people that live in this community who are tired of the constant oppression, the constant abuse they have been served." Reporters quickly turned to another interview.

Whereas the uprising generalized across the working class, the riots were led by a new group of the urban poor. Members of a new underclass of the near permanently unemployed, cut adrift by the Reagan-driven destruction of social services and the collapse of manufacturing jobs, existing largely outside of the circuits of production and consumption, this class lives at the very margins of the market and of society. At the time of the uprising, the LA court bureaucracy was referring to cases around impoverished Black males as "NHI"—"No Humans Involved." As Sylvia Wynter writes, Rodney King was a member of these new Black masses, who, in distinction to the Black middle class that had grown since the sixties, "have come to occupy a doubled pariah status, no longer that of only being Black, but of also belonging to the rapidly accelerating Post-Industrial category of the poor and jobless." People the state considered NHI led the LA uprising, and in thinking through and fighting alongside their rebellion, Wynter argues, we can begin to overturn the current system that constructs "humanity" in such a way as to exile them from its protections and care.[10]

Many Black radicals in the sixties foresaw this economic and social process of double dehumanization: radical movement journals such as *Soulbook*, *The Movement*, *The Crusader*, and *Inner City Voice*, to name only a few, wrote consistently of the danger of coming automation and Black isolation and alienation. Recognition of this class transformation is what prompted the Black Panther Party to organize the people Marxists had traditionally denigrated as the innately reactionary "Lumpenproletariat."

The LA riots were the first uprising in the United States of this new postindustrial underclass, which Marxist theorists have referred to as "surplus populations"—people outside the process of the production of value, people who aren't even needed to drive down wages like the usual mass of unemployed proletarians are. These people whom capitalism regards as surplus do not and cannot make demands of a traditional industrial workplace, so their movements are invisible or opaque to many so-called revolutionaries who believe revolution can only emerge from a shop floor. And this disregard is furthered by the fact that the form of organization favored by this new population of declassed poor is not the union but the criminal gang.

IN THE WEEKS BEFORE THE RIOT STARTED, TWO WARRING SETS WITHIN the Crips and a major crew of the Bloods negotiated a truce. The truce was finalized at a peace summit at the Imperial Courts Project gym in Watts the day before the riots began, ending a gang war that had gone on for two decades in which hundreds of people were killed. They called the truce to build capacity to fight their real enemies, the police. This truce was a significant factor in the growth of the uprising, as the gangs' high level of organization and pseudomilitary training would come in handy in battling the police and opening up new areas of rebellion. As the fires burned, most of the other gangs in LA declared peace as well.*

As Gerald Horne traces in his history of the Watts Uprising, *Fire This Time*, three major organizational trends emerged in the wake of Watts: the revolutionary activism of the Black Panther Party (and other

---

*Ryan Gattis's *All Involved*, a widely renowned 2015 novel that frames the LA rebellion as a moment of total lawlessness in which gang members settled scores and murdered people indiscriminately—consistently implying that the only thing keeping gangsters from going on killing sprees is the presence of the police—is a horrific inversion of these facts and gets the meaning and effect of the riots on LA gang violence almost exactly wrong.

Black radicals), "cultural" Black nationalism, and criminal gangs. As
COINTELPRO ruthlessly destroyed the revolutionary groups of the sixties and seventies, they left cultural nationalism like the Nation of Islam
and gangs as the only forms of organization in the ghetto.[11]

To describe gangs as one dominant form of working-class organization is not to romanticize them. By bringing the international drug
trade through their communities, they manage to produce money and
employment for their "surplus populations" at the expense of dramatic
social damage in the form of addiction and violence. Deeply hierarchi-
cal, built on a sometimes almost cult-like devotion, and focused indelibly
on obtaining money, these are most certainly not revolutionary organizations—though you could also describe many trade unions the same way.

Another similarity the gangs have to the unions is that, as a form of
working-class organization with clear leaders and a cohesive disciplinary
apparatus, the state will, in moments of rebellion and upheaval, turn to
them to negotiate concessions in return for an end to riots. To this end,
the gangs in LA released a list of demands—most novel of which was the
proposal that a gang member with a video camera should be assigned to
every police patrol to keep them honest, but which also included more
traditional demands about jobs, social centers, amnesty for rioters, and
so forth.

The political role gangs play was even more pronounced in the 2015
Baltimore uprising: after street gangs and the Nation of Islam effectively
teamed up to stop looting and repress rioting, media broadcast the spectacle of gang leaders sitting in on a city council meeting. They hadn't
actually been welcomed into the official power structure of Baltimore,
and they haven't achieved a lasting place in the council, but during an
uprising, any group that proves itself able to repress and dampen resistance is temporarily given a seat at the table. Political parties, unions,
gangs, nonprofits, and any other organizational forms that imagine their
route to power goes through the state often stab uprisings in the back and
even ally with the police if it seems to serve them.

Despite propaganda to the contrary, gangs' existence in the ghetto is
not only tolerated but also approved by the state, as they turn economic
and social violence largely inward while giving the state an unlimited

excuse for intervention and repression.* We see this in the widespread police practices of gang injunctions, gang databases, and mass arrest sweeps,
the most famous of which was the 2016 Bronx 120, when NYPD arrested
120 Black and Latinx youths in a series of massive raids; a huge number of
arrestees were unaffiliated. Gang injunctions name certain blocks, street
corners, or neighborhoods as "hotbeds" of gang activity, allowing police to
act with even more impunity in impoverished urban areas, banning public gathering and prima facie criminalizing any young folks they want to
harass on the street. Gang databases, meanwhile, are little more than lists
of the poor urban youth who have had any interactions with law enforcement, inventing gangs whole cloth to churn people more seamlessly into
the prison-industrial complex. But in uprisings against the police, gang-
bangers frequently become frontline soldiers, doing the most dramatic
and dangerous tasks in a riot. This danger—that peace between the gangs
could mean war on the pigs—became a reality during the LA rebellion.

And so, in the aftermath, the LAPD immediately focused on breaking
the gang truce. They attacked and broke up intergang unity rallies, shut
down "truce barbecues" going on all summer, and infiltrated deep into
the various gangs, working to instigate conflict. Nevertheless, the truce
held, and a grassroots-led movement of gang de-escalation spread across
the country, one of the main material victories of the riots. This led to an
immediate, dramatic drop off in gang violence in LA: homicides fell 44
percent in the first two years of the truce. Police, of course, took credit
for this drop, all the while working to undermine the peace. Though the
police couldn't dismantle the truce directly, they did in the intervening
years manage to loosen and weaken gang organizational structure and
discipline.

The police work romanticized in HBO's TV series *The Wire*—studying the ins and outs of gang politics, personalities, and hierarchies in
order to arrest lieutenants and crush leaders—is a fantasy version of the

---

*This excuse, however, is just that—gang violence is as much a myth the police use as
an actual cause of their action, and, were it not for gangs, they would use something else.
As we have seen, police violence in Black neighborhoods is one of the few constants in
American history, and gangs and the drug war are merely the most recent iteration of the
ongoing explanation of that violence.

process of dis-organizing the gangs the police developed in LA after the riots and that spread to police departments across the country. Twenty-five
years later, most gangs in the United States now are small, decentralized,
highly localized groups of kids beefing over a few blocks, nothing like
the massive, tightly organized, pseudo-paramilitary forces formed in the
seventies and eighties.

Meanwhile, that form of gang organization and violence grew in
Latin America. These gangs were often direct products of US government policy. The most famous example is in El Salvador, where hundreds of thousands of refugees fleeing the US-backed, -militarized, and
-funded twelve-year civil war between left-wing guerillas and the government crossed into the United States throughout the eighties. Living here
in poverty, and already once exiled by US policy, many boys joined gangs
as a way of staying safe in the streets of US cities, only to be sent back to
El Salvador under a Clinton-era scheme—initiated in 1995, only three
years after the end of the civil war—that deported any immigrants convicted of gang felonies.

So, boys, some of whom had no memory of El Salvador and many
of whom didn't even speak Spanish, were sent back to a "home" country they had fled as children or even infants, places where they often
had no or only distant family. They then re-formed gangs based on those
they'd participated in in the States as a way of surviving their new, equally
hostile environment. These gangs have since become massive, terribly
violent, powerful actors. MS-13, one of the gangs transplanted directly
from LA, has, in yet another turn of this self-reinforcing cycle, become a
favorite racist bogeyman of the US anti-immigrant Right.

In other places, such as Colombia, Guatemala, Mexico, and Af-
ghanistan, the enforcers of right-wing state structures put in place by or
emerging after US destabilization become drug warlords, cartels existing
as basically sovereign powers, pseudo-states funded by the more or less
infinite demand for drugs and immigrant laborers in the United States
and Europe. The war on terror is merely a continuation, into different
theaters, of tactics, strategies, and effects developed during the war on
drugs, which was itself an extension of the war on Black communities of
resistance.

THE 2000S WERE A TERRIBLE DECADE OF SOCIAL DISSOLUTION AND oppression in the United States. The "stability and prosperity" of the middle classes in the nineties were built on widespread increases in consumer debt, not increased wages; "welfare reform" had doomed millions to deeper poverty; NAFTA and other globalization trends continued to smash unions and pull blue-collar jobs out of the country; and mass incarceration had been expanded and accelerated to all-time highs by tough-on-crime "new Democrats."

Movements fared badly, too. The alter-globalization movement, a bold, increasingly powerful, and militant association of anarchists, labor radicals, and other activists that made world headlines by rioting to shut down the World Trade Organization (WTO) in the 1999 Battle of Seattle, was utterly shattered in the reactionary aftermath of the September 11 terrorist attacks. In their wake, George W. Bush's administration swung the state in an even more deeply authoritarian direction, consolidating incredible powers in the White House, vastly expanding surveillance, implementing more border and police apparatuses, and starting a forever "War on Terror" in the Middle East.

Massive antipolice riots in Cincinnati, Ohio, in 2001 and smaller anti-Nazi rioting in Toledo, Ohio, in 2005 could not stem the rightward swing and received little attention nationally. The biggest show of organized resistance to Bush's regime, the 2003 protests against the Iraq War—which featured the largest single day of protest in world history—was simply shrugged off and failed to transition into an ongoing antiwar movement. And the immigrant rights movement, appearing on the scene with a massive strike and day of action, the Day Without an Immigrant on May 1, 2006, thereafter strayed increasingly toward patriotic, respectability-focused, and Democratic Party–centered reform strategies.

The nadir of the entire period came in 2005, when Hurricane Katrina hit the Gulf Coast. Katrina wreaked devastation across the South: 1,836 people died in the immediate flooding and chaos, and another few thousand died in the next six months from conditions exacerbated or caused by the storm's destruction. And when the Mississippi River overflowed its banks, destroying the levees and flooding 80 percent of New Orleans, the anti-Black character of the Bush administration became terribly clear.

As the majority Black city drowned, and the waters rose to fifteen feet in many places, the federal government barely responded; a Canadian Search and Rescue team managed to get a support force to New Orleans faster than the Federal Emergency Management Agency (FEMA) did. When FEMA finally arrived, in many cases it actually slowed down rescue and evacuation procedures with bureaucratic power struggles, ridiculous paperwork, and general incompetence.

Kanye West's statement at a televised fundraiser that "George Bush doesn't care about Black people" was as clear a fact as could be. It was an important generational moment, what Mychal Denzel Smith refers to as a "rebirth of Black rage," that was captured, shared, and disseminated widely by millennials using emerging internet technologies.[12] But in those reactionary times, it was as far as the mainstream political conversation about anti-Blackness was going to go.

The municipal government of New Orleans, which had declared a forced evacuation before the storm, was utterly unprepared for the disaster—the police didn't even have enough battery-powered radios to operate once the power went out—and local government totally collapsed. Those too poor, old, or sick to leave New Orleans were left alone, without food, route of escape, or safe haven in the midst of one of the largest natural disasters in US history. Of the nearly 1,836 people who lost their lives, most of them were poor, Black, and elderly.

Seven thousand prisoners, the vast majority Black and almost all arrested for minor crimes and misdemeanors, who were unlucky enough to be jailed at the time of the storm, experienced, as prisoners always do, some of the worst of government malevolence. They survived brutal beatings and pepper spraying by police and jailers and the utter terror of near drowning as they watched the waters rise from within locked cells. Then many were seated outside in handcuffs in the hot sun for days waiting for evacuation, only to spend the next year in prison, regardless of charges, as the governor suspended habeas corpus. This was referred to locally as "doing Katrina time."

But rather than focus on the tragedy or the governmental crimes, media, both local and national, summoned instead the image of the Black looter. They reported sniping at helicopters, widespread arson, the killing of rescue workers, mass rape and murder in the Superdome—"thuggery," they called it. Almost all of these stories were false and had to be retracted. Studies have consistently shown that in the wake of natural disasters people come together and help each other, and crime and violence drop dramatically, and Katrina was no different. But the retractions all came much too late. The enduring story of Katrina was of lawlessness, criminality, riot.

White vigilantes and police officers, stewing in the paranoia and the summer heat, responded with murder and mayhem, though the full extent of their crimes is unknown (much of the evidence appears to have gone carefully unrecorded by police or was destroyed by the coroner and other governmental offices). Oppressive actors, such as property owners, the state, and white supremacists, use natural disasters to "restore" law and order through brutal violence. It is hard not to see in their violence in the face of governmental collapse the shadow of the violence of ex-Confederates in the chaotic early years of Reconstruction, and in particular in the New Orleans riot in 1866, when police and other ex-Confederate whites massacred forty-four Black delegates to the Louisiana Constitutional Convention.

Constructing a narrative of lawless Katrina survivors justified the horrifying actions of police and white residents. Police murdered families fleeing New Orleans, most infamously killing two and seriously wounding four unarmed refugees on the Danziger Bridge and murdering Danny Brumfield in front of the convention center—crimes for which cops were actually prosecuted, although only a decade later. When two Black men went to a police outpost looking for an ambulance to take their friend Henry Glover, dying of a gunshot wound, to the hospital, police instead arrested and brutally beat the two men, left Glover to bleed to death in the back of the car, then drove the car to a levee and lit it on fire so as to not deal with his body.

These cases garnered a lot of media attention, and so prosecutors focused all their energy and resources on them. But similar crimes went pointedly uninvestigated. In white, middle-class Algiers Point, a militia formed "to protect the neighborhood from looters and criminals" that in fact hunted Black refugees. One vigilante, Wayne Janak, interviewed in a documentary made after the storm, described killing Black survivors as follows: "It was great! It was like pheasant season in South Dakota. If it moved, you shot it." Another, Nathan Roper, says police gave them support and instruction to kill: "If they're breaking in your property, do what you gotta do and leave them [the bodies] on the side of the road." The emergence of "Stand Your Ground" laws, the first of which came into being in October 2005 in Florida, another state badly damaged by Katrina, codified into state laws these forms of white supremacist vigilante murder.

Because these victims might have been "looting"—though they were almost certainly just trying to get to the evacuation point in Algiers—their deaths were disregarded, and the militiamen, who proudly described their actions *on video*, went unpunished. Journalist A. C. Thompson interviewed Tulane University historian Lance Hill (author of *The Deacons for Defense*, cited extensively elsewhere in this book) about the situation: "Because of the widespread notion that blacks engaged in looting and thuggery as the disaster unfolded, Hill believes, many white New Orleanians approved of the vigilante activity. 'By and large, I think the white mentality is that these people are exempt. . . . I think that if any of these cases went to trial, and none of them have, I can't see a white person being convicted of any kind of crime against an African-American during that period.'"[13]

The New Orleans PD intentionally kept very few records during the disaster, and the coroner also seems to have destroyed and covered up information about bodies that came through his office.

Thus "looting," real or imaginary, becomes an instant marker of the "NHI" category described by Wynter. From the NYC blackout to LA to Katrina, looting became the prototypical crime of the Black, poor, and surplus, an act that immediately exiled its perpetrators from the human community and sentenced them to death, an action that proved the righteousness of their disposability. It's no wonder, after such violent categorization, that people in movements today want to disavow looting or distance "real protesters" from looters.

But we must not reproduce that mark of NHI on our comrades, our siblings in the struggle. Instead, we must join them to overthrow the world that would see anyone so marked.

OUT OF THE FLAMES OF FERGUSON

HISTORY IS A FUNNY THING. A CVS STORE IN BALTIMORE, A BROOKlyn Duane Reade, a St. Louis QuikTrip: these are not meant to be historical places. In fact, an entire science, incorporating marketing, psychology, architecture, and interior design, is devoted to giving corporate spaces like these a sense of the timeless, infinite present of consumption and stripping them of the possibility of change, of difference, of politics, of history. But struggle can turn even the most consciously constructed banality into a place of rupture, community, transformation, and liberation.

That's good, because in the last forty years capitalism has spread its corporate banality across the whole of society, to say nothing of its terrible violence and destruction. But we are once again in the midst of a global period of struggle, which threatens to destroy and overturn those spaces, to fill the world instead with life, love, beauty, and adventure, with solidarity, care, and peace. At the time of this writing, in April 2020, we are in a worldwide quarantine lockdown against the coronavirus, looking down the barrel at an economic collapse on par with that of the Great Depression. Worldwide struggles, and the fascist forces unleashed to destroy them, seem certain to intensify.

When street vendor Mohamed Bouazizi lit himself on fire on December 17, 2010, in protest of humiliation and harassment at the hands of municipal authorities, he initiated a wave of struggle that would spread across Tunisia, through the whole of North Africa, and eventually out to the entire world in what would be called the Arab Spring. The Arab Spring's most significant victories came in the fall of the Tunisian government of Ben Ali and dictator Hosni Mubarak in Egypt. Major movements also sprang up in Yemen, Bahrain, Libya, and Syria, while massive protests occurred in over a dozen other countries.

The fires spread to Europe that summer as huge social movements shook Spain and Greece, and the largest riots the UK had seen in decades unfolded after the police murder of Mark Duggan. From there, the wave jumped the pond to the United States with the Occupy movement, then bounced back to Africa with the #OccupyNigeria uprising. In Montreal a militant student strike soon engulfed the entire city in protest, and the villagers of Wukan, China, rose up, kicked out their local government, and declared themselves a commune. Massive social movements seemed poised to topple governments in Turkey and Brazil in 2013, and Bosnia in 2014.

Political and social instability has meant opportunities for the Right as well. The successful 2013 military coup in Egypt and Turkish president Recep Tayyip Erdoğan's manipulation of a failed 2016 coup have seen increasingly authoritarian powers put in place: protest has been outlawed and repression comes at the barrel of a gun. The United States and UN Security Council helped escalate the Arab Spring into a war in Libya to take out Muammar Qaddafi, and the uprising in Syria was quickly overtaken by a civil war in which most actors disdained and repressed the social revolution. Brazil and Thailand saw right-wing movements appropriate the language and tactics of the 2011–2013 "movement of the squares," while in Ukraine a squares-style political revolution was largely co-opted by bourgeois liberals and right-wing Ukrainian nationalists. Coups have been dismantling the legacy of the Pink Tide socialists in Latin America. And Far Right parties and politicians have won electoral victories in India, Japan, Argentina, Brazil, the UK, Hungary, the United States, and the Philippines.

But still, liberation struggles spread. Many see the revolutionary experiment in Kurdish Rojava as the Spanish Civil War of our time. In the summer of 2014, Palestinians again rose up against the Zionist occupation in Jerusalem, and solidarity marches and actions proliferated globally. Movement has exploded in France: 2016 riots against a vicious reactionary labor law were joined by the *Nuit debout* movement—a movement of the squares that seemed to arrive three years past that tactic's expiration date. The year 2017 saw weeks-long antipolice #JusticepourTheo uprisings, and in 2018–2019 the Gilet Jaunes (Yellow Vests) movement, featuring the most destructive rioting in Paris since 1968, as struggle blazed across the entirety of France, including the neocolonized African island nation of Reunion.

In 2016, a huge strike wave engulfed China, including a massive wild-cat strike across Walmart factories throughout the country: strikes, despite being outlawed, have been increasing in size and number year on year in China, as have protests. The 2017 Gasolinazo movement in Mexico followed in the footsteps of #OccupyNigeria, as, just as Nigerians had exactly five years previously, widespread rioting and unrest flared against cuts in gasoline subsidies, including significant looting and highway and border shutdowns. Gasoline price rises also drove a huge rebellion in Sudan, which eventually saw the government of President Omar al-Bashir toppled. The second half of 2018 included increasingly dramatic struggles erupting across Haitian society, and these have continued into the present. As this book was nearing completion, the world has seen another wave of action akin to the struggles of 2011, as Chile, Iraq, Iran, Lebanon, Algeria, Jordan, India, Indonesia, Colombia, Bolivia, Kazakhstan, Ecuador, Hong Kong, Puerto Rico, and Hawaii have all had massive uprisings, many verging on revolutionary upheaval.

And in the United States, alongside the struggles in Puerto Rico and Hawaii, the historic #NoDAPL pipeline struggle, the largest prison strike in American history, the generalization of militant antifascism, the anti-ICE movement, and the movement that directly gave rise to this book, the antipolice uprisings of the Movement for Black Lives, have all continued to agitate.

These American movements have been on the defensive under the administration of Donald Trump. His first act in office was to push

through the Dakota Access Pipeline (DAPL), and his police state agenda
has emboldened police officers and Immigration and Customs Enforcement (ICE) agents: the first days after his election huge gains in correc-
tions and military-industry stocks kept market indexes from suffering a
drop. The question of reforms, both of police departments and of the
prison system, seems moot. But, as Angela Davis puts it, "We cannot
simply call for reform. The entire history of police, the entire history of
prisons is a history of reform."[1]

A new energy of resistance is building across the country: the rate
and spread of struggle, at least as of this writing, seems to be intensifying,
as a wave of labor actions and rent strikes surges in response to the new
economic crisis. Combined with the impossibility of reform—symbol-
ized most recently in the Democratic Party's defeat of the Bernie Sanders
campaign—it brings with it the growing sense that a more imaginative
solution is required. Abolition of the police and the prisons, as part of
the destruction of the state and the communist transformation of society,
seems to be the only path out of an otherwise fascistic future.

But as we enter a new period of heightened struggle, we must learn
the vital lessons of our history if we hope to truly shape our future. There
is quite simply no freedom without an end to white supremacy and settler
colonialism, without the victory of Black and Indigenous liberation. Capitalism, settler colonialism, and whiteness are so deeply intertwined that
any resistance against capitalism that fails to take on white supremacy is
doomed to repeating the failures of the past or, perhaps more horrifyingly,
to a reactionary victory that would innovate and reinvigorate capitalism
with new forms of settler domination under the guise of revolution.

Nevertheless, one revolutionary contradiction that always faces these
movements in the United States is that the majority of proletarians are
neither Black nor Indigenous, but are white, Latinx, or Asian. Those
people, oppressed by various forms of discrimination and left behind by
capital, are already primed to turn their rage against the system into rage
against Black, Indigenous, and revolutionary movements, and they are
vulnerable to capture by fascist, state, and other reactionary actors. We
saw this reactionary capture when Asian American activists took to the
streets to defend Chinese American cop Peter Liang, who was convicted

in 2016 for the 2014 murder of Akai Gurley in a housing project stairwell; in the victory of Donald Trump among white exurban and Rust Belt voting blocs; and in the spread of the militia and three-percenter movements in the rural West. (The alt-right was much more homogenously urban middle and upper class.)

This danger is greatest among white proletarians: as this book has argued, an attack on the systems of property is an attack, ultimately, on that axiomatic property whiteness, and this property-in-whiteness is the only property many poor white people know. They see this piece of property threatened by the abolition of whiteness and react with disgust at the idea that they might be privileged by it—many are after all suffering in deep generational poverty—at the same moment that they move to defend it. The tendency among many leftists to disown rioting, property destruction, and looting, in particular, and to attack "identity politics" more generally as a way of appealing to liberals and the white working class is ultimately a defense of whiteness, a way of building a rotten and reactionary solidarity on behalf of the system.

A material appeal to these non-Black or non-Indigenous proletarians cannot come in any form that downplays the seriousness, centrality, and power of white supremacy and settler colonialism or that disavows the leadership and righteousness of Black and Indigenous freedom fighters. To ignore the situation of these proletarians completely, however, threatens to leave in the rear a mass base for reactionary politics, raising the specter of civil war. The struggle for the abolition of the police, prisons, and borders offers one potential path through this contradiction, the struggle against pipelines and ecological destruction in the name of Indigenous sovereignty linking up with Appalachian pipeline defense offers another, and the multiracial looting and rioting in solidarity with Black Angelenos in LA in 1992, yet a third.

A revolutionary movement must reduce the value of whiteness to zero while simultaneously demonstrating the possibility of better lives for all of us stuck under its horrifying system—no small task, but not an impossible one, either. The very least revolutionaries can do is not disown and disavow these moments of uprising but instead recognize in them the wisdom and power of the Black revolutionary tradition, turn toward these moments of rupture with joy, attention, and solidarity, and fight to spread them to every corner of this globe. One tiny piece of that, which this book hopes to contribute, may well be recognizing the revolutionary history and potential of looting.

When the rebels of Ferguson stood up for Michael Brown, when they fought back against continued police violence, domination, and control, they gave birth to the most militant sustained struggle seen in the United Stated since the seventies. They rose up both in the midst of a broad international moment of struggle and crisis and out of the long Black radical tradition in its specific American forms and its Black Atlantic internationalism.

WHEN DARREN WILSON GUNNED DOWN MIKE BROWN FOR THE CRIME of being Black in the middle of the street, Wilson's actions represented no great break with American history, no change in the nature of American policing. When the Ferguson Police Department left Brown's body lying in the middle of the road for four hours, they practiced an anti-Black white terrorism as old as the country. But when Brown's friends, family, and community rose up and fought back, when they rioted, looted, marched, occupied, and organized in the streets of Ferguson, they pulled us toward a definitive break with that history.

The riots in Ferguson gave birth to a new era of militant resistance in America, the reemergence of the long movement for emancipation and Black liberation. Where previous rioting, from Miami in 1980 to LA in 1992 to Cincinnati in 2001 to Oakland in 2009, had burned out in intensity after a few nights, rioting in Ferguson was sustained for nearly two weeks, with protests, marches, and street organizing continuing thereafter for months. Massive rioting recurred in November, when a grand jury refused to indict Darren Wilson (despite the fact that, if a prosecutor wants, a grand jury could "indict a ham sandwich," as Sol Wachtler, chief judge of the New York Appeals Court, once claimed).

The rioting in Ferguson became national news with the looting and burning of a QuikTrip gas station on the first night after Mike Brown's death. But the riots went far beyond looting and arson. Shooting back at the police—armed self-defense—and Molotov cocktail attacks on troop carriers were tactics of the movement, though they were barely reported.[2]

This lack of reporting has obvious explanations on both sides, as discussed in the previous sections on armed self-defense. For the organizers focused on the outward appearance of the movement, already worried about media framing of Black criminality and violence, the fact of shooting at police threatens to completely derail the argument of movement nonviolence and innocence. For the police and the media, widespread, organized retaliatory shooting absolutely cannot be reported on because it represents an utter breakdown of respect for police power and threatens to spread and generalize that disregard, to give rioters in other cities ideas. Shooting at police is only reported (and, in these instances, exaggerated) if and when police or national guardsmen kill rioters, because then it is needed for justification. But it was through the consistent use of guns, along with the creative use of cars to broaden chaos and jam up West Florissant, the main avenue of the uprising, that rioters managed to maintain a mostly cop-free riot and protest zone for two weeks.

Knowledge of the armed aspect of the rioting should no longer be kept a shameful secret but instead should be understood and celebrated as action directly in line with self-defense movements of the Black tradition, from the Underground Railroad to the antilynching defense forces to the armed participants in the southern Freedom Movement.

Rioters had more to contend with than only the uniformed police. Nonviolent de-escalation, coming in the form of various peacekeepers, politicians, and nonprofit organizers, emerged quickly as a policing problem from within the movement. Whereas Al Sharpton and Jesse Jackson were booed off stage and out of town, homegrown peacekeepers were harder to deal with. Though some, particularly in the early days, blocked looting or arson in the hopes of advancing the struggle ethically, others did so on behalf of the police, the system of property, or their own political power. In Ferguson, local politician Antonio French, the New Black Panther Party (NBPP), and ministers were the most active peacekeepers. Raven Rakia describes their actions: "Instead of focusing on the violence of the police, peacekeepers are focused on silencing and quelling the crowd—to the point where they pinpoint the issue being a person throwing a plastic water bottle at a police line in riot gear, equipped with helmets, body armor and armored trucks."[3]

Again, nonviolence emerges to put a brake on Black resistance, to discipline and silence people rising up, while providing cover for the intense violence of the state. We can no longer let the police, that despicable occupying army, seem "natural," nor let anyone paint resistance to the settler state as an enemy of peace. Their peace is the peace of the grave.

In Ferguson, such "peacekeepers" provoked immediate and direct antagonisms. Many protesters saw clergy directly informing the police. In at least one crucial instance, peacekeepers formed a wall in front of the cops, preventing attempts by protesters to break police lines because they were unwilling to charge into the clergymen.

Whereas socialist and pan-African Black nationalisms animated some of the most important movements from the twenties through the seventies, the most visible nationalist organizations have proven to be reactionary forces in the current wave of struggle that use riots as opportunities to demonstrate their leadership and expand their control. NBPP and Nation of Islam (NOI) leaders proudly bragged in press conferences that it was *they*, and not the police, who were enforcing the curfew and "controlling" protesters in Ferguson.

The most egregious example of their peacekeeping came in Baltimore. During the 2015 uprising for Freddie Gray, the Nation of Islam brokered a peace between gang leaders, not to fight police as in LA 1992, but instead to stop the riots. TV crews caught scenes of NOI members, obvious in their suits and bowties, chasing looters out of stores and then protecting the stores from further looting. The NOI appealed to gang members' natural leadership as men in the community, and, "united as Black men"—in many instances forming a human shield for the police—they quickly snuffed out instances of looting. Appeals to patriarchy can always be used to protect private property, because without property patriarchy is much weaker: the originary and only property guaranteed to all men are, after all, the wife and children in his family. Here again we see how often anti-militancy is patriarchal.

And then there are the co-opters of a more subtle variety, the "leaders" and nonprofiteers who try to build careers off of media appearances, who try to channel spontaneous uprisings into single-demand-based protest models that can appeal to funds and funders, into electoral or reformist campaigns more easily controlled. And then there are the writers, thinkers, activists, and revolutionaries—like me—who, in the name of pushing the struggle forward, wrench it into theories, arguments, and texts incapable of truly recapturing the fire and always, as such, threatening to extinguish it like a wet blanket.

As the flames rose above the Ferguson QuikTrip, those who would put out the fires were, for the moment, outgunned by those who fought for Michael Brown. In their moment of rage and mourning, they heard that famous cry from Watts echoing down the decades: Burn, baby, burn. After NYPD officer Daniel Pantaleo's acquittal for the murder of Eric Garner, the flames leapt from Ferguson to New York and the Bay. Then to Baltimore, Baton Rouge, Milwaukee, and Charlotte.

It seems likely that, with the even further emboldened and empowered police under pig-in-chief Trump, and the global wave of mass resistance and insurrection, a massive antipolice uprising is in the offing. Maybe this summer, maybe next. Maybe when this book is published it will already have happened.* When it does, we need to stand fast beside looters, rioters, and street fighters and struggle with them against the liberal commentators, de-escalators, nonprofiteers, right-wing trolls, vigilantes, and, of course, the police. We need to argue for and defend every tactic that might help us to overturn this miserable world of white supremacy, anti-Blackness, cisheteropatriarchy, capitalism, empire, and property.

Justice for Mike Brown, for Freddie Gray, for Oscar Grant and Tanisha Anderson! Justice for Keith Lamont Scott, Sandra Bland, Sylville

---

*Author's note: I handed this book's final manuscript to the publisher on May 29, 2020. On May 27, the Minneapolis riots for George Floyd began. As final touches were put on the manuscript, late in the night as the 13th precinct burned to the ground, solidarity uprisings had spread to Louisville, LA, Denver, Portland, Columbus, and Phoenix. I hope by the time this book comes out to have already met some of you in the streets. As I write this, I have no idea what political world this book will emerge into, and that's beautiful.

Smith, Tamon Robinson, and Renisha McBride, for Kimani Gray, Chyna Gibson, and Mercedes Successful! Justice for Trayvon Martin, Sean Bell, Amadou Diallo, George Floyd, Troy Davis, Philando Castille, Jamar Clark, Alton Sterling, Manuel Dias, and Joel Acevedo! Justice for Tamir Rice, Korynn Gaines, Eric Garner, and Miriam Carey! Justice for all those named and unnamed, those millions whose misfortune it has been to be alive at the same time as America!

We will fight, and we will win, and build a world deserving of their memory.

Acknowledgments

For a variety of reasons, some due to my deep and cultivated laziness, most due to frustrating factors outside my control, it took five years between beginning this book and publishing it. In those five years I've lived in three different cities in two different countries. To try to name all the people who have inspired me, helped me, supported me, struggled beside me, and thought and theorized with me in that period would be impossible: I could only end up leaving someone out, and it would break my heart to do so. Instead, if you think you might be one of the people described above, know that you are. Thank you so much, this would've been impossible without you.

Next I want to acknowledge the rebels of Ferguson who taught me to strengthen my critique and understanding of anti-Blackness, white supremacy, capitalism, and the police, who inspired me to deepen my commitment to abolition, revolution, and rebellion, who reignited the fire that's been burning as long as this settler colony has existed but have felt in recent decades that it had been reduced to embers. The last six years have been cruel to many of those activists and fighters, some of whom have been murdered under mysterious circumstances. I hope this book honors their memory and acts as a gift of gratitude to all who take the streets.

I also want to thank the people who helped the original essay come together. To Hannah, Rob, Monalisa, and Ayesha, who worked on the original piece in 2014 in different capacities, thank you so so much. This piece ended up changing my life, and it wouldn't have done so without all of your edits, your time, your energy: while writing the book, I would frequently reflect on the edits and interventions you made. And to the rest of the team at the *New Inquiry*: thank you for the years of support, inspiration, and mutual creation. You are some of the most talented writers, editors, and thinkers I've ever known. It's so great to know, all these years later, that a new generation of editors is keeping the project alive.

Thank you to Rachel for suggesting I pitch the essay to an editor as a book (and then, when I was too lazy and disorganized to do it, kicking my ass into gear), and thank you to Katy for (eventually) being that editor. Your deft editing and constant support over the last year have made the previous four of frustration seem more than worth it, and you helped me believe that there was something here when I was on the verge of giving up. Thanks to the whole Bold Type team, Jocelynn, Miguel, and James. And special thanks to Ian, who rescued the manuscript from stagnation and helped put it into their capable hands.

I'd like to thank my family, chosen and bio-fam, who have been there for me through this whole process. My parents and brother have been cheerleaders and supporters despite my decidedly antisocial topic of interest. Thank you so much. Thanks, too, to Lala and Robespierre, who nestled in laps, luxuriated in sun puddles, climbed all over the various keyboards on which this was written, and generally demonstrated that the best life is one without work, by example (and occasional demands for attention) gently encouraging me toward that kind of life. And thanks, finally, to Sophie, my best friend, my beautiful comrade in struggle, in thought, my sexy partner in crime, my bestie for life. I love you so much. I can't imagine what my life would look like had you not come into it. I do know, however, that without your love, your support, our stupid jokes, and your absolutely inspiring ability to hold me and all our friends accountable to our own best selves, I never could have finished this book. Thank you.

Notes

INTRODUCTION

1. *Oxford English Dictionary*, 2nd ed. 20 vols. (Oxford: Oxford University Press, 1989), s.v. "loot."

2. *Oxford English Dictionary*, "loot."

3. Delio Vasquez, "The Poor Person's Defense of Riots," in *Taking Sides*, ed. Cindy Milstein (Oakland, CA: AK Press, 2015).

4. Neal Keating, "Rioting & Looting: As a Modern-Day Form of Potlatch," *Anarchy: A Journal of Desire Armed* 39 (1994).

5. Stokely Carmichael, "Black Power and the Third World" (address of the Organization of Latin American Solidarity, Havana, Cuba, August 1967).

6. Assata Shakur, *Assata* (Chicago: Lawrence Hill Books, 1988), 212.

7. Tyler Reinhard, "hey, step back with the riot shaming," *Mask Magazine*, no. 7 (July 2014).

8. For more, see Bobby London, *Looting Is a Political Tactic*, on her website thisisbobbylondon.com.

9. Terrence Cannon, "Riots, SNCC, and the Press," *The Movement* 3, no. 7 (1967).

10. Evan Calder Williams, "An Open Letter to Those Who Condemn Looting," *AudioZine* (2012).

11. Williams, "An Open Letter."

12. Sylvia Wynter, "'No Humans Involved': An Open Letter to My Colleagues," *Knowledge on Trial* 1, no. 1 (1994): 42–71.

13. Sophie Lewis, *Full Surrogacy Now* (London: Verso Books, 2019).

14. Joshua Clover, *Riot. Strike. Riot: The New Era of Uprisings* (New York: Verso Books, 2019).

15. Malcolm McLaughlin, *The Long Hot Summer of 1967: Urban Rebellion in America* (New York: Palgrave Macmillan, 2014).

16. Huey Newton, "The Correct Handling of a Revolution" (speech, 1967).

17. Patrick Wolfe, *Traces of History* (London: Verso Books, 2016).

18. James Baldwin "White Man's Guilt," *Ebony*, August 1965; Christina Sharpe, *In the Wake: On Blackness and Being* (Durham, NC: Duke University Press, 2016); Mumia Abu-Jamal, "The Battles of History," *Workers World*, September 10, 2017, www.workers.org/2017/09/33140/.

19. The concept of "otherwise" as used throughout this text is indebted to the work of Ashon Crawley, as in the essay "Otherwise, Ferguson," and further elaboration of the concept in *Black Pentecostal Breath*.

20. Mauritz Hallgren, *Seeds of Revolt* (New York: Alfred A. Knopf, 1933).

21. I want here to mark my deep gratitude to open internet archives like Freedom Archives, the Anarchist Library, History Is a Weapon, Marxists.org, and more focused archives such as Rutgers the Newark Experience, Collective Punishment mapping project, and a few pirate communities I won't name here for their security. My work is guided by a number of incredible books and thinkers. The most central of those academics and theorists to this project are W. E. B. Du Bois, Sylvia Wynter, Barbara J. Fields, Armistead Robinson, Kristian Williams, Ida B. Wells, Russell Maroon Shoatz, Cedric Robinson, Saidiya Hartman, Assata Shakur, Anthony Paul Farley, Eric Foner, Christina Sharpe, Jeremy Brecher, Barbara Ransby, Huey Newton, J. Sakai, Jeanne Theoharis, and Komozi Woodard. Equally important are the theorists of Ferguson, Baltimore, Oakland, Charlotte, and Minneapolis.

CHAPTER ONE. THE RACIAL ROOTS OF PROPERTY

1. Cedric Robinson, *Black Marxism*, 2nd ed. (Chapel Hill: University of North Carolina Press, 2000).

2. Eduardo Galeano, *Open Veins of Latin America* (New York: Monthly Review Press, 1971).

3. J. Sakai, *Settlers* (Chicago: Morningstar Press, 1989), 8; Eric Williams, *Capitalism and Slavery*, 2nd ed. (Chapel Hill: University of North Carolina Press, 1994), 7–9.

4. Patrick Wolfe, *Traces of History* (London: Verso Books, 2016).

5. Lerone Bennett Jr., *Shaping of Black America* (New York: Johnson Publishing, 1975), 18.

6. Robin Blackburn, *The Making of New World Slavery* (London: Verso Books, 1997); Anthony Paul Farley, "The Apogee of the Commodity," *DePaul Law Review*

53, no. 3 (2004): 1229; Theodore Allen, *Invention of the White Race*, Vol 1 (London: Verso, 1994).

7. Barbara Jeanne Fields, "Slavery, Race and Ideology in the United States of America," *New Left Review*, May/June 1990, 102.

8. Quote from Eric Williams, *Capitalism and Slavery*, 2nd ed. (Chapel Hill: University of North Carolina Press, 1994), 14; see also Robinson, *Black Marxism*.

9. Fields, "Slavery, Race and Ideology," 104.

10. Bennett, *Shaping of Black America*, 22.

11. Fields, "Slavery, Race and Ideology."

12. Fields, "Slavery, Race and Ideology," 102.

13. Fields, "Slavery, Race and Ideology," 104.

14. Robinson, *Black Marxism*.

15. Williams, *Capitalism and Slavery*, 108–110.

16. Blackburn, *The Making of New World Slavery*.

17. Frederick Douglass, *My Bondage and My Freedom* (1855; reprint New York: Penguin Classics, 2003).

18. Caitlin Rosenthal, *Accounting for Slavery: Masters and Management* (Cambridge, MA: Harvard University Press, 2018); Simone Browne, *Dark Matters: On the Surveillance of Blackness* (Durham, NC: Duke University Press, 2014).

19. Fields, "Slavery, Race and Ideology."

20. Robinson, *Black Marxism*.

21. Sylvia Wynter, "The Ceremony Must Be Found: After Humanism," *boundary 2* 13, no. 1 (1984): 36.

22. Patrick Wolfe, *Traces of History* (London: Verso Books, 2016).

23. David Roediger, *Seizing Freedom* (New York: Verso Books, 2015), 28; Edward Baptist, *The Half Has Never Been Told* (New York: Basic Books, 2016), 33; Farley, "The Apogee of the Commodity," 1229; Browne, *Dark Matters*, 42.

24. Cheryl Harris, "Whiteness as Property," *Harvard Law Review* 106, no. 8 (June 1993): 1726.

25. Harris, "Whiteness as Property," 1726.

CHAPTER TWO. LOOTING EMANCIPATION

1. David Roediger, *Seizing Freedom* (New York: Verso Books, 2015), 25–26.

2. Robin Blackburn, *The American Crucible* (New York: Verso Books, 2011).

3. J. Sakai, *Settlers* (Chicago: Morningstar Press, 1989), 18.

4. W. E. B. Du Bois, *Black Reconstruction in America* (1935; reprint, New York: Free Press, 1998).

5. Saidiya Hartman, *Scenes of Subjection: Terror, Slavery and Self-Making in Nineteenth-Century America* (Oxford: Oxford University Press, 1997).

6. Hartman, *Scenes of Subjection*, 65–66.

7. Hartman, *Scenes of Subjection*, 65–66.

8. Blackburn, *The American Crucible*.

9. Du Bois, *Black Reconstruction*, 13.

10. Barbara Jeanne Fields, "Slavery, Race and Ideology in the United States of America," *New Left Review*, May/June 1990.

11. John Hope Franklin and Loren Schweninger, *Runaway Slaves: Rebels on the Plantation* (New York: Oxford University Press, 2000).

12. Lerone Bennett Jr., *Shaping of Black America* (New York: Johnson Publishing, 1975), 31.

13. Russell Maroon Shoatz, *Maroon the Implacable* (San Francisco: PM Press, 2014).

14. For more on these strategies of resistance, see Saidiya Hartman, *Scenes of Subjection*, and Alvin O. Thompson, *Flight to Freedom* (Kingston, Jamaica: University of West Indies Press, 2006).

15. The history of these maroon communities has been carefully studied by Russell Maroon Shoatz, who conducts his research from within the modern-day plantation: Graterford State Correctional Institution in Pennsylvania. Shoatz, despite spending twenty-two years in solitary confinement, has written extensively and powerfully about the large maroon communities that existed in the American South. Shoatz was imprisoned in 1972 as part of the "Philly Five," accused and convicted of shooting a police officer in an attack on a Philadelphia police station in 1970. Shoatz, whose book is accurately titled *Maroon the Implacable*, has spent a life in resistance, not only carrying out his scholarship but also escaping twice and organizing with the Pennsylvania Association of Lifers, a group dedicated to ending life-without-parole sentences. As a political prisoner and an absolute enemy of the white supremacist carceral state, he has been kept in solitary confinement for most of his adult life. Along with prison abolition and the history of revolutionary practice, he has recently added his voice to ecological struggles and questions of food security. To support him, buy his book, learn more about his life, and read his incredible scholarship, go to https://russellmaroonshoats.wordpress.com/.

16. On the role of maroons in the Seminole Wars, see Shoatz, *Maroon the Implacable*; Thompson, *Flight to Freedom*; and JB Bird's John Horse project at John horse.com.

17. On role of maroonage in the Revolutionary War, see Shoatz, *Maroon the Implacable*; and Blackburn, *The American Crucible*.

18. Stanley Harrold, "Slave Rebels and Black Abolitionists," in *A Companion to African American History*, ed. Alton Hornsby Jr. (New York: Wiley-Blackwell, 2005), 210.

19. Eric Foner, *Gateway to Freedom* (New York: W. W. Norton, 2016), 15.

20. Nell Irvin Painter, *Sojourner Truth: A Life, a Symbol* (New York: W. W. Norton, 1997), 132.

21. For more on these modes of escape, see *Slave Narratives of the Underground Railroad*, edited by Christine Rudisel (New York: Dover Thrift, 2015).

22. Butch Lee, *Jailbreak Out of History: The Re-Biography of Harriet Tubman* (Chicago: Beguine Press, 2000).

23. Sakai, *Settlers*, 22 (emphasis mine).

24. Quoted in Lee, *Jailbreak Out of History*, 75.

25. Armstead Robinson, *The Bitter Fruits of Bondage* (Charlottesville: University of Virginia Press, 2004), 15.

26. Du Bois, *Black Reconstruction*, chap. 3.

27. Douglass, quoted in Du Bois, *Black Reconstruction*, chap. 4.

28. Du Bois, *Black Reconstruction*, 56.

29. Michael Vorenberg, "Abraham Lincoln and the Politics of Black Colonization," *Journal of the Abraham Lincoln Association* 14, no. 2 (Summer 1993).

30. David Roediger, *Seizing Freedom* (New York: Verso Books, 2015), 37.

31. Du Bois, *Black Reconstruction*, 64.

32. Bennett, *Shaping of Black America* 172.

33. Roediger, *Seizing Freedom*, 17.

34. Du Bois, *Black Reconstruction*, 54.

CHAPTER THREE. ALL COPS ARE BASTARDS

1. Kristian Williams, *Our Enemies in Blue*, rev. ed. (Oakland, CA: AK Press, 2015), 55.

2. David Whitehouse, "Origins of the Police," Libcom.org, 2014, https://libcom.org/history/origins-police-david-whitehouse.

3. Whitehouse, "Origins of the Police."

4. Ben Brucato, "Fabricating the Color Line in a White Democracy," *Theoria* 61, no. 141 (2014).

5. Howard Zinn, *A People's History of the United States* (New York: Harper Perennial, 1980).

6. Williams, *Our Enemies in Blue*, 63–65.

7. Williams, *Our Enemies in Blue*, 56.

8. Williams, *Our Enemies in Blue*, 42.

9. Williams, *Our Enemies in Blue*.

10. Williams, *Our Enemies in Blue*, 77.

11. Lucy Parsons, "The Principles of Anarchism" (lecture, 1905), cited in Gale Ahrens, ed., *Lucy Parsons: Freedom, Equality and Solidarity* (Chicago: Charles H. Kerr, 2004).

12. Mychal Denzel Smith, "Abolish the Police," *The Nation*, April 9, 2015.

13. Michelle Alexander, *The New Jim Crow* (New York: New Press, 2012), 28.

14. Saidiya Hartman, *Scenes of Subjection: Terror, Slavery and Self-Making in Nineteenth-Century America* (Oxford: Oxford University Press, 1997), 80.

15. Angela Davis, *Are Prisons Obsolete?* (New York: Seven Stories Press, 2003), 32.

16. For more, see chapter 2, "Ogeechee Till Death," in Neal Shirley and Saralee Stafford's *Dixie Be Damned* (Oakland, CA: AK Press, 2015).

17. Noel Ignatiev, *Introduction to the United States* (pamphlet published by Sojourner Truth Organization, 1980).

18. Ignatiev, *Introduction to the United States*.

19. Shirley and Stafford, *Dixie Be Damned*, 116.

20. The history of Reconstruction and its failure is a crucially important one that is unfortunately outside the purview of this book. For more on Reconstruction, see W. E. B. Du Bois, *Black Reconstruction in America* (1935; reprint, New York: Free Press, 1998); Saidiya Hartman, *Scenes of Subjection*; and Eric Foner, *Reconstruction: 1863–1877* (New York: Harper & Row, 1988).

CHAPTER FOUR. WHITE RIOT

1. Naomi Murakawa, *The First Civil Right: How Liberals Built Prison America* (Oxford: Oxford University Press, 2014).

2. Paul Ortiz, *Emancipation Betrayed* (Berkeley: University of California Press, 2005).

3. Equal Justice Initiative, *Lynching in America: Confronting the Legacy of Racial Terror*, 3rd ed., 2017, https://eji.org/reports/lynching-in-america/.

4. Ortiz, *Emancipation Betrayed*.

5. Amy Louise Wood, "Lynching Photography and the Visual Reproduction of White Supremacy," *American Nineteenth Century History* 6, no. 3 (September 2005).

6. Ida B. Wells, *Lynch Law in Georgia and Other Writings* (Atlanta: On Our Own Authority! Publishing, 2013),113, 114.

7. Hazel Carby, "On the Threshold of Woman's Era: Lynching, Empire, and Sexuality in Black Feminist Theory," *Critical Inquiry* 12 (Autumn 1985): 270.

8. Wells, *Lynch Law in Georgia*.

9. Wells, *Lynch Law in Georgia*.

10. J. Sakai, *Settlers* (Chicago: Morningstar Press, 1989), 35.

11. Sakai, *Settlers*.

12. "The Solstice," Ultra, April 27, 2014, www.ultra-com.org/project/the-solstice/.

13. Walter C. Rucker and James Nathaniel Upton, eds., *Encyclopedia of American Race Riots* (Westport, CT: Greenwood Press, 2007).

14. Wells, *Lynch Law in Georgia*.

15. Wood, "Lynching Photography."

16. Scott Ellsworth, *Death in a Promised Land: The Tulsa Race Riot of 1921* (Baton Rouge: Louisiana State University Press, 1992).

17. Harry Haywood, *Black Bolshevik: Autobiography of an Afro-American Communist* (Minneapolis: University of Minnesota Press, 1975).

18. Ellsworth, *Death in a Promised Land*.

19. Ellsworth, *Death in a Promised Land*, 106.

20. Ellsworth, *Death in a Promised Land*, 105.

21. "Against Innocence" was published before Mike Brown's murder, so Wang doesn't mention him in the text.

22. Jackie Wang, "Against Innocence," *Lies Journal* 1 (2012).

CHAPTER FIVE. LOOTED BREAD, STOLEN LABOR

1. This is the central thesis of Frances Fox Piven and Richard A. Cloward, *Poor People's Movements* (New York: Vintage Books, 1979), which is a foundational text for this chapter.

2. E. P. Thompson, "The Moral Economy of the English Crowd in the Eighteenth Century," *Past and Present*, no. 50 (February 1971).

3. Joshua Clover, *Riot. Strike. Riot: The New Era of Uprisings* (New York: Verso Books, 2019).

4. Michael B. Chesson, "Harlots or Heroines? A New Look at the Richmond Bread Riot," *Virginia Magazine of History and Biography* 92, no. 2 (April 1984).

5. Nell Irvin Painter, *Standing at Armageddon: A Grassroots History of the Progressive Era* (New York: W. W. Norton, 2008), 37.

6. Noel Ignatiev, *Introduction to the United States* (pamphlet published by Sojourner Truth Organization, 1980).

7. Joseph G. Rayback, *A History of American Labor* (New York: Free Press, 1966), 136.

8. Jeremy Brecher, *Strike! Revised and Updated Edition* (Cambridge, MA: South End Press, 1997), 15.

9. Brecher, *Strike!*, 15.

10. Painter, *Standing at Armageddon*.

11. Brecher, *Strike!*, 102.

12. Brecher, *Strike!*, 114.

13. Louis Adamic, *Dynamite: The Story of Class Violence in America* (Oakland, CA: AK Press, 2008), 235–250.

14. Mauritz Hallgren, *Seeds of Revolt* (New York: Alfred A. Knopf, 1933), 99.

15. Piven and Cloward, *Poor People's Movements*, 49.

16. Hallgren, *Seeds of Revolt*, 133.

17. Piven and Cloward, *Poor People's Movements*, 49.

18. Hallgren, *Seeds of Revolt*, 58.

19. Hallgren, *Seeds of Revolt*, 58.

20. St. Clair Drake and Horace R. Cayton Jr., *Black Metropolis* (Chicago: University of Chicago Press, 1993).

21. Roy Rosenzweig, "Organizing the Unemployed: The Early Years of the Great Depression 1929–1933," in *Workers' Struggles, Past and Present: A "Radical America" Reader*, ed. James Green (Philadelphia: Temple University Press, 1983), 86.

22. Rosenzweig, 87.

23. Rosenzweig, 173.

24. Rosenzweig, 174.

25. Piven and Cloward, *Poor People's Movements*, 73.

26. Piven and Cloward, *Poor People's Movements*, 76–77.

CHAPTER SIX. NO SUCH THING AS NONVIOLENCE

1. Jeanne Theoharis and Komozi Woodard, eds., *Groundwork: Local Black Freedom Movements in America* (New York: New York University Press, 2005).

2. This quotation was taken from an online presentation by Robin D. G. Kelley.

3. William Smith, *The Invisible Soldiers: Unheard Voices* (documentary, VHS, 2000).

4. C. E. Wilson, "Whatever Happened to the Negro's Friend?" *The Liberator* IV, nos. 5+6 (June 1964).

5. Timothy Tyson, *Radio Free Dixie: Robert F. Williams and the Roots of Black Power* (Chapel Hill: University of North Carolina Press, 1999).

6. Smith, *The Invisible Soldiers*.

7. Tyson, *Radio Free Dixie*, 37.

8. Tyson, *Radio Free Dixie*, 48.

9. Ellen Schrecker, "McCarthyism: Political Repression and Fear of Communism," *Social Research* 71, no. 4 (2004).

10. Keeanga-Yamahtta Taylor, *From #BlackLivesMatter to Black Liberation* (Chicago: Haymarket Books, 2016).

11. Schrecker, "McCarthyism," 1045.

12. Brian Purnell, "Drive Awhile for Freedom: Brooklyn CORE's 1964 Stall-In and Public Discourses on Protest Violence," in *Groundwork: Local Black Freedom Movements in America*, ed. Jeanne Theoharis and Komozi Woodard (New York: New York University Press, 2005).

13. Gerald Horne, *Fire This Time: The Watts Uprising and the 1960s* (Boston: Da Capo Press, 1995).

14. Rosa Parks, "Tired of Giving In: The Launching of the Montgomery Bus Boycott," in *Sisters in the Struggle*, ed. Bettye Collier-Thomas and V. P. Franklin (New York: New York University Press, 2001).

15. Parks, "Tired of Giving In."

16. Danielle McGuire, *At the Dark End of the Street: Black Women, Rape, and Resistance* (New York: Vintage Books, 2011).

17. Tyson, *Radio Free Dixie*, 212.

18. Charles Cobb, *This Nonviolent Stuff'll Get You Killed* (New York: Basic Books, 2014), 123.

19. Chana Kai Lee, "Anger, Memory, and Personal Power: Fannie Lou Hamer and Civil Rights Leadership," in Collier-Thomas and Franklin, *Sisters in the Struggle*.

CHAPTER SEVEN. USING GUNS NONVIOLENTLY

1. Robert F. Williams, *Negroes with Guns* (New York: Marzani & Munsell, 1962).

2. I regret that I do not have the space to really discuss the Deacons, who are vital to any radical history of the civil rights movement. Lance Hill's *The Deacons for Defense* (Raleigh: University of North Carolina Press, 2006) is an excellent book and a great place to start learning their history.

3. For more on Baker's life and her inspiring style of organization, read Barbara Ransby's indispensable *Ella Baker & The Black Freedom Movement* (Raleigh: University of North Carolina Press, 2005).

4. Akinyele Omowale Umoja, *We Will Shoot Back: Armed Resistance in the Mississippi Freedom Movement* (New York: New York University Press, 2013); Charles Cobb, *This Nonviolent Stuff'll Get You Killed* (New York: Basic Books, 2014); Kwame Jeffries, "The Ballet and the Bullet: Armed Self-Defense in the Alabama Black Belt, 1965–66" (paper presented at the American Historical Association 119th Annual Meeting, 2005).

5. Cobb, *This Nonviolent Stuff'll Get You Killed*, 8.

6. Hill, *The Deacons for Defense*, 26.

7. Lorenzo Raymond, "Bloodless Lies," *New Inquiry*, November 2, 2016.

8. C. E. Wilson, "Whatever Happened to the Negro's Friend?" *The Liberator* IV, nos. 5+6 (June 1964).

9. Hill, *The Deacons for Defense*, 8.

10. Williams, *Negroes with Guns*.

11. Peter Gelderloos, *How Nonviolence Protects the State* (Cambridge, MA: South End Press, 2007).

12. Malcolm X, "Message to the Grassroots" (speech, November 10, 1963).

13. Dorothy Height, "We Wanted the Voice of a Woman to Be Heard: Black Women and the 1963 March on Washington," in *Sisters in the Struggle*, ed. Bettye Collier-Thomas and V. P. Franklin (New York: New York University Press, 2001), 86.

14. Height, "We Wanted the Voice of a Woman to Be Heard," 87.

15. Pauli Murray, quoted in Height, "We Wanted the Voice of a Woman to Be Heard."

16. Joy James, "Framing the Panther: Assata Shakur and Black Female Agency," in *Want to Start a Revolution? Radical Women in the Black Freedom Struggle*, ed. Jeanne Theoharis, Komozi Woodard, and Dayo Gore (New York: New York University Press, 2009).

17. James, "Framing the Panther."

CHAPTER EIGHT. CIVIL RIOTS

1. Christina Sharpe, *In the Wake: On Blackness and Being* (Durham, NC: Duke University Press, 2016).

2. For more on the Mississippi movement, read Akinyele Omowale Umoja's excellent *We Will Shoot Back: Armed Resistance in the Mississippi Freedom Movement* (New York: New York University Press, 2013).

3. Sharon Harley, "Chronicle of a Death Foretold: Gloria Richardson, the Cambridge Movement, and the Radical Black Activist Tradition," in *Sisters in the Struggle*, ed. Bettye Collier-Thomas and V. P. Franklin (New York: New York University Press, 2001).

4. Harley, "Chronicle of a Death Foretold."

5. Charles Fuller (as C.H.), "Philadelphia After the Riots," *The Liberator* IV, no. 11 (November 1964).

6. Fuller, "Philadelphia After the Riots."

7. Joshua Bloom and Waldo E. Martin Jr., *Black Against Empire: The History and Politics of the Black Panther Party* (Berkeley: University of California Press, 2013).

8. Gerald Horne, *Fire This Time: The Watts Uprising and the 1960s* (Boston: Da Capo Press, 1995).

9. "Watts: A Conversation: If I Go, I'll Take Whitey with Me," *The Movement* 1, no. 9 (September 1965).

10. Jimmy Garrett, "The Negro Revolt in LA—from the Inside," *The Movement* 1, no. 9 (September 1965).

11. Horne, *Fire This Time*, 83.

12. Huey Newton, *Revolutionary Suicide* (1973; reprint, New York: Penguin Books, 2009).

13. Huey Newton, "The Correct Handling of a Revolution" (speech, 1967).

14. Elaine Brown, *A Taste of Power* (New York: Anchor Books, 1994), 136.

15. Max Elbaum, *Revolution in the Air* (New York: Verso Books, 2002), 21.

16. Martin Luther King Jr., "The Three Evils" (speech, Hungry Club Forum, Atlanta, May 10, 1967).

17. Kevin Mumford, *Newark: A History of Race, Rights and Riots in America* (New York: New York University Press, 2007), 125.

18. Malcolm McLaughlin, *The Long, Hot Summer of 1967: Urban Rebellion in America* (New York: Palgrave Macmillan, 2014).

19. Komozi Woodard, "Message from the Grassroots," in *Groundwork: Local Black Freedom Movements in America*, ed. Jeanne Theoharis and Komozi Woodard (New York: New York University Press, 2005).

20. Woodard, "Message from the Grassroots," 80.

21. McLaughlin, *The Long, Hot Summer of 1967*, 91.

22. Dan Georgakas and Marvin Surkin, *Detroit, I Do Mind Dying: A Study in Urban Revolution* (Cambridge, MA: South End Press, 1999).

23. Georgakas and Surkin, *Detroit, I Do Mind Dying*, 13.

24. Elbaum, *Revolution in the Air*, 25.

25. Keeanga-Yamahtta Taylor, *From #BlackLivesMatter to Black Liberation* (Chicago: Haymarket Books, 2016).

CHAPTER NINE. THE INHUMANITY OF LOOTERS

1. For more on this new urbanized organization of global capital, see *Hinterland*, by Phil A. Neel (London: Reaktion Books, 2018).

2. James Goodman, *Blackout* (New York: North Point Press, 2005), 115; Christina Sharpe, *In the Wake: On Blackness and Being* (Durham, NC: Duke University Press, 2016).

3. This page has since been removed.

4. Manning Marable, "The Fire This Time: The Miami Rebellion, May 1980," *Black Scholar* 11, no. 6 (July/August 1980): 14.

5. Mike Davis, "In L.A., Burning All Illusions," *The Nation*, June 1, 1992.

6. Akinyele Umoja, "From Columbus to Rodney King: The Los Angeles Rebellion and Beyond," *Breakthrough* 16, no. 2 (1992).

7. Aufheben Collective, "The Rebellion in Los Angeles: The Context of a Proletarian Uprising," *Aufheben* 1 (August 1992).

8. Max Anger, "From Gulf War to Class War, We All Hate the Cops," *Anarchy: A Journal of Desire Armed*, no. 34 (1992).

9. Anger, "From Gulf War to Class War."

10. Sylvia Wynter, "'No Humans Involved': An Open Letter to My Colleagues," *Knowledge on Trial* 1, no. 1 (1994): 42–71.

11. Gerald Horne, *Fire This Time: The Watts Uprising and the 1960s* (Boston: Da Capo Press, 1995).

12. Mychal Denzel Smith, *Invisible Man, Got the Whole World Watching* (New York: Nation Books, 2016).

13. A. C. Thompson, "Post-Katrina, White Vigilantes Shot African-Americans with Impunity," *Pro Publica*, December 19, 2008.

CONCLUSION. OUT OF THE FLAMES OF FERGUSON

1. Angela Davis, *Are Prisons Obsolete?* (New York: Seven Stories Press, 2003).

2. Anonymous, "Cars, Guns, Autonomy: On the Finer Points of the Recent Revolt in Ferguson, MO," *Avalanche* 3 (November 2014).

3. Raven Rakia, "Between the Peacekeepers and the Protesters in Ferguson," *Truthout*, September 9, 2014.

Index

265

VICKY OSTERWEIL is a writer, editor, and agitator and a regular contributor to the *New Inquiry*. Her writing has also appeared in the *Baffler*, the *Nation*, *Real Life*, and *Al Jazeera America*. She lives in Philadelphia.